Gender and English Language Learners

**Edited by Bonny Norton
and Aneta Pavlenko**

Case Studies in TESOL Practice Series

Jill Burton, Series Editor

Teachers of English to Speakers of Other Languages, Inc.

Typeset in Berkeley and Belwe
by Capitol Communication Systems, Inc., Crofton, Maryland USA
Printed by Kirby Lithographic Company, Inc., Arlington, Virginia USA
Indexed by Coughlin Indexing Services, Annapolis, Maryland USA

Teachers of English to Speakers of Other Languages, Inc.
700 South Washington Street, Suite 200
Alexandria, Virginia 22314 USA
Tel 703-836-0774 • Fax 703-836-6447 • E-mail info@tesol.org • http://www.tesol.org/

Director of Publications: Paul E. Gibbs
Managing Editor: Marilyn Kupetz
Copy Editor: Ellen Garshick
Additional Reader: Sarah Duffy
Cover Design: Capitol Communications Systems, Inc.

ISBN 1931185131
Library of Congress Control No. 2003115696

Table of Contents

Acknowledgments   v

Series Editor's Preface   vii

CHAPTER 1: Gender and English Language Learners:
Challenges and Possibilities   1
     Bonny Norton and Aneta Pavlenko

PART 1: TEACHING FOR CHANGE

CHAPTER 2: Beyond Straight Grammar: Using Lesbian/Gay Themes
to Explore Cultural Meanings   15
     Cynthia D. Nelson

CHAPTER 3: Gender, Sexual Harassment, and the
International Teaching Assistant   29
     Diana Boxer and Andrea Tyler

CHAPTER 4: Feminist Composition Pedagogies in ESL Tutoring   43
     Jay Jordan

PART 2: STUDENT VOICES

CHAPTER 5: Investigating the Male Voice in a Malaysian ESL Classroom   59
     Subra Govindasamy and Maya Khemlani David

CHAPTER 6: Speaking in Silence: A Case Study of a Canadian Punjabi Girl   69
     Allyson Julé

PART 3: INNOVATIONS FOR ALL

CHAPTER 7: Opportunities for Girls: A Community
Library Project in Uganda   81
     Kate Parry

CHAPTER 8: Creating a Community of Difference:
Understanding Gender and Race in a High School ESL
Antidiscrimination Camp   95
     Lisa Taylor

CHAPTER 9: Explorations of Language and Gender
in a Graduate Technology Course   111
     Sarah Rilling and Rebecca Biles

PART 4: INSIGHTS FROM JAPAN

CHAPTER 10: Transforming Emerging Feminist Identities:
A Course on Gender and Language Issues   127
     Andrea Simon-Maeda

CHAPTER 11: Promoting Critical Reflection About Gender
in EFL Classes at a Japanese University   143
     Scott Saft and Yumiko Ohara

CHAPTER 12: Critical Feminist Engagement in the EFL Classroom:
From Supplement to Staple   155
     Tamarah Cohen

References   171

Index   187

Acknowledgments

We thank Jill Burton for the invitation to edit this collection, and for her insightful comments on earlier drafts. We are also very grateful to Ellen Garshick and Ena Lee for their help with the copy-editing process. Bonny Norton acknowledges and thanks the Social Sciences and Humanities Research Council of Canada for financial support.

Series Editor's Preface

The Case Studies in TESOL Practice series offers innovative and effective examples of practice from the point of view of the practitioner. The series brings together from around the world communities of practitioners who have reflected and written on particular aspects of their teaching. Each volume in the series covers one specialized teaching focus.

◈ CASE STUDIES

Why a TESOL series focusing on case studies of teaching practice?

Much has been written about case studies and where they fit in a mainstream research tradition (e.g., Nunan, 1992; Stake, 1995; Yin, 1994). Perhaps more importantly, case studies also constitute a public recognition of the value of teachers' reflection on their practice and constitute a new form of teacher research—or teacher valuing. Case studies support teachers in valuing the uniqueness of their classes, learning from them, and showing how their experience and knowledge can be made accessible to other practitioners in simple, but disciplined ways. They are particularly suited to practitioners who want to understand and solve teaching problems in their own contexts.

These case studies are written by practitioners who are able to portray real experience by providing detailed descriptions of teaching practice. These qualities invest the cases with teacher credibility, and make them convincing and professionally interesting. The cases also represent multiple views and offer immediate solutions, thus providing perspective on the issues and examples of useful approaches. Informative by nature, they can provide an initial database for further, sustained research. Accessible to wider audiences than many traditional research reports, however, case studies have democratic appeal.

◈ HOW THIS SERIES CAN BE USED

The case studies lend themselves to pre- and in-service teacher education. Because the context of each case is described in detail, it is easy for readers to compare the cases with and evaluate them against their own circumstances. To respond to the wide range of language environments in which TESOL functions, cases have been selected from EFL, ESL, and bilingual education settings around the world.

The 12 or so case studies in each volume are easy to follow. Teacher writers describe their teaching context and analyze its distinctive features: the particular demands of their context, the issues they have encountered, how they have effectively addressed the issues, what they have learned. Each case study also offers readers practical suggestions—developed from teaching experience—to adapt and apply to their own teaching.

Already published or in preparation are volumes on

- academic writing programs
- action research
- assessment practices
- bilingual education
- community partnerships
- content-based language instruction
- distance learning
- English for specific purposes
- global perspectives
- grammar teaching in teacher education
- intensive English programs
- interaction and language learning
- international teaching assistants
- journal writing
- literature in language learning
- mainstreaming
- teacher education
- teaching English as a foreign language in primary schools
- technology in the classroom

◈ THIS VOLUME

Writers in this volume profile the fluid, contested nature of gender and identity, along with their complex interactions with age, race, language, and culture in TESOL classrooms. The issues raised will interest all TESOL practitioners and advance professional understanding and practice.

Jill Burton
University of South Australia, Adelaide

CHAPTER 1

Gender and English Language Learners: Challenges and Possibilities

Bonny Norton and Aneta Pavlenko

❖ INTRODUCTION

Since the mid-1990s, several scholars in the fields of language education, second language acquisition, and bilingualism have addressed the influence of gender on access to linguistic and interactional resources, on the dynamics of classroom interaction, and on language learning outcomes (Ehrlich, 1997; Norton, 2000; Pavlenko, 2001; Pavlenko, Blackledge, Piller, & Teutsch-Dwyer, 2001; Sunderland, 2000). The field of TESOL has also exhibited a growing interest in the impact of gender on ESL and EFL learning, seen in the increasing number of plenaries, panels, discussion groups, and papers on the topic. Yet the nature of the connection between gender and language learning remains elusive, or, rather, different scholars and educators approach it from diverse perspectives. Some studies continue to appeal to variationist and interactional sociolinguistics methodology, treating gender as a variable, whereas others, grounded in critical, poststructuralist, and feminist theory, approach gender as a system of social relations and discursive practices.

It is the latter approach that informs this chapter and most of the contributions to the volume. In what follows, we discuss the feminist poststructuralist view of gender, outline its role in the context of ESL and EFL learning, and show how the contributions to this volume enrich TESOL theory and praxis, illuminating the key features of critical feminist pedagogy in TESOL.

❖ DEFINING GENDER

Most if not all scholars who are interested in the role of gender in language education see themselves as feminist. We do not dispute this, yet we point out that there are multiple approaches to feminism that espouse distinct views of gender and its relationship to language (cf. Gibbon, 1999). Until recently, two approaches have been most influential in the study of language and gender (for a detailed discussion, see Ehrlich, 1997; Pavlenko & Piller, 2001). The view of the two genders, male and female, as different cultures, common for *cultural feminism,* has guided the search for gender differences in language learning and use. The emphasis on patriarchy, typical for *material feminism,* has informed research on male dominance in interaction.

We argue that neither approach can be assumed unproblematically in the field of TESOL because both frameworks see *men* and *women* as undifferentiated and unitary groups, members of which have more in common with each other than with the members of the other group. What are the problems with such a view? To begin with, in its most radical form, such an approach, relying on outdated claims in the field of psychology, conflates *gender* with *sex* and *sex* with brain structure, leading to oversimplified generalizations along the lines of "females are superior in verbal skills, while males are superior in spatial skills . . . females are slightly more feeling oriented, while males are slightly more thinking oriented" (Oxford, 2002, p. 252). In reality, however, current work in neuroscience suggests that human brain functioning is a complex process that is influenced by both nature and nurture and is not easily reducible to female/male differences. Furthermore, as Jaeger (1998) has pointed out, even when such differences are found, "in the normal, intact brain, sex differences in functional cortical organization for language processing are not associated with significant behavioral differences in the everyday tasks of reading" (p. 230) or, for that matter, speaking (see also Bing & Bergvall, 1996).

Second, even in cases where the social nature of gender is acknowledged, the binary approach obliterates the fact that, in many cultures, gender as a system of social relations and as a way of interpreting human anatomy is not constrained to the female/male dichotomy, and humans may belong to three or four different genders (Bing & Bergvall, 1996; K. Hall, 2002; Lang, 1997). Consequently, an imposition of an ethnocentrically biased Western view distorts the understanding of group membership in the culture in question, making the findings about female/male differences nothing more than an epiphenomenon. Furthermore, even in cultures that view gender as a dichotomous system, the social meanings and ideologies of normative masculinity and femininity are highly diverse (Bonvillain, 1995) and cannot be superimposed.

Third and most important, the focus on a female/male dichotomy obscures oppression in terms of class, ethnicity, race, sexuality, or (dis)ability. Acknowledging this oppression forces one to recognize that, in some contexts, men and women within a particular group may be strongly united by the common ethnic, racial, religious, or class background and have more in common with each other than with members of other groups. For instance, White upper-middle-class men and women may both participate in oppressive practices targeting members of sexual, racial, or ethnic minorities. Furthermore, it is never purely men or women who are all-oppressed or all-powerful: It is immigrant women who do not always have access to educational resources, working-class boys and girls who are silenced in the classroom, or young Black men who do not have powerful role models in the school hierarchy (Jones, 1993).

Feminist poststructuralism, a framework outlined by Cameron (1992, 1997b), Luke and Gore (1992a), and Weedon (1987), and espoused by us and by many of the contributors to this volume, emphasizes the intrinsic links between gender and other social identities. We see feminist poststructuralism as an approach to the study of language and education that strives to (a) understand the relationship between power and knowledge; (b) theorize the role of language in production and reproduction of power, difference, and symbolic domination (in particular, in educational contexts); and (c) deconstruct master narratives that oppress certain groups—be they immigrants, women, or minority members—and devalue their linguistic practices.

In agreement with this approach, we see gender not as a dichotomy or an individual property but as a complex system of social relations and discursive practices differentially constructed in local contexts. This poststructuralist view of gender foregrounds sociohistoric, cross-cultural, and cross-linguistic differences in gender construction. In doing so, this approach emphasizes the fact that beliefs and ideas about gender relations and normative masculinities, femininities, or representations of third or fourth gender vary across cultures—as well as over time within a culture—based on social, political, and economic changes. Consequently, we do not assume that all women—or all men—have a lot in common with each other just because of their biological makeup or elusive social roles, nor do we assume that gender is always relevant to understanding language learning outcomes. Instead, gender emerges as one of many important facets of social identity that interact with race, ethnicity, class, sexuality, (dis)ability, age, and social status. In accordance with this view, the contributors to this volume consistently consider gender relations—as well as particular student populations—in their local social, cultural, and ideological contexts.

◈ GENDER AND TESOL

The feminist poststructuralist view of gender outlined above does not allow for easy generalizations about men or women or boys or girls, forcing TESOL professionals to look for new research questions and directions. Below, we contend that there are at least three ways of considering gender and gendering in ESL and EFL contexts without looking for gender differences in language learning processes or outcomes: gendered agency, gendered access, and gendered interaction.

Gendered Agency, Resistance, and Imagined Communities

First, we argue that some gender discourses closely linked to English have great potential to influence learners' investments and decisions. These discourses shape learners' desires as well as their images of themselves; their futures; and their social, educational, and economic opportunities. In some cases, perceived opportunities could strengthen the learners' agency, and in others, they could fuel learners' resistance to English.

Several recent studies indicate that many young women around the world consider English to be intrinsically linked to feminism and are motivated to learn it as a language of empowerment. This trend is apparent in Japan, the EFL context highlighted in this volume. At present many more young Japanese women than men appear to be interested in learning English, training for English language–related professions, and traveling to English-speaking countries (Kobayashi, 2002). For these women, English offers an entry into the job market as well as a possible way of liberating themselves from the confines of gender patriarchy. The latter also holds for older Japanese women in McMahill's (1997, 2001) studies of a feminist adult education English class. These women state that English is much better suited to express their personal emotions, views, and newly acquired critical consciousness.

In turn, in other contexts, learners may find imagined gendered identity options unappealing and give up on learning English. From this perspective, TESOL professionals need to examine gender identity options offered to students through textbooks, classroom materials, and classroom interactions as well as to consider students' investments—or lack thereof—in the light of gendered employment opportunities in the local and global marketplaces.

Gendered Access to Linguistic and Interactional Resources

Our second argument is that in some—albeit not all—contexts, access to linguistic and educational resources and interactional opportunities in English may be gendered. Several studies suggest that, in some English-speaking contexts, a number of gatekeeping practices may constrain immigrant and minority women's mobility and their access to ESL classes, education, and the workplace (Corson, 2001; Goldstein, 1995, 2001; Heller, 2001; Kouritzin, 2000; Norton, 2000). Some of these gatekeeping practices originate in the target language community, and some may stem from the minority community's social practices. For instance, in the English-speaking world, immigrant women may face sexual harassment, which inhibits their interactional opportunities and eventually decreases their chances to learn the language (Ehrlich, 2001). These opportunities may be further hampered by gendered and systemic inequalities, such as lack of governmentally funded day care. Recently, several programs have begun to address the particular needs of such populations. Case studies by Frye (1999) and Rivera (1999) offer descriptions of two such programs, in which low-income immigrant Latina women can increase their English proficiency, acquire literacy skills, and improve their basic education.

On the other hand, even in contexts where classes, professional training, and other linguistic resources are available, access problems may arise due to the minority community's gatekeeping practices. Kouritzin (2000) argues that even the best solutions, such as evening and weekend classes and externally funded day care, do not help women who are culturally required to be home with their children and prioritize their roles as housekeepers, mothers, wives, and caretakers. Moreover, being in the workplace does not guarantee access to English either: The first language may become the dominant language of the workplace (Goldstein, 1995, 2001), and English study may be seen as interfering with productivity or as threatening to less educated male partners (Norton Peirce, Harper, & Burnaby, 1993).

Even in the field of TESOL, access to and distribution of resources may be at times both racialized and gendered. White male scholars are commonly in positions of power, middle-class White women are often either in teaching positions or are building bridges between theory and practice, and racial and ethnic minority members are most often on the other side, namely, in the classroom. Thus, inequities in terms of race, gender, and native or nonnative speaker status need to be remedied not only in the classrooms but also in imagining the ESL cadre, and thus in the processes of hiring and promotion (for a discussion of the experiences of a minority woman teacher of ESL, see Amin, 1999).

Gendered Interaction

Our third argument is that in some—once again, not all—contexts, gender as a social and discursive practice affects interactional dynamics. Gender inequities may structure differential interactional opportunities for male and female learners of different ages, classes, or ethnic backgrounds. Consequently, in some contexts, immigrant and minority girls and women may get significantly less classroom interaction time than either minority boys and men or majority men and women (Corson, 2001; Losey, 1995; see also Julé's chapter in this volume). At the same time, recent studies in language education point away from facile generalizations about permanent female disenfranchisement, showing that in some contexts dominant cultures of learning silence working-class and immigrant boys and men (Heller, 2001; Willett, 1995).

◈ ORGANIZATION OF THE BOOK

In this volume, our aim is to showcase diverse studies that examine gender in language learning from a sociocultural and cross-cultural perspective and offer practical suggestions for critical praxis. The 11 cases represent language learning and teaching communities in a number of regions of the world, including Canada, Japan, Malaysia, Uganda, and the United States. The chapters also include a wide range of contexts, from primary, secondary, and higher education to teacher education and English for specific purposes (ESP).

Given the diversity of the chapters in this volume, determining an organizing principle for the collection was a challenge. After much discussion and reflection, we decided on a four-part organization. The chapters in Part 1, "Teaching for Change," focus on the contribution that teachers can make in addressing gender inequities in language learning. Part 2, "Student Voices," presents research that explores ways in which gender inequities contribute to the silencing of particular students in the English language classroom. Part 3, "Innovations for All," describes a range of innovative programs that are centrally concerned with gender and educational change. Part 4, "Insights From Japan," examines three groundbreaking action research projects that promote critical reflection about gender and language in one EFL context, which is also the source of some of the most innovative work on feminist pedagogy in EFL (Casanave & Yamashiro, 1996; Fujimura-Fanselow & Vaughn, 1991; MacGregor, 1998; McMahill, 1997, 2001; Smith & Yamashiro, 1998; Yamashiro, 2000).

In what follows, we summarize some of the key issues raised by the contributions to each part of the book. We conclude with an examination of the common themes across the 11 chapters.

Part 1: Teaching for Change

In chapter 2, Nelson examines how one teacher, Roxanne, used lesbian/gay themes to explore cultural meanings in her grammar-based ESL class in a community college in the United States. In a lesson on modal auxiliaries, the students, hailing from 13 different countries and ranging in age from early 20s to 70s, were asked to explain the scenario *These two women are walking arm in arm*. The scenario was one of a number of similarly ambiguous scenarios on a class worksheet. In the ensuing discussion, Roxanne coordinated a productive debate on lesbian/gay cultural practices by framing questions in a highly skilled manner. Instead of asking, for example, "Do you think lesbians should hold hands in public?" she asked, "How did you learn to interpret public displays of affection between two women in the United States?" This line of questioning enabled her to focus on the extent to which sexual identities are culturally situated and to demonstrate that what counts as normal is not inherent but socially constructed. The discussion also provided students with great insight into the ways in which modal auxiliaries are used for acts of speculation. Blending grammar teaching with exploration of gay/lesbian issues, Nelson powerfully demonstrates that topics previously seen as taboo have great potential for the teaching of both linguistic and intercultural competence.

Although most research in the field of TESOL focuses on the experiences of English teachers, as in chapter 2, or on those of English language learners who are students, in chapter 3 Boxer and Tyler focus on the relatively powerful position of English language learners who are instructors in U.S. universities. These instructors, called international teaching assistants (ITAs), constitute about 20% of all graduate assistants on U.S. campuses and, according to Boxer and Tyler, are highly likely to confront issues of sexual harassment at some point in their tenure as teaching assistants. Because what is considered sexual harassment differs from one context to another and one culture to the next, Boxer and Tyler conducted quantitative and qualitative research on the perceptions of 12 scenarios by a mixed group of ITAs and U.S. undergraduates, focusing in particular on Chinese-speaking and Spanish-speaking ITAs. Their chapter represents the synthesis of previous research, focusing on cross-cultural pragmatics relevant to ITA training. Their central finding is that ITAs are aware that there are particular conventions for what is considered appropriate or inappropriate behavior with respect to students in the United States and that these conventions are frequently different from those in the ITAs' home countries. However, ITAs are sometimes mystified by subtle distinctions and can overgeneralize differences. In their ITA training program, Boxer and Tyler alert ITAs to relevant legal definitions, invite U.S. undergraduates to discussion groups, and ask ITAs to keep journals of their student-teacher interactions, all with the goal of helping ITAs achieve a successful and positive teaching experience and prevent cross-cultural miscommunication.

In chapter 4, Jordan explores the extent to which feminist composition pedagogy, which has tended to focus on native English speakers, can be applied to the ESL tutoring that takes place in college-based writing centers. In particular, he seeks to raise awareness about institutional and gender-related politics in and around writing centers, and show how these politics can be harnessed for the benefit of students in general and ESL students in particular. A writing center, Jordan argues, is an ideal place for the practice of feminist composition pedagogy in that it is an educational site that views students as a source of knowledge, focuses on both process and product in writing, and seeks to decenter authority, particularly with reference to gendered inequities. In following hooks' (1994) example of making theory out of practice in order to inform and transform practice, he surveyed ESL students and tutors involved in the writing center at the Pennsylvania State University, in the United States, investigating how students perceived the writing center, writing tutors, and the process of writing. Findings from both students and tutors suggest, among other things, that a writing center should be a safe place that does not look or feel like a classroom and that tutors should exercise flexibility in engaging students' native rhetorical abilities while addressing demands for standardized English expression.

Part 2: Student Voices

Drawing on their research in Malaysia, Govindasamy and David (chapter 5) describe a study that investigates gender dynamics in the International Islamic University Malaysia (IIUM), where almost two thirds of the student population consists of women. Govindasamy and David discuss national concern over the dwindling male undergraduate population in the country. The purpose of their study was to determine whether the numerical superiority of the female population marginalized male students and whether the male voice needed to be given greater emphasis in academic decisions. The study was conducted in the English department, where males constituted about 10% of the student population and, in general, did not perform academically as well as females. In their analysis of interactive patterns in the ESL classrooms at IIUM, Govindasamy and David found that the numerical superiority of female students had not minimized the role played by the male students. Subsequent analysis revealed that what differed was the goal orientations of the male and female students, largely influenced by expectations of the society, in which men are expected to be involved in the business world and women in the teaching world. A large majority of the male students indicated in interviews that their motivation to pursue many of the English courses was low because they did not consider the courses to be of practical value. An ESP course, Language for Occupational Purposes, was introduced as a way of meeting the needs of male students at IIUM.

Across the Pacific Ocean, Julé (chapter 6) analyzes interaction in a Grade 2 ESL classroom in Canada, in which all 20 students (11 boys and 9 girls) were of Punjabi descent. Julé focuses on a young girl, Amandeep, who was virtually silent over the 10-month period of data collection. Julé demonstrates that the linguistic space in the classroom was inequitably distributed, with the teacher speaking for about 89% of the time, and the students, for approximately 11%. Of the student talking time, boys spoke approximately 88% and girls about 12% of the time. In terms of student speech acts, boys were markedly more active than girls in responding to questions and offering uninitiated comments. Although most of the girls in the classroom exhibited silent behavior, Amandeep's was particularly noteworthy, and Julé describes three events in which Amandeep sat quietly at her desk while the teacher attended to other students. She suggests that the teacher, who described Amandeep as "a nice, quiet girl" (p. 73) may be implicated in Amandeep's silence. Julé concludes that teachers should pay more attention when girls talk, wait for girls to speak, and structure language lessons to encourage more interaction from girls.

Part 3: Innovations for All

In chapter 7, Parry describes an innovative community library project in a rural region of Uganda. The project, initiated by the headmaster of Kitengesa Comprehensive Secondary School (KCSS), provides both girls and boys with greater access to literacy—particularly in the English language. The goal of the project is to serve not only the children in the school, where the project is based, but also the wider rural community. Parry describes why and how girls, in particular, benefit from and contribute to this library project. Because KCSS is new, poor, and locally based, more girls than boys are students there; parents with resources prefer to send their sons to more established schools. Furthermore, girls are more likely than boys to remain in the local area and will most likely become better caregivers because of their enhanced literacy skills. In addition, Parry found that the girls were more effective than the boys at disseminating library material—the girls were more likely than the boys to read their books aloud, thereby reaching young children and illiterate adults. She concludes that the girls were learning that literacy is not necessarily associated with an alien culture, even if it is in a foreign language, and that it has the potential to improve the quality of rural life.

In another part of the world, Taylor (chapter 8) draws on her research on an innovative antidiscrimination camp in Toronto, Canada, to explore the inextricable links between gender and race. With reference to the compelling stories of two English language learners, Hue and Khatra, she argues that the practice of theorizing ESL learning and teaching is incomplete without a perspective on what she calls *racialized gender*. Taylor describes the leadership camp in which public school students of 15 national origins collectively explored their personal experiences of social difference and discrimination. Through the lens of racialized gender, Taylor argues, Hue and Khatra were able to develop critical understandings of their relationship to their history, their educational experience in Canada, and the issues at stake in "coming to voice in English" (p. 105). Drawing on her research, Taylor offers a number of suggestions for TESOL practitioners who wish to investigate the underlying gendered dynamics of students' language learning and identity negotiation. She notes that language learners need the opportunity to explore their experiences of difference; resources to help explore identity not as something one is but as something one does; and access to discussions that address body image, familial obligations, and personal security in which perspectives are framed by gender relations.

In the final case in Part 3, Rilling and Biles (chapter 9) examine the relationship between gender and technology from their respective positions as instructor and graduate student in a technology course in an MA TESL/TEFL program at a U.S. university. Their action research project was based on the premise that a technology course is an ideal site for developing teachers to learn how gender can affect teacher-student and student-student interactions and that insights from such a course would help developing teachers create safe learning environments for ESL students. They outline the technologies used in the course, such as SyllaBase (2001), e_Chat (Bagneski, 1999), and *Tapped In* (http://www.tappedin.sri.org/); describe the prompts Rilling used to promote discussion on gender and technology; and summarize Biles' responses to each of these learning opportunities. Two central concerns for Rilling and Biles were the extent to which technology could either enhance or compromise the learning community's safety, and how issues of gender and language learning and teaching could be productively examined. They found that the course helped students increase their computer skills while providing greater insight into gender and technology. One particularly interesting finding was the realization that the virtual world, while an imagined reality, is nevertheless a gendered space that evokes real emotions.

Part 4: Insights From Japan

Drawing on her experiences in an all-women's junior college in Japan, Simon-Maeda (chapter 9) describes a feminist course that she developed as part of the Gender and

Language Issues program offered by the English department. In this course, which meets once a week for 15 weeks, Simon-Maeda introduces topics that examine gender inequality from a linguistic perspective, including sexual harassment in the school and workplace, domestic violence, sexism in textbooks and the media, and sexuality. In addition to the lecture format, students complete worksheets and engage in journal writing. Simon-Maeda argues that when learners are given the opportunity to negotiate the meaning of gender and language issues that affect their lives, they can begin to imagine different life trajectories. She uses feminist pedagogical theories and practices to emphasize the importance of establishing dialogic relationships with students by drawing on student experience and carefully monitoring on-task activity. Significantly, she makes the point that she does not expect students to uncritically or passively accept the feminist notions that she espouses, arguing that Western feminists working in non-Western contexts need to be particularly vigilant and reflexive about their pedagogy. Rather, she encourages students to develop an awareness "on their own terms" (p. 137) of how women have come to be positioned in a given context and why they might hold certain views about a particular issue.

In chapter 11, Saft and Ohara describe a 4-day module on gender that they developed to encourage Japanese university students to consider the dynamic quality of gender and to think critically about the position of women in Japanese society. The module, taught by Saft, included an examination of the gendered use of language in English and Japanese, an assigned reading on the position of women in Japan, a discussion of the practice of *onna rashii hanashikata* (a womanly way of speaking in Japanese), and a questionnaire on the module as a whole. Saft and Ohara were encouraged by the module's success, finding that both male and female students engaged in discussion on the topic. They found, however, that some male students remained somewhat resistant to the idea that Japanese women experienced discrimination, whereas the women, more responsive, recognized that both men and women need to be committed to gender equality if women are to have greater options in life. Saft and Ohara conclude that discussions about gender are most successful when students have the opportunity to respond to very specific exercises that relate to their daily lives rather than discuss gender as an abstract topic.

The development of "an explicit critical feminist pedagogy" (p. 155) is the central theme of chapter 12, in which Cohen describes in detail how she incorporates feminist pedagogy in an advanced EFL undergraduate course in a private language university in Japan. This intensive, 6-hour-per-week, year-long course for sophomores offers multiple opportunities for students to investigate the relationship between language and gender. Cohen begins by inviting students to examine the evaluations she has received from the previous year's course. She asks students to summarize particular excerpts from the student evaluations and then consider why she has chosen the particular excerpt for analysis. In this way, Cohen anticipates the initial disorientation students may experience in the course, and prepares them for the challenges and rewards. Cohen describes two teaching sequences that illustrate the ways in which she seeks to engage dialogically with text. The first sequence is based on a Japanese TV news report delivered by a demure young woman and a confident older man; the second is a class exercise on neologisms. Cohen demonstrates convincingly that students can be encouraged to develop the oral, interpretive, and word-attack skills common to many EFL classrooms while gaining a greater insight into gendered dimensions of language learning and use.

◈ COMMON THEMES IN CRITICAL FEMINIST PRAXIS IN TESOL

As suggested above, all the contributors share a desire to promote a more equitable relationship between members of different groups in ESL and EFL contexts. Our own hopes lie with critical praxis, both in and outside the classroom. Although we recognize important differences between diverse critical and feminist pedagogies (and address them in other work; see Norton & Toohey, 2004; Pavlenko, 2004), in this volume we emphasize their common aims with regard to the relationship between language, gender, and education: (a) to demystify normative discourses of gender by clarifying the mechanisms of symbolic domination, (b) to engage students with cross-cultural differences in the meanings of gender and sexuality, and (c) to raise the level of critical and *multivoiced consciousness* (Kramsch & von Hoene, 2001, p. 288). Of particular interest and importance to us are recent attempts to devise critical and feminist pedagogies in ESL (Pennycook, 1999, 2001) and EFL contexts (Casanave & Yamashiro, 1996; Fujimura-Fanselow & Vaughn, 1991; MacGregor, 1998; McMahill, 1997, 2001; Smith & Yamashiro, 1998; Yamashiro, 2000), and we sincerely hope that this volume will contribute to these explorations.

Although the discussion of common themes could proceed in a number of ways, we focus on the distinctive features of critical feminist praxis in TESOL as described by the volume contributors. The features below are those most commonly shared across the studies and are ones that stem from the poststructuralist feminist framework outlined above.

- Instead of working with a fully predetermined and decontextualized curriculum, critical educators organize the curriculum around the needs and lived experiences of particular populations, such as young Japanese women or marginalized college students (chapters 4, 10, 11, and 12). Furthermore, critical feminist praxis in TESOL does not reduce teachers and students to just men and women. Rather, it engages with full individuals, who are positioned not only in terms of gender but also in terms of age, race, class, ethnicity, national origins, immigrant status, sexuality, or (dis)ability (chapters 2 and 8).

- While making instruction relevant to students' lives, critical pedagogies also recognize *hidden identities* (Vandrick, 1997b) and illuminate gender inequalities, incorporating such topics as gay/lesbian issues (chapter 2), dominant gender ideologies (chapter 11), domestic violence (chapter 10), sexual harassment in the workplace (chapters 3 and 10), gender inequities in access to technology (chapter 9), or sexist language used to disenfranchise women (chapters 10, 11, and 12).

- Both EFL and ESL classrooms represent unique spaces where different linguistic and cultural worlds come into contact. They offer unparalleled opportunities for teachers to engage with cross-cultural differences and the social construction of gender and sexuality (chapters 2, 3, 7, and 8) and thus help students develop linguistic and intercultural competence, or *multivoiced consciousness* (Kramsch & von Hoene, 2001). This approach respectfully acknowledges students' and teachers' own diverse backgrounds while engaging them with alternative systems of knowledge, values, beliefs, and modes of gender performance. In turn, familiarity with alternative discourses of gender and sexuality enhances students' ability to differentiate between compliments, joking, banter, and sexual harassment, and to respond in context-appropriate ways (chapters 3 and 10).

- Transformative classroom practices, such as teacher-led discussions, personal storytelling activities, or journal writing, incorporate students' lived experiences and then locate their experiences and beliefs within larger social contexts (chapters 4, 9, and 10). Such practices engage students' imagination and allow them to develop critical consciousness (chapters 3 and 11) and to imagine alternative ways of being in the world (chapters 7 and 10). In this regard, the development of voice and the ability to *impose reception* (Bourdieu, 1982/1991) are central to critical feminist praxis.

- Teachers need to be proactive and well prepared to handle controversial topics while maintaining a positive dynamic in the classroom (chapters 2, 4, 9, and 12). Furthermore, they need to pay particular attention to learners who may be silenced by the dominant culture (chapters 6 and 8) or the local educational context (chapter 5).

- Empowerment in the classroom takes place through the process of teachers and students sharing control and negotiating relationships. Teachers' positions become decentered while students gain greater control of the classroom and the choice and management of discussion topics (chapters 4, 9, and 10). Empowerment can also take place through grassroots local initiatives outside the classroom, such as community library projects (chapter 7) or antidiscrimination camps (chapter 8).

◈ CONCLUSION

We acknowledge our debt to the scholars and educators who have been among the first to express concerns about gender inequities and social justice and address the relationship between English education and gender: Chris Casanave, David Corson, Katherine Davies, Cheiron McMahill, Alastair Pennycook, Jane Sunderland, Stephanie Vandrick, and Amy Yamashiro. We are extremely proud to continue this tradition; we see this volume as a tribute to earlier work and a precursor of studies to come.

◈ CONTRIBUTORS

Bonny Norton is a professor in the Department of Language and Literacy Education at the University of British Columbia, in Canada. Her research and publications address the relationship between identity, language learning, and social change. She is the author of *Identity and Language Learning: Gender, Ethnicity and Educational Change* (Pearson Education, 2000) and co-editor (with Kelleen Toohey) of *Critical Pedagogies and Language Learning* (Cambridge University Press, 2004).

Aneta Pavlenko is an associate professor in the College of Education, Temple University, in the United States. Her research and publications address the relationship between multilingualism, identity, gender, and emotions. She is a co-editor (with Adrian Blackledge, Ingrid Piller, & Marya Teutsch-Dwyer) of *Multilingualism, Second Language Learning, and Gender* (Mouton de Gruyter, 2001) and (with Adrian Blackledge) of *Negotiation of Identities in Multilingual Contexts* (Multilingual Matters, 2004).

PART 1

Teaching for Change

CHAPTER 2

Beyond Straight Grammar: Using Lesbian/Gay Themes to Explore Cultural Meanings

Cynthia D. Nelson

I think that at the time we're talking about same gender relationships I could be insecure, nervous, what are students thinking, um, am I gonna lose them or are they gonna get more engaged, what's gonna happen here. But when I'm beyond those teaching moments I can see how valuable that was whether or not we ever talk about it again. . . . I think the message is we can talk about issues that are often considered taboo or inappropriate. (Roxanne, an ESL teacher)

◈ INTRODUCTION

Why and how are lesbian, gay, bisexual, or transgendered issues and perspectives being raised in English language classes, and what teaching challenges and opportunities arise as a result? This was a central question in my doctoral research, which involved observing ESL classes at three educational institutions in two cities in the United States; interviewing the teachers and adult students about their experiences of lesbian/gay topics in class; and facilitating four focus groups for teachers on sexual identities in ESL, held at a university and at an international TESOL convention (C. D. Nelson, in press). A total of 111 students and teachers participated in that study. This case looks at how one of the teachers used lesbian/gay themes to explore cultural meanings in her grammar-based ESL class at a community college in the United States.

Drawing on class observations, class handouts, and teacher interviews[1] (as well as relevant literature), this chapter augments my previous work on Roxanne's class (C. Nelson, 1999). The earlier article included a transcript from a class discussion accompanied by a commentary of my own moment-to-moment thoughts and impressions while observing. This chapter examines portions of that class discussion but from a different vantage point.

The interest here is in how the teacher framed lesbian/gay themes in a way that led to the exploration of cultural meanings and meaning-making practices. This chapter looks not only at what was said during the class discussion but also why the

---

[1] In some interviews, I used a technique called *stimulated recall* (see Nunan, 1992, p. 94). I showed the teacher a rough transcript of part of a class session and played the selected portion of the audiotape, stopping it whenever the teacher had something to say about what she had been thinking or feeling at the time.

teacher paved the way for it, how she framed her questions to the class, and what concerns she was taking into account. Roxanne's teaching practices are examined with a view to offering practical suggestions to other teachers.

This case illustrates that discussing lesbian/gay subject matter can be a means of illuminating "the workings of language and culture" (C. Nelson, 1999, p. 389)—and that in this endeavor, poststructuralist theories can be of practical use.

◈ CONTEXT

Roxanne's grammar-based ESL class met 10 hours each week at a community college in the United States, as part of a government-funded program for refugees and immigrants. The 26 students were from 13 countries: Brazil, Cambodia, Ethiopia, Gambia, Hong Kong, Japan, Korea, Mexico, Morocco, the Philippines, Somalia, Thailand, and Vietnam. As this combination of countries suggests, the students had notably divergent life experiences. Their ages ranged from early 20s to early 70s, and there were equal numbers of women and men in the class. They had been living in the United States from a few months to a few years, and although many were working and several had retired, most intended to pursue further study.

Roxanne had 20 years' experience teaching English in the United States (from which she hailed) and in Asia. The grammatical and functional objectives for this intermediate-level class had already been determined, but Roxanne had free rein as to how to approach them.

A central concern for Roxanne was that students be treated with respect and dignity in her class. Another priority was to make the class meaningful and relevant to students' day-to-day lives. As Roxanne put it,

> I feel accountable for covering certain grammar structures. At the same time I . . . really want each class to be relevant for all 28 people and useful. I mean right now in their life useful. . . . And make sense to them. And not seem as contrived and from a book as it actually is in terms of what I'm accountable for.

To Roxanne, it was important to make it possible for lesbian/gay themes to be raised in her class. During my 2-week observation period, posted near the classroom was a flier advertising a local event for lesbian/gay rights. The community college was located on the main artery of what was commonly referred to as a gay neighborhood, within a city that had adopted policies prohibiting discrimination on the basis of sexual identity in areas such as employment and housing.

◈ LANGUAGE AND GENDER[2]

Lesbian/Gay Topics in the English Language Classroom

Roxanne was not unusual in her desire to integrate lesbian/gay topics into her teaching. Since the early 1990s, interest has been growing in ensuring that English language teaching (ELT) approaches do not presume, and curricula and materials do

---

[2] Although this chapter addresses sexual identity rather than gender per se, the two identity domains are inextricably linked.

not portray, an exclusively heterosexual world—that is, one in which all students and their interlocutors are necessarily straight, and everything students say, read, and think about pertains only to straight people. Newsletter articles and conference presentations (and, increasingly, academic publications) have described efforts to

- integrate gay and lesbian themes and perspectives into curricula (e.g., Summerhawk, 1998) and teaching resources (e.g., Clarke, Dobson, & Silberstein, 1996)

- address homophobia and heterosexism in the profession and in the classroom (e.g., Benesch, 1999; Kappra, 1998/1999; Vandrick, 1997a)

- consider the needs of students (and teachers) who identify as lesbian, bisexual, gay, or transgendered (e.g., Jewell, 1998; Saint Pierre, 1994)

However, engaging with these aims in ESL classes is unlikely to be simple or straightforward. Some teachers (even gay-identified teachers) may feel they lack know-how on this subject matter. In Ó'Móchain, Mitchell, and Nelson (2003), Mitchell quotes a colleague who explains, "We ESL teachers are not prepared to treat gay eventualities in our language classroom, neither are we trained to design materials that address the issue properly" (p. 129). A related concern is that discussing lesbian/gay topics in class might lead to the airing of "opposing views," which could threaten the "whole group dynamics for the rest of the course" (p. 131), as another teacher quoted by Mitchell puts it.

For some, the question is not how but whether gay/lesbian issues should even be addressed. O'Loughlin (2001) reports that "some teachers have told me they will not broach the topic of homosexuality in the classroom as they are concerned it will be offensive to learners from some cultural backgrounds" (p. 39). O'Loughlin considers this attitude "quite paternalistic," noting that "this silence may . . . betray such teachers' own discomfort in talking about these kinds of issues" (p. 39). He points out that "students of all nationalities are aware that gay people exist"—and, importantly, that "[students] will shape their own views on the subject" (p. 39). Instead of protecting students from potentially controversial topics, teachers need to acknowledge that "learners have agency and are more than capable of exercising it" (p. 40).

O'Loughlin (2001) further argues that instead of adopting a "simplistic . . . narrow, homogenised and overly prescriptive view" about what is or is not considered culturally appropriate, teachers should expose students to multiple "gender roles and behaviours" (p. 39). The aim is not to dictate to students "how to live in 'Australian society'" (in this case) but rather to expose students to the diversity they are likely to encounter in the new country—thereby helping them make "informed choices about what is appropriate for their own lives" (pp. 39–40).

My research strongly indicates that as ESL students interact at school, at work, in the home, with the media, and elsewhere, they encounter gay/lesbian themes—and, furthermore, that discussing these themes in class may give rise to uncertainties and mismatched expectations (C. D. Nelson, in press). Given the prevalence of lesbian/gay themes in everyday encounters, combined with the potential for intercultural misunderstandings inside and outside the classroom, ESL students may benefit when these themes are engaged with instead of avoided, as I argue in Ó'Móchain et al. (2003).

Poststructuralist Theories of Identity and Culture

What might it mean to teach in ways that help unpack the complexities of negotiating lesbian/gay themes in day-to-day interactions? The remainder of this chapter considers this question by looking at poststructuralist theories of identity and culture, and then at Roxanne's teaching practices. Thus the practical suggestions that conclude the chapter are grounded in theory and practice (or theory-in-practice).

Identity

In a modernist or humanist view, people are thought to be "endowed with a stable 'self' constituted by a set of static characteristics such as sex, class, race, sexual orientation" (Lather, 1991, p. 5). But poststructuralist theories (e.g., S. Hall, 1992; Spivak, 1990; Weedon, 1987) have challenged this notion, considering identities instead to be

- constructed and negotiated through social relations
- multiple, able to be foregrounded or backgrounded, and even contradictory
- sites of struggle
- acts of strategy

In short, identities are conceptualized not as nouns but as verbs (see O'Loughlin, 2001, writing about gender).

Following this theoretical shift, the aim is to get beyond what Britzman (1995) refers to as *pedagogies of inclusion* to what I have called *pedagogies of inquiry* (C. Nelson, 1999). With an inquiry approach, the teaching aim is not to include minority sexual identities in order to encourage tolerance. It is rather to acknowledge and explore the ways in which sexual identities are part of day-to-day interactions. The focus is on analyzing linguistic and cultural practices (in this case, those pertaining to sexual identities) with a view to enabling second language learners to participate in those practices more fully, or perhaps more strategically.

Culture

Questions of culture arise in the class discussion featured in this case, so before turning to the classroom, I consider the notion of culture. A modernist view of culture informs much of the literature of ELT, which often uses the term to indicate "concrete, separate, behavior-defining ethnic, national and international groups with material permanence and clear boundaries" (Holliday, 1999, p. 242). However, as with identity, there have been shifts in ways of theorizing culture. As Usher and Edwards (1994) explain,

> Postmodernism breaks with modernism in that the latter is a process of cultural differentiation producing clearly defined boundaries of practice and meaning whilst postmodernism on the other hand is a process of de-differentiation where boundaries break down. Consequently different cultural spheres lose their autonomy. (p. 13, citing Lash, 1990)

With poststructuralism, then, regional or national cultures are not considered monolithic, mutually exclusive, or static but heterogeneous, overlapping, and constantly changing (Holliday, 1999). Cultures are "in a constant process of transformation, redefinition, and reconceptualisation" (Simon, 1992, p. 25), and this process involves struggle and contestation (McLaren & Lankshear, 1993). Thus cultures (much like identities) are considered not entities but processes, and these processes are not mutually exclusive but interactive and mutually inflecting.

In terms of teaching English, Candlin (1989) argues for a "focus on inter-cultural understanding rather than on cross-cultural accumulating" (p. 10). An intercultural emphasis, as opposed to a cross-cultural one, underscores the fact that cultures are neither fixed nor separate from each other. In addition, it keeps the focus grounded in actual interactions. As Sarangi (1995) explains, "While 'cross-cultural' attends to abstract entities across cultural borders, the 'intercultural' deals with the analysis of an *actual* encounter *between* two participants who represent different linguistic and cultural backgrounds" (p. 22).

An intercultural focus pertains not only to interactions between individuals but to the shifting identities of individuals. As S. Hall (1992) puts it,

> Everywhere, cultural identities are emerging which are not fixed, but poised, *in transition* between different positions; which draw on different cultural traditions at the same time; and which are the product of those complicated cross-overs and cultural mixes which are increasingly common in a globalised world. (p. 310)

It is crucial that these ideas be taken into account in ESL. As Norton (1997) points out, although "immigrant learners' experiences in their native country may be a significant part of their identity, these are constantly being mediated by their experiences in the new country" (in Norton's case, Canada) (p. 413). This suggests that it is not enough for teachers to simply invite students to discuss their native countries. Instead, Norton argues, teachers need to provide opportunities for students "to critically examine experiences in their native countries in the light of more recent experiences in Canada or to critically examine their experiences in Canada in light of experiences in the native country" (p. 413).

Something of this sort occurred in Roxanne's class, as the next section describes.

❖ DESCRIPTION

Roxanne generally attempted to embed the grammar points she had to teach within themes that students were raising in class and in their homework. She noted that in their assigned journals, some students were writing about lesbian/gay themes on their own initiative, with no such topics featured in their textbook. Nearly midway through the term, Roxanne decided to incorporate this topic during a unit of work on modal auxiliary verbs. Roxanne's approach to teaching modals was to consider not only their lexicogrammatical aspects but also their social functions—in this case, how modals are used in speculating or drawing conclusions based on perceptions and how this use can be linked to, as she put it, "stereotyping."

SPECULATIONS AND CONCLUSIONS

Directions: For each situation below, think of 3 or 4 different possibilities to explain what is occurring.

Example: Those boys are hitting each other! *They must be fighting. Or, they could be playing around. They might be pretending to hit each other.*

1. She is talking so loudly to that man!

2. I saw my friend José hugging a strange woman on the sidewalk last night.

3. Those two women are walking arm in arm.

[...]

FIGURE 1. Worksheet

The Worksheet

Roxanne wrote a worksheet (see Figure 1) and assigned it for homework. After class I asked her why she included the scenario about the two women (No. 3).

> [It's] a beautiful example because people see, especially on Oxford Street [a pseudonym]. It seemed to be a NATURAL example. . . . Almost across the board if a person's from this country [the United States] they're gonna visit that conclusion or speculation that the women are lesbians. And I think in other countries you could talk for a long time before that particular thing could come up for people.

In planning the next class session, Roxanne was eager to follow up in some way on that scenario—in fact, she explained that "the reason I did the whole worksheet was for No. 3." However, given the (potentially) lesbian subject matter, she was not sure whether "she should or could go deeper."

> I tread softly on saying "So what do you think about that?" . . . It's possible that they're dying to be asked. But it's possible that they . . . don't really feel comfortable with the whole thing. . . . Being the kind of teacher I am where someone would say to me "Can I ask you a personal question?" And I just blush and sweat and freak out. . . . I don't want to be so revealing in this public space. . . . So I'm hoping that this will come up naturally.

Before the next class began, Roxanne said she was feeling "nervous about that worksheet." She wanted to follow up the scenario of two women in some way, but she did not know how students would respond to it or even whether that particular scenario would stand out.

Although Roxanne was open to introducing lesbian/gay themes, or to having a student do so, at the same time she felt somewhat concerned about this. One reason was that she might feel, as she put it, "on the hot seat."

> I don't know . . . if I'm gonna get a homophobic comment. . . . I think people look at me like "What's she gonna do or say?" . . . There's . . . always this fine balance of saying something that resonates where they are . . . and also probably challenges them but . . . not to lose them.

Another concern of Roxanne's was that she might appear uncomfortable.

> I want to let students know that even if I look nervous or blush, that I do want this conversation to happen . . ., so there's this nervousness of mine to try to project across cultures that, uh, I wanna have this conversation. . . . [Because] I'm not comfortable with that topic being so uncomfortable for most of us in the world. The topic of two women in love or two men in love.

Another factor adding to Roxanne's sense of apprehension was that she anticipated a wide range of experiences and viewpoints among the students in relation to lesbian/gay subject matter: "A lot of people in the room have a different starting place about this conversation. . . . Some people live it every day, and some people don't think about it much . . . or don't wanna think about it." She expected that some of the students would themselves identify as gay or lesbian while others would find discussing homosexuality unfamiliar or even undesirable. It might be a challenge to accommodate this mix of perspectives and attitudes.

There was also the question of Roxanne's own sexual identity. In a previous class comprising newly arrived international students who wanted to study "lesbian and gay people," a student had asked Roxanne if she was a lesbian. Roxanne had found this question disturbing and unsettling, and she dreaded the prospect of facing it again in front of another class.

> I'm afraid somebody's gonna, um, judge that part of me that doesn't yet know how to label myself . . . I don't want to, even. So that if the issue came up in class . . . I would already walk into it with sensitivity.

Given her desire to integrate lesbian/gay themes along with her concerns about doing so, Roxanne hoped these themes would be raised in an unobtrusive—what she called a "natural"—way.

Group Work and Class Discussion

Once in class, Roxanne had students form small groups to go through their answers to the worksheet and the reasons underpinning their speculations. As Roxanne circulated, a number of students asked her questions pertaining to the scenario of two women, such as whether it was possible to say *I am loving someone* and *I fall love*. As Roxanne interacted with each of the small groups, the focus was on grammatical structure, not on "how they felt about the situation": "I wasn't really asking 'Why do you say that? What makes you speculate that?' as much as 'So if you wanna express this, this is how you do it.'"

After 15 minutes of small-group work, Roxanne reconvened the class and invited questions about any of the worksheet scenarios. Roxanne fielded grammar questions about some of the other scenarios until finally, mindful that the class session was nearing its ending time, she decided to bring up the scenario of two women walking arm in arm. She did this by linking it to a student's question about using the continuous tense in one of the other scenarios, and she was grateful for "that NATURAL segue."

Roxanne elicited some answers to No. 3 and then guided the class through an analysis of the grammar problems of sentences such as *They could be loving*. Focusing on the grammar was "part of me as a teacher," but also a means of coping with nervousness—"something to hang onto."

As the discussion continued, one student (a man from Gambia) offered his answer: "They could be lesbians." Roxanne then attempted to shift the focus away from grammar and onto the meanings ascribed to same-sex affection in public in the students' home countries versus in the United States. Most students seemed to agree that, in their countries, same-sex affection did not indicate gayness but that in the United States it did. Roxanne then asked how they had learned the local meaning. (For a complete transcript of Turns 159–246 of the class discussion, see C. Nelson, 1999.)

> 155 Roxanne: So I wanna know, how did you find out it was different in this country? Or, it could be different?
> [...]
> 159 Roxanne: How about two men, 30 years old, walking down Oxford Street, they're brothers. Holding hands, yes or no?
> 160 Students: No, no, no.
> 161 Roxanne: How did you learn that?

During the lively 15-minute discussion, an impressive half of the 26 students spoke in spite of the fact that getting and keeping the floor was not easy; most of Roxanne's questions generated energetic responses, with a number of students speaking at once.

The students raised a range of issues and dilemmas about negotiating cultural meanings and meaning-making practices. For example, Raúl, a man from Mexico, said that in his country, it would be dangerous if two men were to hold hands. He contrasted this with the situation in the United States.

> 209 Raúl: It's like, uh, if were in my hometown, we see two people walk, two mens, holding hands. Afraid they're gonna get shot. (little laugh)
> [...]
> 218 Raúl: So normal here to see couples holding
> 219 Roxanne: Yeah.
> 220 Raúl: Same sex together.

Given such sharp contrasts in the cultural practices that are associated with sexual identities, Fabiola, a woman from Brazil, raised the complex question of how to act when returning to her country after living away for some time.

> 228 Fabiola: . . . I . . . be like long time here and when get back, you know go back to my country again, I don't know 1 year after that or something like. And I'm gonna see my friends! I'm gonna HUG them and walking you know! (little laugh) And like, uh, you think people- maybe if you would do this here people "Ah! Maybe they are gay!"

Students noted that sexual identities are linked not only to cultural meanings but to gendered meanings.

> 252 Raúl: I think women will be different. I mean you can see womens everywhere in the world. They can hug and, you know, be kind of so sissy.

Neuriden, a man from Morocco, raised another intercultural dilemma. He was not sure how to interact with children in the United States because touching them might be seen in a sexual way.

264	Neuriden:	In my country they was playing around me. In my country I can play with them, I can touch them.
265	Roxanne:	You can?
266	Neuriden:	But here I was like afraid. (crosses his arms over his chest and laughs)

Raúl brought up the point that cultural differences are found not just between cultures but within them (intraculturally), citing contrasting responses in different parts of the United States to male-male affection in public.

302	Raúl:	It depends on the city.
303	Roxanne:	It depends on the city?
304	Raúl:	. . . Here . . . it's good. . . . You go back to the East Coast, South, and Carolina, they'll BURN you there.

After class Roxanne reported being very pleased with the discussion. She felt the students had engaged with not only the grammatical form but also the intercultural complexities of formulating speculations. She also felt that she had benefited from the opportunity to reflect on her own teaching in relation to gay/lesbian topics.

> It was a great experience. . . . I'm really glad it happened when you were in the classroom too. Because . . . I get questions and more opportunities to think about it, which I think will make it easier for me to do this again. Continue. To not feel so freaked out by things that are part of life.

The students I interviewed were also very positive about this class discussion. (See C. D. Nelson, in press, for an examination of their perspectives, along with the classroom experiences of more than 100 teachers and students at other educational institutions.)

◈ DISTINGUISHING FEATURES

What was particularly innovative or noteworthy about Roxanne's attempts to acknowledge the multiplicity of sexual identities that exists beyond (and within) her classroom?

Taking Risks

On one level, what Roxanne did could be considered quite simple. In a worksheet, she included one scenario about same-sex affection, and in a follow-up class discussion, she initiated a discussion about that scenario, an activity pattern that was typical in her classroom. But as I have explained, Roxanne found these teaching events somewhat challenging because of the gay theme. Despite her own discomfort, she took the risk of making space for, and then pursuing, the lesbian topic.

Although students were writing about lesbian/gay matters in their journals (which only the teacher read), none had yet raised these matters in front of their peers. Although students working in small groups were discussing the same-sex scenario and asking questions about it, when the class reconvened, none brought it up.

If Roxanne had not included that scenario on the worksheet or raised it for discussion in the whole group, even those students who wanted to bring up the subject may have felt it was inappropriate or too threatening to do so in the classroom context. If Roxanne had not taken it upon herself to create an opportunity for lesbian/gay themes to emerge, or if she had not responded with enthusiasm when this occurred, then the intriguing class discussion would probably not have ensued.

Framing Questions Meaningfully and Respectfully

Another distinguishing feature was how Roxanne framed her questions. She sought to make her class meaningful to all the students, respect students' privacy, and avoid distressing them in any way (knowing that some had experienced the traumas of war).

Keeping these objectives in mind, I note that Roxanne did not elicit students' personal experiences of seeing same-sex affection (or of engaging in it themselves). Instead, she posed a hypothetical situation in which students were asked to imagine (not to recall) witnessing same-sex affection ("Those two women are walking arm in arm") and to respond by speculating about what might be going on (see Figure 1). Through a series of questions, the students reached a general agreement that in the United States two women or two men displaying affection in public would tend to be seen as lovers whereas in many other countries this might not be the case. Roxanne then asked the class, "How did you learn that?"

This question gets at how people go about learning what unfamiliar cultural practices mean or might mean. By framing the interpretive process as potentially confusing, or inconclusive, Roxanne emphasized "*ways* of knowing" rather than "*states* of knowledge" (Bernstein, 1971, p. 57). In this way she steered clear of inviting discussion about the controversies that sometimes surround same-sex affection or relationships. She did not ask, for example, "Do you think lesbians should hold hands in public?"

She also managed to generate discussion about lesbians and gay men, but without making it prohibitive for lesbian and gay students to participate in the discussion. In other words, her questions did not construct the entire class as necessarily straight. She did not ask, for example, "When you see gay people walking down the street, how are they different from you?" (This made-up question and the one above may seem unlikely, but teachers in my study posed such questions to their classes, which is why I include them here in contrast to Roxanne's approach.)

Framing Sexual Identities as Culturally Situated

Also noteworthy is that Roxanne framed sexual identities as relational acts that are culturally situated, not as core inner truths that are timeless and universal and can be either expressed or suppressed (see C. Nelson, 1999). The emphasis was on examining local, everyday interactions, not exploring personal feelings or debating social issues (as it was in other classes that I observed). The focus was on how sexual identities are performed or communicated in particular contexts, and how meanings are made through this process. This focus made it possible to talk about the challenging aspects of negotiating *acts of identity* (Le Page & Tabouret-Keller, 1985), especially in intercultural contexts.

The class discussion touched on how sexual identities are open to interpretation and, therefore, misinterpretation, and how their meanings are not self-evident but must be learned. Interestingly, Roxanne did not specifically address sociopolitical questions in asking students how they learned that in the United States, two 30-year-old men holding hands are more likely to be lovers than to be brothers. But at the same time, students' responses to her question underscored the fact that sexual identities are not necessarily valued equally or neutrally but involve power differentials (as one student put it, in some contexts, two men holding hands might get shot whereas in other contexts this hand-holding might be considered normal).

What counts as normal or natural, then, is not inherent but socially created—and these norms are negotiated, managed, and contested. The underlying implication seems to be that sexual identities can be made to seem normal (or not normal). Although Roxanne's intention was not to debate the politics of sexual identities, the way she framed the discussion made it possible to acknowledge, or at least touch on, these aspects—but without courting controversy or setting up an issues-based debate.

Foregrounding the Ambiguities of Identity Categories

Another interesting aspect of teaching lesbian/gay topics involves the possibility that teachers' own sexual identities may be foregrounded in the classroom, which raises complex questions about how teachers are managing or representing their own (sexual) identities in class and what this might mean in relation to their teaching practices.

Whereas many contributors to the grassroots literature on gay/queer issues in language education (cited earlier in this chapter) themselves identify openly and unambiguously as either lesbian, gay, bisexual, or straight, Roxanne did not identify with any of these categories. In the classroom or in the profession, when discussing lesbian or gay (or bisexual, transgendered, queer, or straight) matters, language professionals need to keep in mind that some people (students, their interlocutors, their teachers) do not ascribe to any of these identity categories. This may be because they are questioning or in transition from one category to another, because they object to the practice of classifying people according to sexual identity, or because they simply do not consider this identity domain significant enough to warrant attention.

In Roxanne's case, the openness and ambiguity that she herself felt in relation to sexual identity may have shaped her teaching practices—to good effect. Instead of fixed identities or positionings, the teaching focus was on the ambiguity of sexual identities, which worked well in this lesson about speculating.

Furthermore, the fact that gay themes were somewhat beyond Roxanne's comfort zone may have served more as a resource than a liability, causing her to carefully think through her teaching approach beforehand (while being prepared to take up opportunities as they arose in the moment). This suggests that for teachers, reflecting on their own motives for, and concerns about, engaging lesbian/gay themes in class may enhance their teaching practices.

◈ PRACTICAL IDEAS

Drawing on Roxanne's experiences, this section offers practical suggestions for teachers who wish to acknowledge a range of sexual identities in terms of both what gets talked about in the classroom and whose perspectives get taken into account. The intention in putting forward concrete ideas in the form of questions for teachers to ask themselves is neither to be prescriptive nor to oversimplify complex matters but at least to put something on the table in the hope of sparking collegial discussions.

Create Opportunities for Discussing Lesbian/Gay Matters

Make a point of creating opportunities for students to discuss lesbian/gay issues:

- Have you considered the ways in which sexual identities feature within day-to-day interactions?

- Do your curricula and learning materials include representations across a range of sexual identities (straight, lesbian, gay, bisexual, transgendered, queer)?

- Where might there be openings to acknowledge this multiplicity and invite students to engage with it in some way?

- How might you proactively make spaces for lesbian/gay matters instead of relying on students to do so, as they may be taking their cue from you?

Address Tasks and Questions to Students of Any Sexual Identity

Frame classroom activities so that they are directed to students of any sexual identity:

- When framing learning tasks, activities, assignments, and discussion questions, do you consider to whom these are addressed?

- Are they directed to, and relevant to, students across a range of sexual identities?

- Do the tasks and questions invite the ready participation of all students, whatever their own positionings vis-à-vis sexual identity?

Use Lesbian/Gay Themes to Foster Inquiry

Make sure to use lesbian/gay themes to foster inquiry in ways that further the objectives of the class:

- When lesbian/gay themes arise, are they framed in ways that encourage inquiry, invite multiple interpretations, and take into account intercultural complexities?

- Are taken-for-granted notions problematized, explored, and opened up?

- Is it clear to students that gay themes are being used in ways that further the broader learning objectives of the class?

Maximize Choices

Throughout the process of negotiating lesbian/gay themes, maximize choices for you and the students:

- When exploring bisexual/lesbian/gay themes in class, do you make a point of finding out students' responses as a lesson progresses, to help you plan your next step?

- Do students have choices about the ways in which, and possibly the extent or the intensity to which, they are to participate in gay-themed discussions?

- Do they have choices about how personal or impersonal they wish to be?

Reflect on Your Own Motives and Concerns

Reflect on how your teaching practices are informed by your own motives and concerns with regard to (bi-, hetero-, and homo-) sexual identities:

- What do you hope to achieve by integrating gay, bisexual, and lesbian themes (or by not doing so)?

- How do your own experiences and viewpoints on this subject matter shape your teaching practices?

- Do you have any concerns about broaching the topic or dealing with it when others do so?

- Might the students have similar concerns as they negotiate discursive interactions in class and out of class—and if so, how can you structure learning tasks that will be of practical use to them?

◈ CONCLUSION

Roxanne was able to get beyond straight grammar in two ways: She explored not only grammar but also cultural meanings, and she did so in a way that encompassed meanings pertinent not only to straight people but potentially to anyone. Getting beyond straight grammar allowed Roxanne to accomplish her main aims: to make her teaching relevant to students in their day-to-day lives, and to integrate lesbian/gay issues in uncontrived ways.

By using lesbian/gay themes as a focal point, Roxanne made space to discuss acts of speculating—why they are sometimes necessary and how they are accomplished in English using modals. By asking about the cultural meanings and meaning-making practices associated with sexual identities, she made space to discuss the potentially perplexing aspects of managing intercultural interactions. Thus the ambiguity of interpreting same-sex affection proved a useful means of engaging students in thinking through the bigger-picture issues connected to the grammar point at hand.

This case suggests that keeping the teaching focus on questions of language, culture, and meaning-making practices may make it possible to engage lesbian/gay themes productively. Also helpful in this endeavor is conceptualizing sexual identities as communicative acts or cultural practices that are accomplished in particular contexts with particular effects.

This teacher attempted to achieve a balance between "offering . . . opportunities for open-ended exploration and discussion and . . . fulfilling a responsibility for achieving established curriculum goals" (Mercer, 1995, p. 29). Roxanne managed to engage a student cohort that was multigenerational and markedly international (from 13 different countries) in a lively discussion about lesbian lovers during a lesson on modal auxiliary verbs. And she accomplished this despite her own nervousness with regard to gay themes. Paradoxically, what made this lesson stand out is that it did not stand out. This case demonstrates that integrating lesbian and gay themes in an ESL class can be, well, ordinary. Perhaps that is the extraordinary thing.

❖ ACKNOWLEDGMENTS

For providing some material support during part of this research, I thank Macquarie University for an Australian Postgraduate Award. I also thank the English Language Study Skills Assistance Centre (under the direction of Alex Barthel) at the University of Technology, Sydney. I am grateful to the teacher and students quoted in this chapter for generously agreeing to participate in my study.

❖ CONTRIBUTOR

Cynthia D. Nelson is a senior lecturer at the English Language Study Skills Assistance Centre at the University of Technology, Sydney, in Australia. She was awarded a PhD for her research on sexual identities and language pedagogy, and was a founding member of the TESOL task force that has since become the Lesbian, Gay, Bisexual, Transgender, and Friends Caucus. Her ethnographic play, *Queer as a Second Language,* has been performed at conferences and universities, and her forthcoming book about sexual identities in language education will be the first to explore this topic.

CHAPTER 3

Gender, Sexual Harassment, and the International Teaching Assistant

Diana Boxer and Andrea Tyler

◈ INTRODUCTION

This chapter addresses an issue central to the theme of gender and TESOL—cross-cultural perceptions of sexual harassment within an academic setting. Much existing research on language issues in the domain of higher education deals with problems of nonnative speakers of English who are students in the English-speaking world. In contrast, we study here some of the problems facing international teaching assistants (ITAs) on U.S. campuses.

Exposure of undergraduate students to ITAs is now a common element of the college experience. Nationwide, about 20% of all graduate assistants come from outside the United States. One finding from a large, midwestern university indicates that graduating students had taken an average of 3.1 classes from ITAs (Fox & Gay, 1994). Another estimates that 6% of all university instruction is delivered by ITAs (Plakans, 1997).

Because ITAs find themselves in the powerful role of college instructor, they are faced with specific challenges to their sociolinguistic competence (cf. Canale & Swain, 1980). Understanding and being able to effectively adhere to the norms of appropriateness in verbal interaction is a critical dimension for nonnative speakers who are in positions of power over native speakers. Such is the case on many large U.S. campuses, where graduate students often have primary responsibility as teachers of undergraduate classes and laboratories. Like all instructors in U.S. universities, a high percentage of today's ITAs are likely to confront issues of sexual harassment and, hence, need to understand what language and actions constitute sexual harassment in current U.S. culture.

◈ CONTEXT

Although TESOL and second language (L2) professionals are aware of reports of negative U.S. student reactions to the communication skills of ITAs, they may be surprised to learn that many U.S. females, especially in engineering and the sciences, perceive men from other countries negatively and report difficulties with foreign male students, faculty, and business professionals (Sandler & Hall, 1986). The perception is exemplified by an article in a professional engineering journal advising women to avoid taking jobs in businesses and departments where the men in power are foreign born (Brush, 1991; Fader, 1990).

As professionals who work with international graduate assistants and ITAs, we are particularly concerned about the implications of these perceptions of such students. Although we acknowledge that some men from cultures outside the United States may bring with them negative attitudes toward women in universities and in the workplace, we also believe that some of these negative perceptions may be the result of cross-cultural misunderstanding.

Moreover, evidence is emerging that perceptions of sexual harassment vary from culture to culture. This cross-cultural dimension suggests that it is particularly important for TESOL professionals who deal with ITA training to address sexual harassment. Research on gender and cross-cultural language use has shown that simply being exposed to someone who speaks a different code is often not enough to guarantee improved understanding. Singh, Lele, and Martohardjono (1988) argued that much research in cross-cultural communication has failed to fully take into account the "constrained interpretive schema" (p. 54) of both the native speaker and the nonnative speaker. A key notion is that speakers are largely unaware of the particular filtering of perceptions produced by the constraints of their own schema or societal norms. Individuals with different interpretive schemas can easily assign divergent interpretations to a particular event or conversation without realizing that an equally valid, competing interpretation is possible.

In studies of ITA training specifically, researchers have identified many important cultural differences in expectations for student-teacher relations and classroom interaction. In general, the U.S. classroom and the face-to-face interactions that occur there are perceived as less formal than in many other societies. The overriding message to ITAs is to loosen up, adjust preconceived notions of teacher-student roles, be more personal, and show more interest in the individual student. As ITAs attempt to redefine their notion of appropriate student-teacher boundaries, they also need guidance in understanding the reasoning and cultural values behind these adjustments and clarification of the boundaries of appropriateness.

It is widely known that behavior considered as neutral in one culture might be considered as sexual in another culture. For instance, within the United States, shaking hands with a person of the opposite sex is generally considered a neutral greeting, devoid of sexual implications. Researchers of language and culture are aware that this is not the case in Islamic cultures. However, the public, including typical university faculty and students, is generally not aware of this difference. One ITA reported to us that a new male graduate student from an Islamic country offended the female faculty when he vigorously shook the hands of all the male faculty but refused the extended hands of the female faculty members. When asked by his culturally naive fellow graduate students why he did this, the student reportedly stated that in his society, it was highly disrespectful to female professors for a male student to engage in such intimate physical behavior with them.

Support for the claim that, for some Islamic cultures, a handshake has sexual connotations comes from Jamaluddin, Nongshah, Taufek, and Zulkifli (1986), who state that Malay Muslims "cannot touch the hands of people of the opposite sex except when they are wearing gloves" (p. 27). Our goal in this research endeavor has been to provide a bidirectional analysis of perceptions of select student-teacher interactions that might be interpreted as appropriate by one group and inappropriate by the other, thus creating the potential for cross-cultural misperceptions of sexual intent and consequently of sexual harassment.

In spite of widespread acceptance of the view that interpretation of verbal and nonverbal behavior varies from culture to culture, the prevailing attitude within the general academic community seems to be that common sense determines what behavior and language is sexual or might constitute sexual harassment. For instance, standard statements found in the National Education Association (NEA) and American Association of University Professors guidelines on sexual harassment, which have been adopted by many U.S. universities, are quite general. The assumption seems to be that everyone knows which behaviors are sexual in nature, which are sex neutral, and what constitutes appropriate boundaries between professional and personal.

This chapter explores potential cultural differences in what is considered sexual behavior and different levels of sexual behavior that may be considered acceptable. The findings reported here are both quantitative and qualitative. Using data deriving from statistical analysis and from in-depth ethnographic interviews, we examine and compare the multiple perspectives of graduate teaching assistants (TAs) currently teaching in U.S. universities and compare these perspectives with U.S. undergraduates' perceptions of situations that could be construed as sexual harassment.

◈ LANGUAGE AND GENDER

Divergent Views of Sexual Harassment Constituted in Action and Language

People from the United States do not agree on what actions and language constitute sexual harassment. Several studies (Dziech & Weiner, 1984; Fitzgerald, 1992; Sandler & Hall, 1986) found that women and men tend to disagree on what actions and language constitute sexual harassment and on the seriousness of the problem, with men finding a narrower range of behavior offensive and estimating the effects as far less serious.

This division is also found within U.S. universities. On the one hand, ITAs hear the official line that denounces sexual harassment. On the other hand, they observe some U.S. males acting in quite a different way. A large number of international students are therefore exposed to a number of inappropriate linguistic and behavioral role models.

Reasonable Person Versus *Reasonable Woman*

Sexual harassment generally involves an asymmetrical power relationship in which the person with power tries to introduce sexual issues into the relationship. For example, even the use of terms of endearment such as *sweetie, honey,* or *dear* is indicative of power asymmetry and inserts a possible sexual element into a verbal interaction in the workplace. Similarly, certain compliments, such as those that comment on the addressee's inherent features—for example, color of hair or shape of hands—tend to be interpreted as having sexual connotations in the academic setting. Historically, sexual harassment has been defined by invoking the perspective of the *reasonable person.* More recently, however, North American courts have found it more appropriate to invoke the notion of *reasonable woman* in defining instances of sexual harassment. In writing about this important distinction, Ehrlich (2001) explains that

> a communicative act such as sexual banter may be perceived as more threatening to women than to heterosexual men because women's stock of cultural beliefs may include the proposition that sexual banter is potentially a prelude to violent sexual assault. (p. 115)

Hence undergraduate women may indeed be more sensitive than men to perceptions of potential contexts in which sexual harassment is likely to occur. Traditionally in Western society, men have held institutional power, and the overwhelming tendency has been for women to be the victims of sexual harassment. In the NEA report on sexual harassment in higher education, Fitzgerald (1992) notes that sexual harassment is used to make women feel unwanted and inferior and thus to keep them out of traditional male domains. Reports of the prevalence of sexual harassment in U.S. universities vary with the instrument used to survey the population. Several surveys have found that at least one third of female students report having experienced some form of sexual harassment by male teachers in college (Fitzgerald, 1992).

◈ DESCRIPTION

This case is a synthesis of the findings of two studies. In the first study (Tyler & Boxer, 1996), we carried out a quantitative analysis of perceptions of 12 scenarios by a mixed group of ITAs and U.S. undergraduates. The second study (Boxer & Tyler, 1996) fine-tuned the analysis with in-depth ethnographic interviews with two subsets of ITAs, Chinese speaking and Spanish speaking.

Reactions to Written Scenarios

In the first study (Tyler & Boxer, 1996), the survey participants were 44 U.S. undergraduates (27 females and 17 males) and 20 ITAs from a wide range of countries. Survey participants read 12 scenarios that depicted interactions between a TA and a student, and commented in writing on how they would interpret the TA's behavior. (The scenarios used the label *TA* so as not to lead the participants to think of only ITAs as capable of such language and behavior.)

Four of the scenarios were based on situations reported in the literature on sexual harassment on U.S. campuses (Fitzgerald, 1992) and cultural differences reported in the literature on cross-cultural communication (Nelson & Echols, 1991). Eight were based on reported situations involving ITAs that occurred at a large U.S. state university (Tyler, 1994). The findings showed that for five of these scenarios, ITAs and undergraduates had statistically significant differences in judgment. These five scenarios are the primary focus of the findings reported here. (See Tyler & Boxer, 1996, for a full description of the scenarios in the undergraduate questionnaire and a full report of the statistical findings.)

The survey participants' open-ended responses indicated that the TA's identity, in terms of race, ethnicity, and gender, would play an important role in their interpretation of the TA's behavior. In a series of ethnographic interviews conducted following the questionnaire, participants often stated that their assessments would depend on who the TA was and how the TA delivered the potentially offensive language and behavior.

Video Prompts and Interviews

As the focus of the second study (Boxer & Tyler, 1996), we developed video prompts in which individuals playing the part of the ITA and the undergraduate enacted the scenarios.

Each scenario was enacted twice, once with a male playing the role of the TA and a second time with a female playing that role. We reasoned that the TA's gender might affect the survey participants' judgments. In the United States, some actions, such as disclosing personal information or giving a compliment, are more likely to be performed by women than by men (Boxer, 1993; Wolfson & Manes, 1978) and therefore might more likely be judged as appropriate if the TA is female rather than male.

While the interview participants watched the video enactments, we conducted ethnographic interviews with ITAs from two broad linguistic groups—Chinese speakers from Taiwan and the People's Republic of China and Spanish speakers from Colombia, Uruguay, and Venezuela. We decided on these two groups because of the large numbers of ITAs from these broad cultural groups on the campus where this research was carried out. In addition, we suspected that the views of individuals from these two different parts of the world would contrast sharply. One of the goals of these ethnographic interviews was to ascertain whether the language and behavior depicted in the scenarios would more likely occur in the ITAs' own speech communities than in their L2 environment.

Our interview participants were nine male ITAs (six Chinese speakers and three Spanish speakers) and six female ITAs (three Spanish speakers and three Chinese speakers). Like many large U.S. college campuses, the campus in question employs fewer female ITAs than male ITAs. Moreover, given that the majority of graduate assistants who undergo ITA training are in the scientific or mathematical field, it is not surprising that there were fewer female ITAs. We compared our interview participants' perceptions of the scenarios with each other's perceptions and with those of the U.S. undergraduates.

◈ DISTINGUISHING FEATURES

We present here data from the questionnaires and interviews that have implications for the type of cross-cultural pragmatics relevant to ITA training. Often, what the ITAs said they would not do in their countries, they said they might do or say in the U.S. context, given their perceptions of different rules of speaking. Conversely, many of the ITAs indicated that they might say or do such things as they saw in the video prompts in their countries, but they would not in the United States. In other words, these nonnative speakers understood something about the different rules of speaking that coincide with the different norms of interaction they had experienced. They sometimes overgeneralized these differences so that they overstepped the boundaries of what is considered appropriate in the U.S. college context. The qualitative findings indicated the issue of cross-cultural perceptions of sexual harassment to be much more complex than a simple test of statistical significance would lead one to believe.

Because the survey involved people from many different cultural backgrounds who were grouped together as ITAs, we could not say anything specific about how different cultural groups interpreted sexual harassment. The comments from the second set of interviews, which took place after more focused groups of interview participants viewed the scenarios enacted on video prompts, more clearly illuminated differences that were due to linguistic and cultural norms. In the following we present the five scenarios that were found to elicit statistically significant differences in perceptions between the undergraduates and the ITAs.

Varying Perceptions of a TA's Telephone Call

Scenario A: The TA Calls a Student at Home

> The student is in an introductory class. The TA has apparently tried to present the material in an animated way. The TA encourages students who have trouble with the material to come to office hours, and has even announced special help sessions on the weekends. The student has not done well on the last test but has not come in to talk to the TA about it. Last Saturday, the TA located this student at the house of her/his brother and phoned the student there. The TA got the phone number from the student's roommate. The TA said, "Look, I'm worried about your performance. I'd like to discuss your test with you. We could even meet tonight if you like."

The results of a chi-square analysis showed that ITAs were statistically more likely to find this interaction appropriate than were undergraduates (see Table 1).

All of the Spanish-speaking ITAs, both females and males, indicated that this scenario would be inappropriate in the U.S. campus context. The Chinese speakers, on the other hand, were more willing to accept the appropriateness of the scenario under certain circumstances. For example, one Chinese female thought it would be appropriate in Taiwan for a teacher to suggest such a meeting. She commented, "This would be perfectly normal in Taiwan, tonight is okay."

This suggestion is further corroborated by the comments of some of the male

TABLE 1. UNDERGRADUATES' AND ITAS' PERCEPTIONS OF SCENARIOS

Scenario	Undergraduates	ITAs	x^2	p
A	0.76	0.42	6.41	< .011
B	0.83	0.53	5.81	< .016
C	0.39	0.89	15.92	< .010
D	0.90	0.74	2.65	< .103[a]
E	0.95	0.74	5.40	< .020
F	0.90	0.56	8.98	< .003

Note. 0 = appropriate; 1.00 = inappropriate.
[a]Not significant.

Taiwanese informants. One said that, in Taiwan, the TA could appropriately seek out the student's telephone number and call the student if the student and TA had a good relationship. Another male Taiwanese ITA said that if the student gave the TA the phone number, it would be appropriate for the TA to call the student at home.

Thus, the type of relationship between the teacher and the student would be a factor in determining whether and to what extent this scenario would be perceived as normal or not. Note that the Taiwanese informants did not say that this scenario would be appropriate in the United States but merely that it might naturally occur, under certain conditions, in their country. The above comments indicate the potential for cross-cultural miscommunication based on discontinuities between the two groups of ITAs. Moreover, the comments of the Taiwanese ITAs point to a potential conflict with perceptions of the undergraduates surveyed in the original study.

Varying Perceptions of a TA's Physical Contact With a Student

Scenario B: The TA Puts an Arm Around a Student

> The student has an introductory computer programming class with a lab that meets once a week, at the end of which students have to turn in their program. Before they actually turn it in, they must sit down with the TA and explain certain aspects of the program. If they can't explain them clearly, they could lose some points. This makes some of the students nervous. This particular student finds it difficult to explain things even when she/he has done them properly. The TA tells this student that she/he has lost a few points on the first two labs because of the explanation. Last week, when the student came in for the explanation, the TA pulled a chair up close to the student's and, putting an arm around the student's shoulder, said, "OK, your program seems to run fine. I want you to relax and just tell me what you did." The TA left the arm around the student's shoulder for about 30 seconds while the student began to explain, then sat back and listened while the student finished the explanation. The student explained the program as well as she/he had on the previous labs. When the student finished the TA said, "OK, good job." The next week when the student got ready to explain the lab, the TA again put his/her arm around the student's shoulders while the student began to explain.

The results of a chi-square analysis showed that the ITAs were statistically more likely than the undergraduates to find the actions represented in this scenario acceptable (see Table 1).

A female ITA from Colombia stated that in her country, such behavior would be perfectly acceptable and not out of the ordinary. She hastened to add, however, that this was not the case in the United States, saying that in the United States, there are more defined borders; in Colombia there is less personal space. In sharp contrast, a Taiwanese female informant had the following comment: "Chinese people don't hug. But in the United States it's more common. It seems weirder, though, for a female TA to do this than a male TA."

A Chinese male ITA commented,

> If the TA is male and does that to a female student, maybe once, maybe it's OK. If the TA is female it sends the wrong message for a male student. If a

male TA did this to a female student, occasionally, maybe it's OK. But if it's reversed, maybe it means the TA is interested.

The comments indicate contrasts between Colombia and Taiwan. In Colombia, people have more day-to-day physical contact whereas, in sharp contrast, in Taiwan people in that situation would not hug at all. ITAs from both places felt they had to make an adjustment to attitudes toward physical contact when in the United States. The South American felt she needed to be sensitive to the fact that certain kinds of touching do not connote the same level of intimacy in her area of the world as they do in the United States. Her interpretation of physical interaction in terms of intimacy is different from that of the ITAs from Taiwan. The Taiwanese felt that, within Taiwanese culture, physical contact conveys a certain level of intimacy that may be reserved for family members. However, they also indicated that they believed such touching may be acceptable in the U.S. setting. Hence, both are struggling with a change in the concept of appropriate physical contact. Our U.S. interview participants indicated that such touching was questionable.

Varying Perceptions of a TA's Unannounced Visit
Scenario C: The TA Returns a Book to a Student's Apartment

> The student has a class that meets every Monday, Wednesday, and Friday. The TA borrowed a book from him/her 2 weeks ago. During the last class, which met on Friday, the student asked if the TA happened to have brought the book to class. When the TA said no, the student responded, "OK, no problem." At 9:30 Saturday night, the TA dropped by the student's apartment to return the book. After handing the book to the student, the TA asked the student what he/she was doing. When the student responded that he/she was just reading, the TA said, "I'm not doing anything either."

The results of a chi-square analysis showed that ITAs were statistically more likely to find the language and actions depicted in this scenario acceptable (see Table 1).

An Uruguayan female ITA said, "Okay, the TA forgot the book. It's okay to return it at home, you have to. But don't ask the question about what the other is doing." Apparently, according to this informant, dropping by unannounced to return the book was quite acceptable. The inappropriateness came from the question that intruded on the student's privacy.

A similar response came from two Taiwanese female ITAs. One said, "The greeting and question about what the student is doing are not appropriate." Another said, "Just returning the book is okay, but the questions aren't." These comments converge with the Uruguayan female ITA's comment above. According to these three women from two different cultural groups, it was not the action of dropping by unannounced but the verbal behavior that broke the rules of acceptable behavior between teacher and student.

A Taiwanese male had a somewhat different perspective on this scenario:

> It's not a big problem. It's better to return the book at a scheduled meeting time before, during or right after class or in the office, but if the student lives on campus it's okay. If the student lived off campus it would be kind of weird.

The ITAs seemed to agree that showing up unannounced to return the book was not so problematic; it was the question about what the student was doing that was inappropriate.

In some societies visiting friends and acquaintances without calling ahead is perfectly acceptable and even expected. This is not generally true, however, in most U.S. speech communities. Indeed, research on the speech act/event of invitations (e.g., Wolfson, D'Amico-Reisner, & Huber, 1983) indicates that, in U.S. society, people tend to do a dance of negotiation, in which interlocutors put forth and respond to leads that result in an invitation only through the efforts of both parties. Our U.S. interview participants had a strong negative reaction to the TA's dropping by, especially on a weekend night.

Thus, although Spanish-speaking and Chinese-speaking ITAs had little problem with this scenario, there is a clear mismatch between their views and the U.S. undergraduates' views. Both groups of ITAs, therefore, may create problematic situations if they overgeneralize the acceptability of stopping by a student's house unannounced, even for some professional reason, such as returning a borrowed book.

Varying Perceptions of a TA's Invitation

Scenario D: The TA Invites a Student to Lunch on Saturday

> The student is in a class with an enthusiastic TA. His/her grades are just average, and the TA has encouraged him/her to come to office hours for special help. So far, the student hasn't gone. On Monday, the student got a quiz back. A note was written on the quiz that said, "I'm disappointed that you didn't take up my offer. It's not too late. I'll have a help session this Saturday in my office at 7:30 p.m." When the student got home from studying Wednesday night, his/her roommate told him/her that the TA had called to see if the student was planning on going to the help session. The student didn't go. The following Monday, the student got a quiz back. Again, the student didn't do well. At the bottom of the quiz was another note, "Missed you Saturday. I think it would benefit you greatly if you talked to me individually. How about lunch on Saturday?"

The results of a chi-square analysis showed that ITAs and undergraduates were likely to find the language and actions depicted in this scenario equally inappropriate (see Table 1).

Judgments of the acceptability of this scenario were affected by the participants' gender rather than by their cultural background. Behavior that the women felt was highly inappropriate, some of the males from both language groups found not only not to be a problem but to be positive behavior. This contrast no doubt resulted in no statistical difference between the two groups for this scenario. We include it here to illustrate gender differences in perceptions.

All the female ITAs that we interviewed, both Chinese-speaking and Spanish-speaking, thought this scenario was highly inappropriate. Male informants, on the other hand, had a somewhat different view. A Chinese-speaking male thought the note suggested that the "TA really cared." A Spanish-speaking male said,

It is very clear that the TA is interest in the grades of the student. He or she is worried about him and wants to help him. So that's why he or she became a teacher or a TA.

Varying Perceptions of a TA's Compliment

Just as rules for invitations vary cross-culturally, rules for the speech act of complimenting may also vary. Although a fair number of studies have investigated gender differences in compliment realization (see, e.g., Herbert, 1990; Holmes, 1988; Wolfson, 1989; Wolfson & Manes, 1978), less is known about the use of compliments cross-culturally. Responses to Scenario E, in which a TA makes a compliment about a student's eyes, show a potential area for miscommunication.

Scenario E: The TA Says a Student Has Amazing Eyes

The semester is about halfway over. The student recently got back the first midterm and did rather well. The student generally likes the TA in this course. If he/she had a problem with class material, the student feels the TA would try to help. This week, the student happened to get to class a few minutes early; no other students were there yet, but the TA was. As the student entered the room, he/she greeted the TA and stopped to say a few words. The TA complimented the student on his/her performance on the midterm. Then the TA said, "I never noticed it before, but you have amazing eyes." The student said thanks and began to move to his/her seat. The TA responded, "Eyes are the reflection of the soul. Beautiful eyes reveal a beautiful soul. Your eyes are truly beautiful."

The results of a chi-square analysis showed that the ITAs were statistically more likely than the undergraduates to find the language depicted in this scenario as appropriate (see Table 1).

All ITA interview participants, except the Spanish-speaking males, thought the compliment was inappropriate. The Chinese-speaking male informants thought it so inappropriate as to not even be worthy of lengthy comment. Their responses included "really bad idea to talk about this [laughs]," "NO!" and "too personal." The female Chinese speakers indicated that the compliment would be appropriate only if the student and TA were both female. In contrast, one of the South American males said, "The TA likes my eyes, that's all. She or he thinks I have beautiful eyes. What's the problem?" The Spanish-speaking female informants showed more of a sensitivity to different rules of the first and second cultures. The Uruguayan ITA said that, in the U.S. context, commenting on how a student looks would not be appropriate. A Colombian female ITA said, "It's weird. You must be sensitive to cultural differences with persons who don't know your culture." This view is corroborated by the other Colombian female ITA:

You have to go by the rules of the other country. It's the hardest thing to learn in another language. The teacher is educated and should know this. You must change behavior in a second language in order not to be rude.

The above comments tend to point to a contrast between male and female Chinese speakers and female Spanish speakers, on the one hand, and Spanish-speaking males, on the other. Whereas the South American women did not see this scenario as appropriate, their male counterparts tended to dismiss it as nonproblematic. A further probe of any possible differences in perceptions would require more male, Spanish-speaking interview participants.

Varying Perceptions of a TA's Personal Questions

Scenario F: The TA Asks a Student Personal Questions

> In the first meeting of class, the TA announced that during the first 2 weeks of the semester there would be individual conferences with all students so the TA could get a better idea of the students' background knowledge and interests. When the student arrived at the individual conference, the TA began by asking the following questions: "What do you like to do on Friday and Saturday nights?" "Does your social life leave you enough time for your academic work?" "Are you romantically involved?"

The results of a chi-square analysis showed that ITAs were statistically more likely than undergraduates to find the language and actions depicted in this scenario appropriate (see Table 1).

In general, the Spanish-speaking females perceived this type of questioning as inappropriate: "This isn't the correct approach. It's not the same as 'you're not doing well, I'd like to know the reasons.'" Another commented, "A lot depends on your closeness with the students. It's okay to ask in general, but not specifics."

The Chinese-speaking female ITAs tended to agree with their South American counterparts: "How big is the class? If there are problems during the semester then it's time to discuss." "In China we just do our job; this isn't part of it."

A Spanish-speaking male TA had a different view: "Every personal problem or lifestyle affects the students' profile. The TA needs to know what kind of person is he or she deals with. He or she needs to know how he can help."

With the exception of this one Spanish-speaking male, the ITAs generally agreed that the TA's questions were inappropriate. Again, making conclusive generalizations would require more data from male, Spanish-speaking ITAs.

◈ PRACTICAL IDEAS

The underlying philosophy of our ITA program emphasizes that many of the communication problems that occur between ITAs and U.S. undergraduates stem from cross-cultural differences at all levels of discourse and schema, including differences in culturally appropriate ways of enacting student-teacher roles. Thus, the program stresses co-construction and bidirectionality in communication. The program's goal is to provide support for ITAs with the aim of helping them have a successful teaching experience. We approach issues of sexual harassment from this same philosophy.

Trying to convert ITA values is inappropriate for ITA educators and is likely to lead to distasteful moralizing. Instead, we place issues of sexual harassment in a historical-cultural and legal framework and clarify the behavior that is likely to be perceived as transgressing teacher-student roles in the United States. Thus, we frame discussion of sexual harassment in terms of protecting ITAs from possible cultural misunderstandings and helping ITAs become more effective and successful with all the students, peers, and professors they work with.

In ITA classes, we address the issue of sexual harassment with a variety of activities. We suggest the following.

Alert ITAs to Relevant Legal Definitions

Inform ITAs of legal definitions of problematic behaviors. Follow up with a discussion of the rather vague guidelines for behaviors such as *unnecessary touching,* which, as this case indicates, are not uniformly defined across cultures.

Involve U.S. Undergraduates

Invite U.S. undergraduates to participate in discussions of sexual harassment cases, such as the ones on which our scenarios were based. In some cases, we bring in newspaper clippings that report cases of sexual harassment complaints filed against ITAs.

Discussing real cases with U.S. undergraduates provides the ITAs with the opportunity to hear how the undergraduates are likely to interpret actions and to ask questions and gain clarification on the undergraduate perspective.

Ask the ITAs to Keep a Teaching Journal

Have ITAs keep a teaching journal in which they comment on aspects of student-teacher interactions in the classes they are teaching and on aspects of interactions they observe in the university at large. Such journal entries have raised important points relating to sexual harassment. For instance, one ITA majoring in sports science related a series of incidents of perceived sexual harassment involving a fellow graduate student, who had complained to the ITA about their professor's inappropriate touching when using her as a model for proper stance in tennis. This journal entry formed the basis of a discussion that clarified the definition of *unnecessary touching,* the importance of the potentially offending behavior occurring more than once, and the genuine distress his friend felt in the situation.

◈ CONCLUSION

The qualitative findings described above point to considerable agreement in perceptions of sexual harassment between the Chinese-speaking and Spanish-speaking ITAs. The ITAs' comments seem to indicate that English language teaching professionals need to move away from thinking that simply because Latinos are friendly or outgoing, require less personal space, do more touching, and generally exhibit more intimate behavior (and language) than their U.S. counterparts, they will transfer these norms to the U.S. campus context, where the behavior could get them into trouble. Differences are drawn not necessarily along cultural lines but also along gender lines. What females may see as problematic within one linguistic and cultural system may be generally seen as nonproblematic by males from the same system.

A number of the comments made by the interview participants indicated that they were aware of cultural differences between their home culture and the target culture but still did not clearly understand the norms of the latter. They may have been developing an *interculture*—one that does not match the norms of either the home culture or the target culture—analogous to the interlanguage continuum. These nonnative speakers may have been developing hypotheses about acceptable rules of speaking and nonverbal behavior that may or may not conform to the L2 norms. Some nonnative speakers may see U.S. culture and classroom interactions as less formal and more interactive than those in their own culture and thus may overstep the norms. Others, frightened by a heightened awareness of sexual harassment, may go too far in the other direction, refusing to develop any kind of closeness with the students in their classes for fear of being wrongly accused.

The consequences for ITAs judged to have crossed appropriate boundaries are serious. In addition to being put on probation by universities and publicly accused of unethical actions, ITAs found guilty of sexual harassment have lost all departmental funding and been permanently denied enrollment in departmental classes. Once this occurs, letters of recommendation ITAs need to move to a different department or university are difficult to obtain, and ITAs may find that their academic careers in the United States are finished.

What is sure is that U.S. workplaces and campuses are no longer tolerant of language and behavior that may be construed as sexual. Particularly because so many international graduate students on U.S. campuses are in a position of power over U.S. undergraduates, issues of sexual harassment are likely to become increasingly important.

What constitutes sexual harassment is often confusing to males and females, native speakers and nonnative speakers. Those who are novice teachers particularly need to be aware and exercise exceptional care in cases of a power differential, such as that which is inherent in the teacher-student relationship. Beyond the scope of classroom discourse in U.S. higher education, our findings have implications for other groups around the world interacting with speakers of American English. As sensibilities change and as women become an increasing presence in an international workforce, the potential for serious miscommunication increases. Cross-cultural misfires concerning potential perceptions of sexual harassment have repercussions not only in the educational but also in the business and diplomatic spheres.

Some of our ITAs have stated that their solution to the problem of sexual harassment is to keep a definite distance from students of the opposite sex. The consequence of such a stand is that ITAs may treat a certain class of students with more camaraderie and give them more overt encouragement than they do others—for instance, by encouraging certain students but not others to come to office hours. All students—regardless of their gender--ought to have equal access to the instructor's guidance and receive equal rewards for their academic work. This issue should be central in ESL programs that train ITAs.

In some disciplines, such as engineering, as much as 70% of the graduate student population is international. Today's ITAs will constitute a large percentage of the U.S. professors in the future. Whether or not ESL speakers interacting with Americans believe Americans are overly sensitive on the issue of sexual harassment, they will find themselves subject to current U.S. sensibilities, particularly if their interactions occur within the United States. An understanding of the issue will be increasingly important in U.S. higher education and beyond.

◈ CONTRIBUTORS

Diana Boxer is a professor and chair of the Department of Linguistics at the University of Florida, in the United States. She teaches and publishes in the areas of discourse and pragmatics, second language acquisition, and gender and language. She is the author of *Applying Sociolinguistics: Domains and Face-to-Face Interaction* (John Benjamins, 2002) and co-editor (with Andrew D. Cohen) of *Studying Speaking to Inform Second Language Learning* (Multilingual Matters, 2004).

Andrea Tyler is an associate professor in the Linguistics Department at Georgetown University, in the United States. Her courses have largely focused on applications of discourse analytic, pragmatic, and cognitive theories of language to issues in second language learning and teaching. As a result of her research on ITA discourse, she received the 1994 TESOL–Newbury House Outstanding Researcher of the Year Award. She has published in numerous journals, including *Language, Journal of Pragmatics, TEXT, Studies in Second Language Acquisition,* and *TESOL Quarterly*. She is the coauthor (with Vyvyan Evans) of *The Semantics of English Prepositions: Spatial Scenes, Embodied Meaning, and Cognition* (Cambridge University Press, 2003).

CHAPTER 4

Feminist Composition Pedagogies in ESL Tutoring

Jay Jordan

◈ INTRODUCTION

Of all students who approach undergraduate writing centers, those who often appear most in need of extra writing practice and instructional and tutorial support are the same ones whose needs are least theorized. ESL students arrive in writing centers with widely varying experiences with written English, and their facility with spoken English may not accurately predict their writing ability. Additionally, the stress they may experience as a result of their immersion in a majority English-speaking community and their often unstable and politically charged U.S. residency statuses point to needs that much native-English-speaking (NES) student tutorial pedagogy does not anticipate.

Students' frustration is frequently exacerbated when they receive papers in their writing classes marked with comments like "Grammar!" in the margins. This feeling may not abate when their tutors select from the techniques that have been canonized over decades of writing center pedagogy. A significant amount of the training literature undergraduate and graduate student tutors are exposed to assumes that student and tutor can work together as partners. They may set agendas, brainstorm, negotiate meaning, and plan revisions. Tutors may even adopt a minimalist approach, allowing the student as many opportunities as possible to take over the tutorial. The success of such power-sharing tutorial pedagogies has been demonstrated in many settings, but how well do they translate to situations in which the tutor and student do not share the same level of English proficiency? Is there a potential power difference that precludes ESL students from collaborating with their often NES tutors?

This case arose out of my own need to ask those questions after two semesters' work as a writing tutor for ESL students. In reflecting on that work, I follow hooks' (1994) example of making theory out of practice in order to inform and transform practice. That is, I critique ESL interactions in the writing center as a NES writing tutor trained in composition for native English speakers in order to make sense out of my work with students whose language needs are undertheorized in my field. (The *Bedford Bibliography for Teachers of Writing* [Bizzell, Herzberg, & Reynolds, 2000] includes several pages of annotated citations on the topic, but many are provided by ESL theorists or appear in publications, such as *TESOL Quarterly*, that have little readership outside the field of TESL/applied linguistics.)

The obvious way to fill this knowledge gap was to draw from work in ESL composition, but that field has addressed writing classrooms extensively while leaving the space and practice of writing centers mostly unnoticed. Searches of the *Linguistics and Language Behavior Abstracts* (1973–2002) and *MLA Bibliography* (1963–2002) turned up two articles each that address ESL writers and tutoring or writing centers directly (see, e.g., Harris, 1997; Ritter, 2000) and more than 200 on ESL writers and writing generally, a significant majority of which address writing classrooms. It would have been shortsighted to exclude from my research the large body of work on ESL writing in classrooms. In fact, I believe that the fields of ESL composition and English for native speakers have many insights to offer each other, and I hope this project can contribute. The growing ethnic, national, and linguistic diversity of the student bodies at many colleges and universities in the United States challenges the division between these two disciplines, which makes knowledge sharing increasingly necessary.

To that end, I see potentially productive applications of feminist composition pedagogies—which have largely been preoccupied with NES writers—to ESL writing. Since feminism's earliest entry into composition studies, feminist scholars have focused their attention on how English teaching—and especially composition teaching—have historically been undervalued in many colleges and universities (see especially Holbrook, 1991; Jarratt, 2001; Miller, 1991). These scholars have uncovered the development of attitudes toward composition as a secondary discipline more connected to the *service* of teaching than to the rigorous *work* of other academic subjects. But they have also discovered that these same attitudes simultaneously construct teaching as necessary to students' development as academics and citizens.

Thus, composition has, paradoxically, become established as a required course and ignored as remedial or merely preparatory. Feminist teachers have taken advantage of this discrepancy in attitudes by closing the doors of their largely unnoticed classrooms and opening the floor to student work that may not otherwise find outlets in college and university courses that stress proficiency in solely academic expression. In doing so, they have recognized the abilities and authority that often-marginalized students already have as writers before entering writing classrooms (Anzaldúa, 1999; hooks, 1994). I believe that the conscious, carefully theorized deployment of feminist pedagogies in ESL tutoring sessions can allow ESL writing students to develop authority based on their experiences and competencies outside the academy while developing the writing competence necessary to succeed within the academy.

❖ CONTEXT

The site for my research was the Undergraduate Writing Center at the University Park campus of the Pennsylvania State University (Penn State), a 40,000-student, publicly supported, land-grant university located in the mostly rural central region of Pennsylvania, in the United States. Although a significant portion of the student body is White, of European descent, and Pennsylvanian, a growing number of undergraduate students arrive at Penn State from other countries and language backgrounds, often attracted to the university's renowned programs in engineering, the sciences, and business administration. The university saw a 94% increase in international student enrollment between 1993 and 2002 and a concomitant increase in ESL student enrollment (*Statistical Data on International Students,* 2002).

Like many other colleges and universities in the United States, Penn State requires all entering undergraduates to demonstrate competence in academic writing. This requirement takes the form of four first-year writing classes. Basic Writing and Rhetoric and Composition are offered by the English department for NES or near-NES students. The university's Program in Linguistics and Applied Language Studies staffs the ESL equivalents of these classes. The Writing Center provides approximately 40 hours of appointment-based and walk-in peer tutoring assistance per week for NES and ESL students during the fall and spring semesters.

As new tutors during the semester prior to this study, my colleagues and I met weekly to discuss student progress and particular concerns and to read articles about the practice of tutoring. Several of these articles, especially Latterell's (2000), made connections between writing center practices and gender that, I discovered, were not necessarily based on how many men versus how many women were tutoring or what happened when tutors and students of different genders worked together. Instead, I began to see that a feminist conception of teaching and tutoring might generally address the politics of working in the marginalized space of the writing center.

I decided to enroll in a seminar exploring feminist pedagogies. I was interested in thinking about how gender dynamics might work through the university's paradoxical attitude toward composition teaching—an attitude that carried over into perceptions of writing center work. I saw an initial possibility for resolving this paradox in Kramarae's observations that women "find ways to talk 'out of order'" in "bathrooms and hallways of offices" and "in the lunch areas of factories" (cited in Foss, Foss, & Griffin, 1999, p. 48). In these borrowed and largely ignored spaces—outside and between spaces of often male-dominated power—Kramarae believes, a "women's world" can be constructed as a healthy alternative to a "men's world" (p. 47). I saw a parallel to writing centers, and I became especially interested in exploring the potential of this insight for ESL tutoring situations that, for my colleagues and me, were becoming more common but not necessarily any more comfortable for us or our ESL students.

◈ LANGUAGE AND GENDER

In Composition

To chart my exploration, I first contextualize the issue of gender and, especially, feminism in composition more fully.

In colleges and universities, the 19th-century division of labor along gender lines in factories and other businesses translated to the artificial division between service courses—institutionally perceived as feminine and often staffed with women—and advanced, theoretical courses—perceived as predominantly masculine and taught largely by men (Holbrook, 1991, pp. 202–205). Composition, as a nurturing introductory course that coaches beginning students in academic English, the lingua franca of supposedly more rigorous, higher level work, clearly fell on the feminine side of this division. But this identity is more complex than it initially appears. Composition's coaching function clearly serves a vital role, even if *serves* is the operative term: For male professors and administrators, the prevailing belief that women were good at menial labor meant that women could at least do some work in the "niche composition found in the English hierarchy" (Holbrook, 1991, p. 207).

Beyond composition's supportive yet fundamental position in the academy is its broader importance as a gatekeeper. Miller (1991) argues that composition's task of teaching written communication has simultaneously earned it the role of supporting more advanced classes and "assur[ing] the continuation of our civilization" (p. 42). The effect of this complex entrenchment is that the feminization of composition has proven difficult to overcome.

In Writing Centers

Housed in or staffed and supported by composition programs in English departments across the United States, writing centers have shared the feminized status of those programs (Bean, 1999). But writing centers actually appear doubly feminized. In the universities whose writing centers I have both tutored in and sought assistance in as an undergraduate and graduate student, the spaces occupied by writing centers have been physically separated from composition faculty and administrative offices, sometimes even being located in entirely separate buildings. These centers have often had to beg for funding not from "the provost" (p. 127), as Bean suggests, but from English departments. At least one writing center has resorted to registering students who use an adjacent computer lab in order to provide evidence of consistent facilities usage and justify continued funding. Both the writing center's physical space and the perceptions of the work done there—even the perceptions of others who work in the discipline of composition—are limited (North, 1984).

Whereas North (1984) sees the writing center's sometimes sparse furnishings as an unquestioned limitation, M. W. Nelson (1991) finds that ESL students in her pilot group-writing program comfortably used the "ragged old overstuffed chair that [a] tutor found for $5 at Goodwill" (p. 30). Harris (1997) confirms that, despite prevailing conceptions in ESL and native English composition studies that ESL students come to the writing center looking for another opportunity to be told "what to do" (p. 223), they overwhelmingly expect sessions that open with "friendly conversation" (p. 227) and that proceed on the basis of "advice" (p. 227)—all within writing centers that are built on the idea of putting students and tutors at ease.

Whatever the furniture looks like in any given writing center, the space of the center is self-consciously not a classroom: Small tables replace desks and podiums, bookcases and eclectic selections of readers and handbooks replace required texts, and critical conversation can replace evaluation. The writing center, then, can be an ideal space for the practices Jarratt (2001) identifies as characteristic of feminist composition pedagogy: an attempt to decenter or share authority, a view of students as sources of knowledge, a focus on process as a part of writing at least as important as product, and a critique of society's gendered power relations, which, among other things, attempt to dictate what kinds of work should be done in composition (p. 115).

In Composition Pedagogy

Since the early 1990s, several teachers and scholars have been opening feminist pedagogies to account for intersections between gender—feminism's primary preoccupation—and class, race, and language competence issues brought to the attention of teachers by substantial demographic changes in many classrooms. Anzaldúa (1999) has led the challenge with her invocation of the *mestiza,* a female figure whose overwhelmingly defining characteristic is her position in the *borderlands.* By that term, Anzaldúa means not only the geographical borderlands of her upbringing in south Texas, but also the metaphysical borderlands occupied by people everywhere who are attempting to live, speak, and write their way into unfamiliar cultural and social situations.

Anzaldúa (1999) describes in traumatic detail the experience of feeling forced to separate from her native languages and assume just one of the many identities she considers to be hers. As noted by Foss et al. (1999, p. 113), she also discusses her cultivation of *la facultad* (literally, the ability)—a sensitivity to realities below surfaces and to different ways of being that seems very much like a rhetorical skill that writing teachers are concerned with in their composition courses. Although she directly addresses the situations of women, she believes she shares *la facultad* with "the homosexuals of all races, the darkskinned, the outcast, the persecuted, the marginalized, the foreign" (Anzaldúa, 1999, p. 60). She also believes that communication is enriched in the borderlands by code switching, the practice of moving in and out of different languages to compensate for the fact that the standard or preferred local speech frequently fails to capture the intended meaning. A clear—and humorous—example is her mother's chiding her about sounding like a Mexican, which is a message that English alone cannot quite convey: "I want you to speak English. *Pa'hallar buen trabajo tienes que saber hablar el inglés bien. ¿Qué vale toda tu educación si todavía hablas inglés con un* accent?" (To find good work, you have to speak good English. What's the use of all your schooling if you continue to speak with an accent?) (p. 75).

Despite the attractiveness of metaphors of conversation and the value of code switching, students will, eventually, encounter evaluations of their ability to write standardized, academic English, and any writing center pedagogy must be honest about that. Thus, it must be flexible—perhaps more so than Jarratt's (2001) list implies. As some feminist scholars note, there are dangers in establishing a static feminist pedagogy that uncritically attempts to turn power over to students. Such a pedagogy can become "as expected and institutionally dictated as the most classically delivered 'masculine' lecture" (Treichler, 1994, p. 88), thus replacing one set of dictates with another (also see Jarratt, 2001). As liberating as the idea of student empowerment is, it can cause tutors to overlook students' need to complete writing projects successfully, as *success* is defined in their high-stakes gatekeeping composition courses (Benesch, 2001; Gore, 1992; Latterell, 2000). This problem can be especially pronounced in ESL writing tutoring situations in which tutors intent on simply helping students feel comfortable and on listening in relatively passive, conversational roles may miss opportunities to make the rules and codes of the academic writing culture more apparent (Delpit, 1988). Thus, a feminist composition pedagogy in a writing center must acknowledge that opening power relations for ESL students may mean being more directive than tutors steeped in traditional writing center and feminist practices are used to being.

◈ DESCRIPTION

The Writing Center

In addition to providing as-needed walk-in and appointment-based assistance, Penn State's Writing Center houses a credit-bearing tutorial (English 5) in which students in any of the university's writing courses may enroll. English 5 differs from the Writing Center's other tutorial assistance in that (a) it is facilitated by graduate students and fixed-term, nontenure-track instructors from the Department of English rather than undergraduate peer tutors, and (b) it involves a 35-minute meeting per student once a week rather than hour-long, as-needed blocks.

English 5 is popular: During the semester in which I conducted this study, funding and staffing constraints limited enrollment to 160 students, down from as many as 220 in previous semesters. Graduate students who staff English 5 usually tutor 8–17 students per week. In a given semester, roughly one fourth of the total number of students receiving tutoring for credit are ESL students, including most of the students involved in the university's College Assistance Migrant Program, which offers support for entering students from families with migrant or seasonal work backgrounds—all of whom speak English as a second language (*College Assistance Migrant Program,* 1999). During the semester of this study, 46 students in the credit-bearing tutorial identified themselves as ESL students.

Note that graduate students in English are the sole source for English 5 tutors. Graduate students from the Program in Linguistics and Applied Language Studies are available approximately 8 hours per week for appointment-based tutoring sessions, but their teaching obligations keep them from further involvement. Furthermore, English graduate students are not trained in ESL teaching: The English Department offers no ESL-related seminars or practica, and the courses that train graduate students for composition teaching and tutoring include no more than a lesson's worth of material and discussion on ESL issues. This situation, of course, is not unusual. Matsuda (1999) tells the history of the disciplinary divide between ESL composition and composition for native English speakers and of the development of separate Conference on College Composition and Communication and TESOL camps that, in turn, moved ESL considerations almost entirely out of English curricula. Many English students, like me, encounter ESL learners only in comparatively informal, extracurricular settings, such as through volunteer opportunities, before meeting them in the Writing Center.

The Survey

Even though I could see clear connections between what feminist scholars were expressing and what I was observing in the Writing Center, I felt it would be hypocritical to ask about the possibilities of applying feminist composition pedagogies in ESL tutoring situations without asking the people involved in that tutoring. I conducted a survey of ESL students' opinions about their interactions with Writing Center tutors (see the Appendix). I based my survey method and questions on Harris's (1997) survey of 85 ESL students at Purdue University. Like Harris (p. 222), I was concerned about the tendency of many ESL students to be more guarded in face-to-face interviews than in written responses—a characteristic I had noticed in many of my own tutoring sessions with them—so I asked my questions on paper and requested anonymous answers.

Although I was, from the start of this project, interested in the extent to which student responses might support or question the application of broadly conceived feminist pedagogies, I did not ask questions specific to students' encounters with feminism. Because I was anxious about skewing their responses or confusing them by explaining connections between my survey and a feminist project, I asked open-ended questions that addressed issues—such as space, student-teacher and student-tutor interactions, and critical awareness about writing assignments—that I knew to be relevant to the possibilities of feminist pedagogies. In addition to asking about age, native language, and duration and location of formal English training, my questions included the following:

- How is what a writing tutor should do different from what a writing teacher should do?

- What things that you and your tutor do are most effective in helping you with your writing? What things are ineffective?

- Do you discuss your opinions about your writing assignments with your tutor? Why or why not?

- Do you feel more comfortable with your tutor than you feel with your writing teacher?

I decided to survey only the ESL students enrolled in the English Department's credit-bearing tutorial because I wanted to focus on students who had the most regular interactions with tutors and to ensure the return of as many surveys as possible.

During the last few weeks of the semester, after students and tutors had spent at least 12 sessions together, I distributed surveys to tutors, who then agreed to distribute them to the ESL students in their classes. I received 10 completed surveys from students whose first languages were Cantonese, Korean, Mandarin, Russian (two; one from a student from Ukraine), Spanish (one Colombian and one Panamanian), Tigrina (Ethiopian), and Vietnamese (two). Eight respondents indicated their gender as female, and two, as male. Students' formal education in English in and outside the United States ranged from 4.0 to 24.0 years, with a mean of 11.2 years.

After the end of the semester, I asked the tutors to respond to substantively the same questions because I was interested in the similarity of students' and tutors' perceptions of their experiences and because I wanted to preserve in some way the dialogues I knew students and tutors had had during the semester. I received lengthy responses from 4 of the 10 graduate students who staffed the Writing Center.

◈ DISTINGUISHING FEATURES

The generalizations drawn from the survey may be useful to tutors of ESL writers.

A Tutorial, Not a Class

I addressed the issue of the educational experience in the program by asking in the survey both about differences between tutors and teachers and about differences between the Writing Center and writing classrooms. Almost all the students responded that they felt at least as comfortable in the Writing Center as in their classes. Several noted that they felt more comfortable with their tutors, for several reasons:

> because she [the tutor] does not hold the power to grade me.

> even though I make a big big mistake, I will willing to change it after I talk to my tutor.

> But with my teacher, I will feel that I am forced by my teacher to change.

> Being with my tutor is an one-on-one conversation, whereas with my teacher it is like I am talking for the class if I ask a question in class.

Tutors responded similarly, indicating that they shared with the students they worked with a desire to take advantage of the one-on-one time (albeit often very brief) the tutorial afforded them. Furthermore, they confirmed that they were not interested in evaluating students' work; one tutor went as far as to say confidently that "in a tutorial, the student can offer ideas that will not be challenged."

Discussion of Assignments

One survey question asked whether students expressed their opinions about writing assignments to their tutors. I included this question because I had noticed that both ESL and NES students often seemed uninterested in the more or less directive writing tasks they were assigned. Although I did not want to create the sense that the Writing Center could be a kind of complaints department for writing assignments, I wanted to know how far the students' comfort in tutoring sessions extended. Interestingly, all the students who responded that they expressed to their tutors their opinions about writing tasks connected their perspectives on assignments with developing invention skills:

> I do discuss my opinions with my tutor to go through the process of creating more solid ideas.

> If I didn't like the topic, the tutor might help me to find other ways or things and make me to interest in it.

> I think if I discuss about the writing assignments, even if I don't like them, I can come up with more ideas.

Tutors responded variously to this question. Several indicated that students often seemed to misunderstand the assignments they had been given and that part of the tutorial was productively given over to explaining the requirements. Thus, reflecting critically on assignments prior to jumping into the writing can help students clarify the overall writing task as well as generate ideas.

Students' Pace and Students' Levels of Need

Common among several respondents was the view that tutors should help students take advantage of the greater one-on-one time a tutorial offers relative to a writing class. They felt that tutors should slow the pace at which they review the writing process with students and try not to get frustrated. Even if the student's goal is a more correct product, individual sessions can take diversions to explore, allow, and encourage that student's creativity. The correct form can be one goal, but it does not have to be the only one.

The tutor's encouragement of a more active role for the student in setting a tutorial agenda might also serve this exploratory purpose. Ritter (2000) notes that her attempt at negotiating with her ESL students "slows the conversation and allows the student more time to process information" (p. 108). This process is reminiscent both of Anzaldúa's (1999) code switching, which slows the understanding of the non-Spanish-speaking audience, and of hooks's (1994) suggestion that imperfect or slowed understanding may

> subvert that culture of capitalist frenzy and consumption that demands all desire must be satisfied immediately, or . . . disrupt that cultural imperialism that suggests one is worthy of being heard only if one speaks in standard English. (p. 174)

A Flexible Curriculum and a Patient Approach

How, then, to reconcile the engagement of students' native rhetorical abilities with the demands of writing curricula that emphasize standardized English expression? Respondents to my survey suggested flexibility. They showed a strong awareness of the importance of mechanics, and they tied their learning of mechanical competence to overall rhetorical competence and meaning making. They wrote that tutors should help students with mechanical correctness, but that they should also help students create, organize, and revise at higher levels of discourse.

According to one student, an effective tutor "helps me to think critically" and develop "writing techniques . . . that gives me the knowledge for future writing reference." Students cited "writing style" and "creativity" as areas they want to focus on in sessions. One student who was insistent about mechanical concerns wrote that "these things change between languages" and that sentence-level work was necessary for "comprehension and development," expressing a view of mechanics informed by a desire for effective overall communication.

Following Harris's (1997) lead, I asked students if they had any general advice for NES tutors of ESL students. Harris noted that the responses to her request for advice stressed that ESL students understand their differences and their potential authority, which I confirmed in my sample. Again, responses varied noticeably even in this small group, but what emerged was the suggestion that tutors should, above all, have patience—an idea best expressed in one of the students' own words: "Different people have different problems in different areas of English. So just try to communicate with them to find out what they most need help with." Implicit in most responses was the idea that students, too, will demonstrate patience, and that they want to find as many opportunities as possible to discuss their writing processes: "It is important to have people talk to us about our work, the more the better."

◈ PRACTICAL IDEAS

The students' and tutors' responses to the survey and the results of my other research have led me to several suggestions for tutors. Because I share with several of the feminist scholars I cite in this chapter, and especially with Vandrick (1994), the belief that "feminist pedagogy is not a specific set of practices; [that] each classroom, each teacher, each group of students, is different" (p. 84), the suggestions are necessarily less a how-to guide than a call to be more conscious of institutional and gender-related politics in and around writing centers and of how those politics might be best manipulated for the benefit of students.

Ensure That the Writing Center Does Not Look or Feel Like a Classroom

Although not all writing centers will resemble the comfortable, well-worn one in M. W. Nelson's (1991) study, they will most likely look markedly different from classrooms. Tutors (and writing center directors) can emphasize this productive distinction by reducing the physical distance between them and the students as much as is comfortable. Greeting students individually as they arrive and sitting next to—rather than across from—them during sessions may make students feel at ease, which is especially critical for ESL students.

Tutors should ensure that writing centers feel different as well. My fellow tutors and I have frequently set agendas for the next session with students and just as frequently have suspended or abandoned them altogether based on new concerns the students expressed or new feedback we needed to give. Whereas spontaneity may, at times, be incompatible with an ESL writing teacher's need to address various points of academic writing in a classroom setting with as many as 25 students, it is a hallmark of one-on-one interactions in the writing center. It is also key to keeping tutoring sessions open to the idea that both tutors and students need to take over at different times.

Give Students a Chance to Reflect Critically on Their Assignments

If tutors and students can create a space and practices that encourage comfortable, spontaneous interaction, tutors may find themselves dealing with students' expressions of misunderstanding of or frustration with writing assignments. Such situations can be precarious because tutors can easily be caught between students and writing instructors.

As several students suggested, however, working through frustration can be especially helpful in guiding understanding of assignment expectations. For instance, tutors should ensure that students bring assignment descriptions with them to sessions and, to clarify what the assignment requires, should consider talking through alternative writing topics or alternative ways to approach the topic. Implied in such clarification is open communication among tutor, student, and teacher. In fact, tutors should take the initiative to establish a regular communication channel and a system of documenting outgoing and incoming messages—whether by e-mail or paper memorandum. Above all, students should be encouraged to share their critical perspectives on writing tasks not only because of the link to invention uncovered in this study but also because students' appraisal of writing situations is crucial to their development as writers.

Recognize Language Differences as Language Strengths

Anzaldúa's (1999) recognition of the value of code switching is provocative for thinking about tutors' interactions with ESL students. The question any ESL tutor in a writing center faces is whether what is on the page represents a deficiency or a richness of expression that varies from academic English but that may reveal rhetorical sophistication. (hooks, 1994, pp. 40–41, is clear on this point, calling for recognition that students will use different cultural codes in a given setting.)

Once tutors have decided (as I believe they should) that any ESL student's work warrants reading beyond surface features in an attempt to draw out meaning, they may be guided by any or all of Jarratt's (2001) suggestions about feminist pedagogies. In her group writing program, M. W. Nelson (1991) collected preenrollment writing samples from entering ESL students. She then instructed the teacher-tutors to have the students free write once the course started. Specifically, teacher-tutors told students to write without worrying about being monitored for mechanical problems or for content that seemed "too personal" (p. 32). Both the students' fluency and their accuracy in using standardized English mechanics improved. They were working through their native rhetorical abilities to produce better English prose than they would have produced if their teachers had been monitoring their grammar all along. Nelson does not specifically label her methods *feminist,* but her work attempts to examine how ESL composition classes ignore students' competencies and skills in favor of a traditional standard. This focus aligns her work with that of Jarratt (2001) and Anzaldúa (1999).

Given M. W. Nelson's (1991) finding that ESL students' fluency and mechanical skills improve when they are left to write without worry about correctness, tutors should strongly consider making time for unsupervised free-writing activities both early in their relationships with ESL students and as new assignments come along.

Tutors can also ask students to provide pretutoring samples of their writing, then compare these samples with later free writing to judge progress. Students as well should review their progress to encourage their active and continuing participation in the tutoring relationship.

Use Tutorial Time to Slow Down Writing Processes and Make Them More Transparent

Many tutors may not have much time to spare during tutoring sessions, but tutors should not forget that the goal of these sessions is to help students develop sustainable writing practices. To that end, tutors should slow down the rush to finish and polish a product as much as possible. This showing may help students develop an appreciation for their writing processes and allow students to draw on their diverse language abilities to approach assignments in innovative ways.

Tutors could benefit greatly from consciously untangling reading from evaluating as they review students' drafts. In doing so, they might look for reorientation among the diverse rhetorical devices ESL students may use and ask the students for guidance (Land & Whitley, 1989).

Do Not Hesitate to Help Edit or to Work on Mechanics

At some point, ESL students working in most writing centers will face a deadline for handing in writing for evaluation. In wanting to focus on process instead of product, tutors and writing center administrators may—at the ultimate expense of the students—ignore the classes that send students to the writing center (North, 1984, p. 438).

Students whose writing teachers have indicated that mechanics weighed heavily in a bad grade may be uncomfortable working on organization before grammar, as one tutor suggested in a response to my survey. A feminist composition pedagogy that prompts a tutor to default to a larger-level-discourse-concerns-first strategy may be counterproductive in such a situation by sacrificing an honest consideration of the student's particular need for a static, tutor-centered session.

◈ CONCLUSION

If the suggestions in the Practical Ideas section seem contradictory, it is because a feminist pedagogy that takes itself and students seriously must offer options useful at particular sites for particular students rather than offer static rules. On the surface, offering these options may look like a reworking of the old writing center idea of doing whatever works. Far from that, however, this case is a call to writing tutors to embrace feminist composition pedagogies that, by being self-critical as well as critical of gendered power relations, "perceive educators and students as expressing authority that is varied, temporary, and mutually dependent" (Latterell, 2000, p. 118). The same student may walk into the writing center on 2 different days with two different sets of concerns. As I have discovered, this is especially true of ESL students, who must balance their concerns and competencies in order to be successful in U.S. academic settings.

As I was tabulating student responses and checking enrollment statistics in the Writing Center, I encountered an interesting problem that pointed to the implications of a growing ESL presence in writing centers and composition classrooms. I recalled that, although Penn State has separate writing classes for ESL students, at least a couple of the ESL students I had tutored had been placed instead into the composition courses for NES students. Thus, I could not rely on enrollment figures from the ESL composition courses to tell me how many ESL students were taking the tutorial.

This observation suggested more than a need to recheck numbers. The divide between composition for native English speakers and ESL composition persists now largely as a formal separation between academic disciplines. The students and the cultural and social changes they represent are wearing away the distinctions. Writing administrators and tutors have known for some time that NES and ESL students have attended writing centers together in larger numbers and with increasing frequency. Yet institutional constraints have often limited the ways writing centers serve more and more complex student populations. The limited, marginal, feminized position and practice of writing centers can become an empowered one, reflecting and utilizing the power and potential flexibility of feminist pedagogies that have long been prevalent in composition. These pedagogies not only serve NES students but may also benefit ESL tutoring situations.

◈ ACKNOWLEDGMENTS

I am grateful to Julie Story, assistant director of Penn State's Center for Excellence in Writing, for much of the specific information about the Undergraduate Writing Center.

◈ CONTRIBUTOR

Jay Jordan is a doctoral candidate in English at The Pennsylvania State University, in the United States. His research focus is on interconnections between composition for native English speakers and ESL composition theories and pedagogies. He has taught, tutored, and led writing workshops for NES and ESL students in the United States and in Poland.

◈ APPENDIX: SURVEY

Dear Participant,

I am conducting a survey in order to gather information about ESL students' interactions with tutors in the Undergraduate Writing Center at Penn State University, as well as students' opinions about the effectiveness of the tutoring help they receive. Please do not write your name on this survey; your answers will be used only for the purposes of this research project and will remain anonymous. Your decision whether or not to participate in this survey or to stop participating will in no way affect your grade in any course.

Please try to answer all questions as completely as you can.

Thank you very much for your cooperation.

Jay Jordan

1. What is your sex?   FEMALE   MALE   (Circle one.)

2. What is your age? _____

3. In which country were you born? _____

4. Which language did you learn to speak first? _____

5. When did you start learning English? _____

6. When did you come to the United States? _____

7. What other English writing classes have you taken (at Penn State, other colleges or universities, or in high school or secondary school)? Briefly describe the kinds of writing assignments you did in those classes.

   _____
   _____
   _____   _____
   _____

8. Which writing class are you currently taking?

   ESL 4   ESL 15   English 4   English 15

For each of the following questions, you are free to use all of the space provided and to turn the page over and use the other side.

9. Give examples of what you think an ESL writing tutor should do. Why did you list these things?

    _____
    _____
    _____
    _____

10. How is what a writing tutor should do different than what a writing teacher should do?

    _____
    _____
    _____
    _____

11. Of the things you and your tutor do during your sessions, which things do you believe are effective in helping you with your writing? Why?

    _____
    _____
    _____
    _____

12. Which things that you and your tutor do are ineffective? Why?

    _____
    _____
    _____
    _____

13. Do you discuss your opinions about your writing assignments (for example: whether you like them, think they are a waste of time, etc.) with your tutor? Why or why not?

    _____
    _____
    _____
    _____

14. Do you feel more comfortable with your tutor than you feel with your writing teacher? Please explain your answer.

    _____
    _____
    _____
    _____

15. What advice in general do you have for tutors of ESL writing students?

    _____
    _____
    _____
    _____

PART 2

Student Voices

CHAPTER 5

Investigating the Male Voice in a Malaysian ESL Classroom

Subra Govindasamy and Maya Khemlani David

⬦ INTRODUCTION

Although Malaysian society can be generally classified as traditional and patriarchal, some of its institutions of higher learning are female dominated. A case in point is the International Islamic University Malaysia (IIUM), a government-sponsored university, where the case described in this chapter was based. At IIUM, almost two thirds of the student population is female, and female lecturers represent 40% of the teaching population (*IIUM Directory,* 2002). This numerical imbalance is more marked in the humanities than in the sciences. In the Department of English Language and Literature (DELL), for example, 60% of the ESL teaching faculty (both senior and junior staff) is female, and 80% of the junior lecturers are female.

In light of this learning and teaching context, a question that may arise is how male students are performing in this female-dominated academic setting. In other words, has the numerical dominance of female students inhibited the active participation of male students in the ESL classroom? Has the male voice become distant in this emerging academic setting? An investigation of this nature is particularly significant now because the Malaysian government is deeply concerned about the nation's dwindling male undergraduate population. A related concern is the academic performance of males in DELL. In the case described here, we set out to determine whether or not male students (a) perform well academically, (b) display a high level of motivation, and (c) are active in ESL classes.

If the female students, with their numerical superiority, outdo the male students in all three academic areas, there is reason to support the claim that the latter's voice is indeed fading. But if the men manage reasonably well in the three areas in spite of their smaller numbers, the national concern that the male voice has become distant has no basis. In order to investigate the issue, we studied the academic performance, classroom culture, and goal orientations of English majors at IIUM.

⬦ CONTEXT

IIUM and DELL

IIUM is a center of higher learning for aspiring, bright Muslim students from Malaysia and other parts of the world. Its inception was a result of the commitment of member nations in the Organization of Islamic Countries and the efforts of

Malaysia's Muslim leaders. It offers traditional academic courses in such areas as medicine, physical sciences, human sciences, religion, architecture, law, business, and accounting, with an Islamic perspective.

DELL is a unit within the Faculty of Human Sciences in IIUM. Demands on the students in the department are heavy: In addition to 54 credits of university courses, students majoring in English must complete 78 credit hours in the department, including 12 courses in linguistics (sociolinguistics, semantics, pragmatics, language acquisition, grammar, morphology and syntax, research methodology, and advanced writing courses) and 14 courses in literature (British, U.S., Malaysian, and Islamic).

The Students

Our study focused on the male students of DELL, who hold minority status in the program. Of the 360 undergraduate students in the department in the June–November 2002 semester, only 10% were male. It is not uncommon to find only two or three male students in a particular course. Occasionally, however, a class has a larger number of male students. Although such classes are atypical, by studying them we were able to examine the experience of a larger pool of male participants.

Research Methodology (RM), a compulsory course, was the subject of this case. The RM course combines qualitative research, writing, and presentation of findings. The course was designed to enable graduating students to acquire professional skills needed for their future employment and to develop students' ability to engage in independent research. The predominant belief among the faculty members in the department was that RM was sufficiently professional in its orientation and that the skills taught were adequate for graduating students who were entering the job market. The findings of this study would either confirm or reject this belief. We also observed interactions among students in two ESL classes to elucidate any differing trends in interaction between the male and female students.

◈ LANGUAGE AND GENDER

Traditionally, one area of research on gender in education has examined possible differences between female and male characteristics, ability, and performance. For example, Foote (2000) studied confidence levels among female and male respondents and found that women were as confident as men when making item-specific judgments but were less confident when answering ambiguous and demanding questions.

Another study by P. Wolfe (1998) concluded that boys tend to dominate interaction when the content has a high level of difficulty whereas girls tend to dominate when the content is less demanding. Govindasamy, Mohamed, and Zain (2000) observed that girls were usually less visible than boys in the classrooms they studied and were often bypassed because boys' movement and voices were more likely to attract the teachers' attention. The study also suggests that the faculty were more likely to listen to male students, credit men for ideas presented, and develop discussion around men's comments.

Hsiao (1998) found that Asian boys were more flexible, more creative, and more active in class participation. Her findings support the view that male-dominated classroom interactions are the norm in the region. She notes that male students clamored to answer most of the teachers' questions during classroom discussions. On the other hand, Marcelo and Suarez-Orozco's study of immigrant children in the United States (cited in Campo-Flores, 2002) reveals that female students' performance was better than that of their male counterparts, as the former were more adept at straddling cultures.

◈ DESCRIPTION

We believed that a two-pronged investigation—of the academic achievements and classroom performance of male and female students—would shed light on gender-related issues in the IIUM's ESL classrooms. To investigate academic achievement, we relied on documentary evidence of graduating students' overall academic performance over the period 1995–2002.

To find out whether one group dominated the other in classroom discussions, we recorded and tallied the distribution of frequency of turns in six sessions of two freshman ESL classes, one with more male students (19 male and 8 female), and the other with more female students (32 female and 8 male). The first three observations were during class discussions on relatively concrete topics, and the last three, during class sessions dealing with relatively abstract topics. We observed freshmen in order to capture students' behavior before they became acculturated to the practices of the institution. In addition, we interviewed randomly selected students from both classes.

We also interviewed 51 (43 female and 8 male) final-year students about their goal orientation. We chose final-year students because they would be more concerned about gaining employment than their junior counterparts. If the academic achievement and the interactive patterns in classrooms do not explain the performance of IIUM students, motivational factors may do so: The course content may not be stimulating enough, or students may regard it as less useful for their vocational interests. If there is a good fit between the learners' goal orientation and the course content, especially in the selection of teaching material, the source of discontent may be more personal than academic and institutional. At a minimum, investigating course content as a motivational factor may rule out the possibility that poor performance among students is due to course content.

◈ DISTINGUISHING FEATURES

Academic Performance of Females and Males

According to IIUM convocation program books, each year from 1995 to 2002, more females than males earned top honors (first class and second class upper). In 1998 and 2002, in fact, none of the male students received top honors.

These findings based on annual achievements may not give a true picture of the academic achievements of the two groups, as the female students were numerically dominant during the 8-year period (81 male vs. 314 female students). Thus we reconstituted the data for the same period using intragroup achievement (see Table 1). For second upper honors, female students had more than a 12-percentage-point advantage over their male counterparts. More male students than female students earned lower honors (64.2% vs. 52.6%).

TABLE 1. ACADEMIC PERFORMANCE OF MALE AND FEMALE STUDENTS, 1995–2002

Honors	Male students		Female students	
	n	%	n	%
First class	1	1.2	2	0.6
Second upper	28	34.6	147	46.8
Second lower	52	64.2	165	52.6
Total	81	100.0	314	100.0

Because we lack more refined data on performance differences between the two groups and on those students who either did not complete their studies or failed to complete the minimum requirements for graduation, we do not regard the slightly better performance of females as indicating academic superiority. Accepting that the marginally superior academic achievement of female students indicates the undermining of the male voice would require corroborating evidence.

Patterns of Interaction in the Classroom

To establish that male and female students differ in academic performance, we looked at interactive patterns in the classroom. In particular, we examined turn taking during learner-based group discussions (a feature of classroom interaction that provides an immediate insight into the nature and dominance of student groups) and participation in discussions of more and less abstract topics.

Turn Taking

Nonparticipant observation of interaction during group discussions revealed that male students dominated discussion in the male-dominated class and that females dominated in the female-dominated class ($p < 0.05$ on the SPSS t-test measure; see Table 2).This dominance of one group over the other is to be expected, as the numerical superiority of male students in one class and that of the females in the other would produce some difference unless one group were culturally and socially impeded from expressing their opinion. This finding establishes that the university's religious environment has not prevented the female students from developing their potential, as is the case in many Muslim nations. An incidental finding is that both male and female students participated a little more actively in the smaller class (27 students) than in the larger one (40 students) (see Table 2).

Our finding that the males dominated interaction in the class where they were numerically superior but less so in the female-dominated class contradicts Hsiao's (1998) findings, based on a study of Asian children. Hsiao's study portrays boys as more flexible, more creative, and more active in class participation. She notes that male students clamored to answer most of the teachers' questions during classroom discussions. In contrast, we found that the male students appeared generally more reluctant to participate than the female students. In each of the six sessions of the female-dominated class we observed, the males' level of participation was low, and their interactive strength was very close to that of their numerical strength (20%).

When a male respondent in a female-dominated class was asked about male

TABLE 2. TURNS BY MALE AND FEMALE STUDENTS DURING DISCUSSIONS IN MALE- AND FEMALE-DOMINATED ESL CLASSROOMS

| | Male-Dominated Class[a] | | | | Female-Dominated Class[b] | | | |
| | Males | | Females | | Males | | Females | |
Session	n	%	n	%	n	%	n	%
1	243	77.1	72	22.9	54	21.8	194	78.2
2	228	62.8	135	37.2	66	24.1	208	75.9
3	260	61.2	165	38.8	72	26.1	204	73.9
4	221	54.3	186	45.7	62	22.3	216	77.7
5	184	55.1	150	44.9	80	26.3	224	73.7
6	189	53.8	162	46.2	84	24.1	264	75.9
M (individual)		11.6		18.1		8.7		6.8
M (group)		60.7		39.3		24.1		75.9
SD		8.9		8.9		1.9		1.9
Correlation		−1.0				−1.0		
t-value		2.959				−34.017		
p		.032*				.000*		

[a] 19 males (70.4%), 8 females (29.6%). [b] 8 males (20%), 32 females (80%).
*Statistically significant.

performance during participation in such discussions, he quipped, "The girls don't control us. They're usually better prepared. Usually they do their homework. We allow them to talk more [laughs]. But when we talk, they don't intrude. We manage without doing a lot of work."

Another male respondent confided that he did not feel threatened by the large number of girls in his class. However, he felt singled out by the ESL lecturer. This respondent explained, "Somehow, because we are few, the lecturer remembers our names more easily. She always calls us first to answer any questions. The girls escape. Difficult to remember the 32 names. Easier to know us."

The studies mentioned earlier confirm this observation that teachers were more likely to listen to male than to female students. Apparently, numerical dominance of women may not automatically bring about control of interaction and contribute directly to a loss of the male voice.

Confidence in Dealing With More and Less Abstract Topics

The third, fourth, and fifth class sessions we observed covered topics that were relatively more abstract than the topics in the first three sessions. Contrary to the findings of P. Wolfe (1998) and Foote (2000) cited above, in our study the female undergraduates dealt with abstract discussion topics as well as males did. The female students remained confident regardless of the topic. This finding, we reasoned, may be due to the female students' numerical superiority in the department as well as in the university.

Goal Orientations of Male and Female Students

We also examined the goal orientations of male and female students in their final semester of study (i.e., those enrolled in the RM course) with regard to the types of writing, interactive, and other skills that they would need to find jobs after graduation. Students were asked to rate the value (to them) of a set of writing, conversational, and job-related skills (some taught in the RM course, others not) by choosing either the statement *I really need this skill for enhancing my employment prospects* or the statement *I may need this skill for enhancing my employment prospects* for each skill. We told the students that for a given skill, choosing the first statement (*I really need . . .*) indicated a high rating for the skill and that choosing the second (*I may need . . .*) indicated a low rating.

The Importance of Writing Skills

For written communication skills, male and female students differed significantly in the skills they rated as important and those they rated as less important ($p < 0.05$). The male students rated writing research papers, business letters, résumés, commentaries, and e-mails, and summarizing and paraphrasing as important subskills (see Table 3).

TABLE 3. MALE AND FEMALE STUDENTS' RATING OF WRITING SKILLS (%)

Skill	High[a]		Low[b]	
	Males	Females	Males	Females
Editing	37.5	44.2	62.5	55.8
Writing research papers	62.5	41.9	37.5	58.1
Writing business letters	62.5	41.9	37.5	58.1
Writing reports	37.5	37.2	62.5	62.8
Writing résumés	75.0	60.5	25.0	39.5
Writing proposals/project papers	37.5	44.2	62.5	55.8
Writing commentaries	62.5	34.9	37.5	65.1
Writing e-mail	75.0	79.1	25.0	20.9
Doing creative writing	37.5	41.9	62.5	58.1
Writing summaries	62.5	41.9	37.5	58.1
Paraphrasing	62.5	46.5	37.5	53.5
M	55.7	46.7	44.3	53.3
SD	15.2	12.5	15.2	12.5
Correlation	0.559		0.559	
t-value	2.241		−2.241	
p	0.049*		0.049*	

[a] I really need this skill for enhancing my employment prospects. [b] I may need this skill for enhancing my employment prospects.
*Statistically significant.

On the other hand, the female students considered only two of the skills (writing e-mail and writing résumés) as highly important. That the female students ranked writing e-mail highly is not surprising: The students may see e-mail as the fastest and most efficient way to communicate with others. As graduating students, they may realize that they need to know how to write good résumés to get jobs.

When asked why female students generally gave low ratings to skills such as paraphrasing, editing, writing research papers, writing business letters, and writing commentaries, one female respondent stated, "I don't want to work in the business world. I'm worried about that. I don't have many skills. People [i.e., the employer] may scold me. I want to teach English in a private school. It is easier."

Male students appeared less worried about their ability to function in the corporate sector. In fact, all eight of them wanted to be employed in this sector. One respondent said, "I want to be a businessman, get a lot of money, buy a big car and house like my elder brother. It's not difficult . . . . No, I don't want to teach."

The Importance of Oral Communication Skills

Both groups rated most of the oral communication skills as important (see Table 4). The male students rated one skill—speaking fluently and confidently with other fluent speakers—relatively lower than the females did. This rating appears contrary

TABLE 4. MALE AND FEMALE STUDENTS' RATING OF ORAL COMMUNICATION SKILLS (%)

Skill	High[a]		Low[b]	
	Males	Females	Males	Females
Interacting during social conversation	75.0	86.0	25.0	14.0
Participating in problem-solving discussion	75.0	88.4	25.0	11.6
Giving opinions and suggestions	62.5	86.0	37.5	14.0
Raising questions and objections	75.0	88.4	25.0	11.6
Describing graphs, charts, etc.	62.5	76.7	37.5	23.3
Evaluating information	62.5	93.0	37.5	7.0
Presenting oral reports	75.0	95.3	25.0	4.7
Negotiating intelligibly	62.5	93.0	37.5	7.0
Speaking fluently and confidently with other fluent speakers	37.5	95.3	62.5	4.7
M	65.3	89.1	34.7	10.9
SD	12.1	5.9	12.1	5.9
Correlation	−.233		−.233	
t-value	−4.864		4.864	
p	0.001*		0.001*	

[a] I really need this skill for enhancing my employment prospects. [b] I may need this skill for enhancing my employment prospects.
*Statistically significant.

TABLE 5. MALE AND FEMALE STUDENTS' RATING OF EMPLOYMENT-GAINING SKILLS

Skill	High[a]		Low[b]	
	Males	Females	Males	Females
Computer literacy	75.0	97.7	25.0	2.3
Business communication skills	75.0	90.7	25.0	9.3
Pedagogical skills	37.5	95.3	62.5	4.7
Job-related skills (apprenticeship)	75.0	95.3	25.0	4.7
Spoken English course	75.0	95.3	25.0	4.7
M	67.5	94.9	32.5	5.1
SD	7.5	1.1	7.5	1.1
Correlation	−.097		−.097	
t-value	−3.556		3.556	
p	0.024*		0.024*	

[a] I really need this skill for enhancing my employment prospects. [b] I may need this skill for enhancing my employment prospects.

*Statistically significant.

to the male students' desire to enter the corporate sector, a career sector that would seem to require good interaction skills.

The Importance of Employment-Gaining Skills

The third group of skills examined included computer literacy (e.g., the ability to use computer-based presentation software), language for conducting and participating in meetings, speaking skills, teaching skills, and other job-related skills. The female students rated all the skills highly, including pedagogical skills (see Table 5). The male students rated the teaching skills low but rated expertise in other areas as important.

The findings of the study reveal that the goal orientation of the male and female students differed, largely influenced by expectations of the society—that is, that men should be involved in the business world and women in the teaching world. However, on a positive note, the pedagogical skills that female students most valued can be obtained at IIUM at the postgraduate diploma level in the Faculty of Education. On the other hand, the university does not offer the occupational skills valued by the males.

◈ PRACTICAL IDEAS

Offer a Course That Responds to Students' Perceived Needs

Responding to requests from the students, the department introduced an English for specific purposes course (Language for Occupational Purposes [LOP]) with the primary purpose of enhancing graduating students' skills. LOP focuses on skills that RM does not cover, namely, speaking persuasively on informative topics, negotiating deals, participating in and conducting meetings, writing business letters, writing memos, composing e-mail, and performing other job-related, interactive tasks.

Have Students Serve Internships

One feature of the LOP course is a short internship in a business organization. Students observe the kinds of communication that take place in various business firms and, on their return to the classroom, present detailed reports to the lecturers.

One of the students' greatest discoveries was that, although Malay is the national as well as the official language of the country, 90% of the interactions and communications in the 16 business organizations participating in the project were conducted in English. This was an amazing revelation to them. The students were also surprised to see that even Malays conducted business in English (see also David, 2000). They noted the varieties of English that were spoken: from the more formal medium used by the executive staff to the pidginized variety used by the manual and support staff.

Have Students Conduct Meetings

Another course activity tests students' linguistic creativity by allowing them to script and conduct formal meetings in public spaces in the university. This activity involves a great deal of research, writing, discussions, rewriting, and role playing. Inevitably, students have to stretch their linguistic resources to participate. Participation helps them uncover concepts and practices and increases their fluency. This approach gains strength from the theoretical assumption that routines contribute immensely to language and skill acquisition (Foster, 2001).

◈ CONCLUSION

We wanted to ascertain whether the numerical superiority of the female population in public universities in Malaysia has made the male voice distant. If enough evidence showed that the male voice was fading, we would conclude that future academic decisions needed to attend to the male voice. However, our analysis of the students' academic performance and of the interactive patterns in the ESL classrooms does not support the view that the numerical superiority of female students has minimized the role played by the male students. Subsequent analysis revealed that the goal orientations of the male and female students differed considerably. The cultural expectation that males must be engaged in business and industry whereas females should be employed as teachers appears to have played a key role in the students' goal orientations, as graduating male students wanted to be employed in the corporate sector.

Apparently, the courses offered by DELL have been too academic. Their academic nature may have been partially responsible for the below-par academic performance of the male students. Many acknowledged that their motivation level was low and that their courses did not have any practical value. They also anticipated that the department would provide courses that might be of greater help in procuring skills that are valued in the job market. Cultural expectations and their influence on goal orientations, an intrusive and not very well understood factor, appear to be an important factor influencing our results. In light of this observation, our results do not validate the concern that the dwindling male population in Malaysian universities may have triggered a fading of the male voice. Students may have preferences, and the faculty should to be sensitive to their needs.

◈ CONTRIBUTORS

Subra Govindasamy is an associate professor in the Department of English Language and Literature at the International Islamic University Malaysia. He has researched extensively on English grammatical/discourse features using the semiotic model of analysis. His research interests include issues in language acquisition, a systems approach to instructional design, bilingualism, language policy, and language planning.

Maya Khemlani David is a professor and deputy dean in the Faculty of Languages and Linguistics at the University of Malaya. She has conducted research on language choices of minority ethnic communities and the effects of changing language policies on the various ethnic communities in Malaysia. She is the author of *The Sindhis of Malaysia: A Sociolinguistic Account* (Asean, 2001) and the editor of *Methodological and Analytical Tools in Language Maintenance and Shift Studies* (Peter Lang, 2002) and *English Language Teaching in a Second Language Setting* (Peter Lang, in press), and has published in numerous books and journals.

CHAPTER 6

Speaking in Silence:
A Case Study of a
Canadian Punjabi Girl

Allyson Julé

◈ INTRODUCTION

All students live within the complexities of their gender, social class, and ethnic identity. These factors do not appear in isolation but intersect and influence each other in powerful and personal ways. In focusing on one Canadian girl of Punjabi ancestry, this chapter brings out general issues and concerns to language education and gender studies, particularly regarding the use of linguistic space within a language learning classroom. That Amandeep is a girl and is of Punjabi origin may affect language opportunities in her ESL second-grade classroom (on the former, see Sunderland, 1994, 1995, 1998; Vandrick, 1999a, 1999b; Yepez, 1994; on the latter, see Angelo, 1997; Bannerji, 1993, 2000; Bhopal, 1997; Brah, 1987; Ghuman, 1994).

This case looks at Amandeep's experiences within her language classroom across one school year. The central aims are (a) to discuss how an ESL classroom connects with current research on gender and language teaching and (b) to examine the possible construction of silence in one female student. In analyzing Amandeep's failure to claim the floor in her language lessons, I discuss what in the language classroom might have contributed to her silence and, in particular, what teaching methods were used when she appeared quiet. Two areas not considered here are her language experiences elsewhere, such as at home or with neighborhood friends, and the enormous complexity surrounding the construction of a gendered identity that comes from society at large, the media, and her family or friends. There are a multitude of ways to be a girl. The focus here is on describing and understanding one girl's silence in a particular context.

Schools and classrooms are pervasive language environments, and this is a fundamental reason for studying classroom talk, particularly concerning language learning classrooms where language use is a main objective. In fact, for many ESL children, classroom conversations may be the central educational process or a major portion of it (Adelman, 1981; Aries, 1997; Stubbs, 1976; Vandrick, 1999a, 1999b). In light of the tremendous amount of talk that children encounter daily and the ways in which talk may encourage or be antagonistic toward their participation, an analysis of classroom talk is one important means of exploring a female ESL student's silence.

Stake (1995) and Flyvbjerg (2001), as well as other educational ethnographers, see such qualitative educational research as increasingly concerned with the distinctive complexity of a single case or a single main character and with coming to understand those particular circumstances. They agree with, for example, Geertz (1973) and Gumperz (1982) that such case studies are naturalistic, phenomenological, and largely narrative in nature. And although some observers may criticize such an intimate focus as based too heavily on interpretation of one isolated experience, the field of ESL education must be concerned with the intimate classroom experiences of particular participants (Hammersley, 1992, 1998, 2000).

◈ CONTEXT

Amandeep's School

Amandeep was born in Canada to Punjabi immigrants from India who came to Canada to work on the local produce farms. Like the parents of the other students in her class, her parents are working class. Though Amandeep's cultural roots are in the Punjab, she has never visited it and has always lived close to her school. When she started school at age 5, she spoke no English at all. By all accounts (i.e., speech, written ability, reading ability, listening, and comprehension), at age 7, the time of the study, she was fluent in English and spoke it spontaneously with her classmates—as they all did with each other.

What is particularly interesting is that Amandeep's ESL classroom was located in a Canadian Punjabi Sikh school where all students shared a Punjabi Sikh heritage. Such a culturally specific school is unusual in Canada. Amandeep's school is one of three Punjabi schools in British Columbia. These schools enroll children of Punjabi ancestry and use the set curriculum while offering Sikh studies and Punjabi language classes.

The teacher, Mrs. Green, is a White native speaker of English. She saw herself as a dedicated teacher and expressed consistent concern for the students and their language development. The class had 20 students: 11 boys and 9 girls. In assisting with research at this same school a year earlier (see Toohey, 2000), I had met the students and knew them well before they entered Mrs. Green's Grade 2 class (Julé, 1998, 2001, 2002).

The Punjabi Sikh Community in British Columbia

Amandeep's ethnic group presents a potentially important case for educational research on possibilities for language acquisition primarily because of the Punjabi Sikh community's growth in British Columbia (Angelo, 1997). Regular local news coverage of the Punjabi community has included reports of and discussions on the arrest and trial of British Columbia's Punjabi Sikh terrorists (Bains, 2003) and the arrest of two Vancouver Punjabi Sikh teens for a fatal beating of a classmate (Mickleburgh, 2003). In addition, a Punjabi immigrant to Canada, Ujjal Singh Dosanjh, became premier of British Columbia in 1999, making him Canada's first visible-minority leader (Brooke, 2001). Why this distinction fell to the Punjabi community sparked much notice, particularly in light of the fact that other ethnic groups (e.g., Chinese, Blacks, and Aboriginal nations) have been in Canada much longer. In spite of their presence and contributions to British Columbian society, the Punjabi community has had little representation in academic study, and the establishment of Punjabi Sikh schools in the area has been largely ignored by educational researchers (Alexander, 1996; Brah, 1987; Brah & Minhas, 1985; Cumming & Gill, 1992; Gupta & Umar, 1994).

◈ LANGUAGE AND GENDER

The Power to Speak

Linguistic and interactional patterns that are systematically used more by one gender than the other may offer some insights to ESL educators. Language structures that are specific to classrooms are of particular interest in the larger gender and language debate and also offer insights into the ESL classroom.

One of the themes running through the work of Walkerdine (1990) was that classrooms are sites of struggle—for girls, often passive struggles. Such struggles may result from the particular power relations within the classroom and may be partly witnessed in a lack of speech. One of the various interpretations of silence (see Jaworski, 1993) is that it suggests lack of power or legitimacy to speak. This chapter rests on this possibility.

Gendered Differences in Classroom Talk

Of particular help in understanding Amandeep's silence is what Mahony (1985) first termed *linguistic space.* Mahony found that it was normal for a teacher to ignore girls for long periods of time, for boys to call out, and for boys to dominate classroom talk (i.e., linguistic space) and the classroom space.

Some evidence of gendered differences in classrooms derives from examinations of the amount or proportion of talk time in teacher-led lessons. According to Corson (1993), many studies confirm that teachers may be unaware that they treat boys differently from girls and that they allow and create different access to linguistic space. Many teachers disbelieve the evidence when confronted with it. Indeed, ESL teachers commonly defend their methods with the sincere disclaimer that they "treat them all the same" (p. 144).

Thornborrow's (2002) research highlights the ways that teachers control classroom participation through teacher talk and sees the amount of time teachers spend talking as creating and maintaining asymmetrical power relationships. Teacher-led classroom talk is often organized around initiation–response–follow-up (IRF) exchanges, in which the teacher controls the dynamics of classroom discourse: "The teacher takes turns at will, allocates turns to others, determines topics, interrupts and reallocates turns judged to be irrelevant to these topics, and provides a running commentary on what is being said and meant" (p. 176). Stanworth (1981) and Mahony (1985) argue that giving extra time to male students sends the implicit message that boys are simply more interesting to the teacher. The extra attention paid to boys (much of it corrective) results in girls' relative silence in the same classrooms.

On girls' silent classroom participation, Spender (1980) wrote,

> Both sexes bring to the classroom the understanding that it is males who should "have the floor" and females who should be dutiful and attentive listeners . . . . Within educational institutions girls are quickly made aware that their talk is evaluated differently from boys. (p. 149)

Other findings on gender and the amount of language do not seem to vary much, even as the participants and context of the interaction vary in age, social class, ethnicity, level of schooling, subject matter, and gender of the teacher. In Graddol and Swann's (1989) research, both female and male teachers tended to pay less attention to girls than to boys at all ages, in various socioeconomic and ethnic groupings, and in all subjects. Also, in general, girls appear to receive less behavioral criticism, fewer instructional contacts, fewer high-level questions, less academic criticism, and slightly less praise than boys. Teachers also have been found to direct more open-ended questions at boys in the early years of schooling and more *yes/no* questions at girls (Graddol & Swann, 1989). Boys tend to be first to jump into classroom discussions because of the teachers' nonverbal cues, particularly their gaze attention. This eye contact appears to be important in systematically offering boys more opportunities for participation. Arguably, teachers themselves may gender their classrooms and create talkative male performers and quiet female students as a result.

Silence

Goldberger (1997) reports that "silence is an issue not just for a subset of women . . . but is a common experience, albeit with a host of both positive and negative connotations" (p. 254). *Silence* is defined simply as the absence of speech and, therefore, identifying it in transcription work may be complicated, and interpreting it, even more so. Silence is ambiguous and may be understood only through an interpretation of context. Lakoff (1995) admits that not all silence is necessarily about power, but she advises researchers to consider this possibility. She isolates two female speech patterns as related to silence: interruption and lack of topic control (cf. West & Zimmerman, 1983, 1987). Lakoff suggests that if one is interrupted, in a sense one is silenced by being stopped; if one does not have ideas picked up by others, one is silenced by being ignored.

Gal (1991) differentiates self-imposed and externally imposed silence, a distinction that may be difficult to perceive from the outside. Evidence suggests that many female students feel silenced and unheard, a painful and frustrating experience. To be ignored when speaking is the equivalent of being told that one knows nothing and has nothing to say worth hearing. Ignoring spoken contributions, by not making eye contact or a sound of recognition, may be a powerful way of silencing girls.

◈ DESCRIPTION

At the time of the study, Amandeep had had 2 full years of English instruction (kindergarten and Grade 1) and was involved in her third (Grade 2). Her relationships with the teacher and with other members of her classroom did not appear to be meaningful to her, which may be significant in understanding her silence. Even before I embarked on my research, it was clear to me that Amandeep's particularly striking patterns of silence deserved some attention.

Over the 10 months I spent in the classroom, I noticed that many of the girls shared Amandeep's silent behavior. In this sense, many of the girls could have served as the main character in this case, but I chose Amandeep because of her striking silence. Her behavior initially struck me as quiet; she also appeared lonely in that she often played alone and seemed to create opportunities to be by herself. She did not often call out answers yet was pleased to privately show me her work on display. I wondered if she was simply shy or quiet or if she was performing a particularly accepted role as a girl in this classroom. When I asked the teacher this question in an interview, her response was, "She is a nice, quiet girl." I wondered, however, if Amandeep was being constructed as a "nice, quiet girl." If so, how? How could I document and explain such silence?

Over the 10 months, I visited Amandeep's ESL classroom 29 times and collected 43 hours of observation, resulting in 28.5 hours of videotaped data. After transcribing the data in their entirety, I isolated and analyzed segments of the class's morning literacy lessons in a stratified random sample to isolate lessons involving teacher-led discussions. I then chose monthly samples as a way of scanning lessons throughout the school year. I pulled 10 segments of teacher-led lessons, counted the words of teacher talk and student talk, and converted the word counts to percentages to account for the use of linguistic space. Afterward, I documented the types of speech acts to gain a sense of linguistic context (Cameron, 2001; Searle, 1969).

◈ DISTINGUISHING FEATURES

Division of Linguistic Space in the Classroom

Teacher's and Students' Talk

The finding of teacher-dominated lessons in classrooms is not surprising (i.e., most teachers speak more than the students in their classes do); however, the overwhelming and consistent amount of teacher talk in this ESL classroom is curious because it was a language learning classroom. In each of the 10 segments analyzed, the teacher used, on average, 90% (78–97%) of the linguistic space (see Figure 1). The students, on average, used 10.6% of the remaining talk (2–22%). Boys used almost 10% of the linguistic space, with girls accounting for less than 2% of the words spoken.

This lack of linguistic space for the girls supports the earlier findings of male domination of classroom talk (Graddol & Swann, 1989; Mahony, 1985; Stubbs,

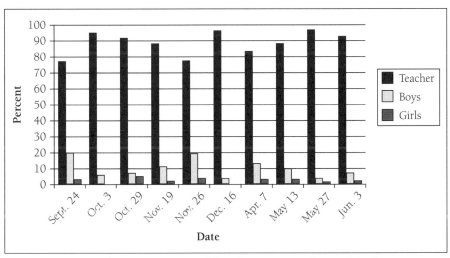

FIGURE 1. Division of Linguistic Space of the Classroom: Teacher and Students

1976). In this regard, the particular ethnicity represented here seems unremarkable concerning gender divisions of public talk. Punjabi or not, boys seem to speak more than their female classmates in teacher-led lessons.

Boys' and Girls' Talk

Many of the full-class lessons in this ESL classroom regularly involved interactions between the teacher and the male students, with the girls observing. In these class discussions, the children's linguistic production was minimal (0–3%), and the girls' production almost nonexistent (1.3% of the total discussion time).

Of the linguistic space occupied by students, boys spoke most of the time (88.3%), and girls much less (11.7%). Amandeep was completely silent, and the other nine girls seem to have been similarly quiet. Consistently throughout the 10 months of observation, the ratio of boys' to girls' use of linguistic space in this classroom was close to 9:1 (see Figure 2). The disproportion of linguistic space for the girls in Amandeep's classroom did not shift as the year progressed; instead, the lack of linguistic space remained a constant for Amandeep and the other girls in her class.

As evidenced in Figures 1 and 2, the use of linguistic space was not divided equally. On average, the teacher spoke 89.4% of the time (78–97%). The students, on average, used 10.6% of the remaining talk (2–22%). Of this, boys spoke most of the time (88.3%). Girls used 11.7% of the linguistic space left over to the students. In other words, girls spoke during only 1.3% of the total discussion time with the teacher (0–3%). Amandeep was completely silent, and the other nine girls appeared to be similarly quiet.

Type and Direction of Speech Acts

A reasonable interpretation of the findings on linguistic space in Amandeep's classroom is that the teacher was gendering the classroom talk by privileging the boys over the girls in some way. To explore this question, I classified each

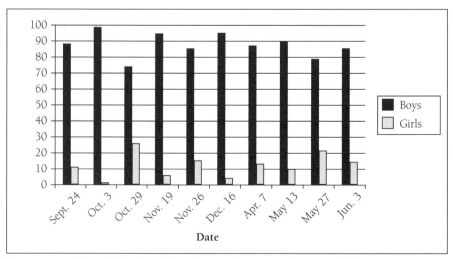

FIGURE 2. Division of Linguistic Space in the Classroom: Boys and Girls

participant's utterances into *speech acts* (Searle, 1969) (see Tables 1 and 2). The categories I used arose from my extensive observations of the classroom over the 10 months. In creating some categories that seemed best to match the classroom discussions, I followed an ethnography-of-speaking model, in which speech acts are organized into types relevant to a particular setting.

The teacher's most frequently used speech act was questioning (79 occurrences). She generally directed her questions to the class as a whole (67 times), sometimes to the boys (11 times), and only once directly to a girl. She often repeated students' comments as recognition of their contribution (59 times), most often in response to a boy's comment (44 times) and only a few times to a girl's (5 times), almost a 9:1 ratio.

The teacher question–response–evaluation pattern confirms other research describing classroom speech acts (Thornborrow, 2002). In this classroom, the conversation took place almost entirely between the teacher and the boys: Of the 79 questions she asked, 57 were answered by boys.

The teacher also used explanation and instruction in her talk, followed closely by negative (31) or positive (24) responses. Most of her responses were directed to boys over girls (24 vs. 9, a ratio of 2.5:1). Negative responses were directed to boys more often than to girls (20 vs. 4, a ratio of 5:1) as were positive comments (14 vs. 5, a ratio of almost 3:1). The teacher offered praise 4 times: once to the whole class, 3 times to a boy, and never to a girl.

The students' speech acts were usually responses to the teacher's questions; this teacher's IRF sequence matches Thornborrow's (2002) study of teacher practice. However, the boys in this study were the usual and consistent responders to such a method (21 answers vs. 3 by girls, a 7:1 ratio). The students themselves asked only two questions (one by a boy and one by a girl).

TABLE 1. TEACHER'S SPEECH ACTS BY CONTENT AND DIRECTION

	Direction			
Content	To the class	To a boy	To a girl	Total
Question	67	11	1	79
Repetition of a student's comment	10	44	5	59
Explanation	32	1	0	33
Negative response to a question	7	20	4	31
Instruction or guidance	28	0	0	28
Positive response	5	14	5	24
Direct order	1	10	2	13
Ignoring student's comment	0	10	2	12
Criticism	0	8	2	10
Praise or reinforcement	1	3	0	4
General comment	3	0	0	3
Storytelling	2	0	0	2

TABLE 2. STUDENTS' SPEECH ACTS BY CONTENT AND SPEAKER

Content	Speaker			
	Group	Boys	Girls	Total
Response to a question	15	57	8	80
Uninitiated comment	0	21	3	24
Question to teacher	0	1	1	2
Storytelling	0	1	0	1

The Silencing of Amandeep

The following three excerpts are samples of classroom moments that reveal the silencing of Amandeep. To isolate these moments, I selected all the sections of the transcripts that revealed Amandeep as present in the room. Because she spent so much classroom time saying nothing, silent classroom moments were prevalent and impossible to transcribe. I therefore selected three brief samples in the data that exemplify typical moments for Amandeep: She sits quietly at her desk while her teacher attends to students, pausing to offer corrections or assistance.

(The class is busy working quietly.)
Teacher: When you find the next page you'll have to start right away! The *p*s I want you to make the bubble first and then start the back. Remember on the *d*s, the little guys, you do the ball first and then the stick. Ball first and then the stick. Ball first and then the stick. Then it comes out really nicely. (Begins assisting students individually. She pauses at Amandeep's desk and addresses her.)
Teacher: Put your name on the top. This one right here. Show me . . . . (She moves on.) (Classroom Visit 5)

(Camera pans back to the teacher helping students with their work.)
Teacher: Do not put two the same (in a singsong voice). If you want to trade your book, you can do that for a minute, while we just finish up here. (Amandeep continues sitting at her desk, offering no response, and this goes unnoticed.) Remember please that you pick two from here, two from here, and then you pick one more from either space. It doesn't matter. Whatever you want, but you need five altogether.
(Clip ends. The teacher moves past Amandeep, who appears to need help with the assignment.) (Classroom Visit 7)

(Students work on their own. The camera focuses on Amandeep, who prints and then erases her work. The teacher can be heard in the background, circulating and checking and correcting students' work. After about a minute, the camera pans out to show most students getting up and walking away from their desks, evidently finished. Amandeep continues working on her own. After another minute, Amandeep finishes and gets up. She does not ask for help, nor does the teacher offer any.)

(Clip changes to boy standing on his own, reading a book aloud. After a few seconds, the teacher approaches him to ask him how he is.) (Classroom Visit 27)

I found no evidence of Amandeep's calling out or responding to classroom instructions or questions. Her usual form of interaction with her classroom teacher was silence. Amandeep appeared not to be having a rich discourse experience in this ESL language classroom, and the teacher seemed not to notice Amandeep. She was not talkative during class discussions or even in small-group talk, so she may have been easy to ignore. But this ignoring may also have caused silence in Amandeep: Her silence may have been an understandable response to her classroom environment. Such a possibility implicates other language teachers who view the silence of students as desirable or ethnically based behavior and therefore beyond engagement.

◈ PRACTICAL IDEAS

Pay Attention When Girls Talk

Amandeep clearly did not have or take the linguistic freedom in the classroom to demonstrate her *communicative competence* (Hymes, 1972). Perhaps Amandeep kept a low profile in the class because of the particular ways the teacher limited her participation. Amandeep rarely participated in conversation and rarely joined the narratives of others. This may be because she was temperamentally quiet or because of the teacher's lack of response or attention. Amandeep's silence ultimately appeared to be her most consistent speech strategy.

In primary ESL classrooms, gender may be a factor influencing silent participation, and ESL teachers should be particularly sensitive to this possibility. The main finding of this study provides descriptive statistical evidence of how gender may correspond to access to linguistic opportunities in a language classroom. The teacher's participation in silencing girls is compelling, and teachers would do well to pay more attention to the quiet girls in their classrooms and consider gender as a factor in predicting language use.

Wait for Girls to Speak

ESL classrooms must be organized in such a way that gender is recognized as a factor in speech production. ESL teachers should look at how—and when—girls talk in classrooms. Paying attention to girls who are speaking and attending to what they are saying may go a long way in supporting female ESL students. Not all ESL teachers habitually wait longer than usual for girls' replies or specifically ask girls to participate in conversations; such sensitivities can be taught in teacher education programs. Even in primary ESL classrooms, gender is a powerful variable, and primary ESL teachers must also organize their ESL classrooms and discussions with this in mind.

Structure Language Lessons to Encourage Girls to Speak

ESL teachers might consider structuring talk-related activities and preparing girls for classroom lessons and discussions before the lessons begin. Teachers may use talk as a preliminary activity to other classroom assignments, yet they often talk through the entire lesson in an attempt to govern the learning rather than permit students access to the linguistic space.

Teachers may need to recognize that speech itself can determine learning opportunities; if girls are kept quiet, this silencing may compromise their language learning potential. The argument that ESL girls may be shy and quiet of their own accord is irrelevant (as well as unsubstantiated); the systematic silencing or ignoring of girls in order to engage the boys may need further attention.

Research needs to continue if the TESOL field is to address the processes at work in ESL classrooms that limit the potential of any students. "Who is talking?" is a critical question for the ESL teacher. The stereotyping of Punjabi girls (and other groups) as quiet is simply an inadequate response. The realities of one ESL classroom suggest that teaching methods, particularly IRF, may be contributing to the silence of certain students.

◈ CONCLUSION

This study shows that teaching methods are a significant variable in language use. In the relationship between Amandeep and her teacher, the teacher may have limited Amandeep's speech through the practices of instruction and interaction: by denying or failing to provide her access to linguistic space.

Certainly Amandeep's particular case is dependent on local understandings, and a complete analysis would require a much fuller narrative than this one. But such local complexity may implicate all ESL classrooms, each filled with distinctive and complex issues and personal stories. What all ESL classrooms share with Amandeep's is the variable of gender and its potential power to influence speech acts. A recognition of gender challenges accepted ways of thinking about primary ESL settings as benign or neutral. Sometimes girls are not permitted reasonable access to linguistic space in classrooms.

ESL teachers need to be concerned with the linguistic opportunities of all students. However, as Amandeep's case demonstrates, some students (perhaps mainly females) may need particular attention.

◈ CONTRIBUTOR

Allyson Julé is a Canadian currently serving as senior lecturer at the University of Glamorgan, in Wales. She has taught English and applied linguistics at Trinity Western University, in Canada, as well as run film studies workshops at the English Language Institute of the University of British Columbia, in Canada. Her research interests are gender and language use in classrooms as well as the Punjabi Sikh experience in Canada and elsewhere.

PART 3

Innovations
for All

CHAPTER 7

Opportunities for Girls: A Community Library Project in Uganda

Kate Parry

◈ INTRODUCTION

In 1969, the United Nations Educational, Scientific, and Cultural Organization's (UNESCO) Regional Office for Education in Asia lamented, "Although they have learned to read, many literate people continue to behave as illiterates because their society and the behavior of its members is still pre-literate" (quoted in Phillips, 1970, p. 26). The lament is echoed in much of Africa today, where educators and other professionals regularly bewail the lack of a reading culture. Part of the problem, as the UNESCO report suggests, is that too many people still cannot read at all, but illiteracy rates have declined over the years and are now well under 50% in many areas. In such areas, a reading culture is lacking not so much because people cannot read but possibly, at least in part, because they have too little access to written material.

In Uganda, for example, a substantial proportion of the population, especially in the younger cohorts, has been to school (Uganda Bureau of Statistics & ORC Macro, 2002, p. 13), and there is a growing realization of the importance of information (Byamugisha, 2001). In addition, a growing number of institutions—publishers, nongovernmental organizations, and government agencies—are producing written material for rural people. The problem is that there are no adequate means of disseminating this material. Although "signs of literacy" (K. Parry, 2002, p. 151) are often seen in rural communities—notices advertising goods and services, boards identifying local schools, handwritten announcements of meetings—people have little access to books or newspapers. They hardly ever have occasion to read extended text, so their reading skills are little used and naturally atrophy (cf. Abadzi, 1994; Omoding-Okwalinga, 1985).

The community library project described here is an attempt to build on, and build up, the literacy skills that exist in one rural community by providing books that are both interesting and accessible to the local people. Because in that environment most printed matter is in English, it is also a means of building on and building up knowledge of the English language.

Such a project, being locally based and outside the formal education system, is particularly significant for girls and for the women that they will become. At all levels of schooling girls are at a disadvantage in Uganda: Not only are fewer girls than boys sent to school in the first place (UNESCO, 1995, p. 36; Watkins, 2000, p. 93), but more of them leave school before completion (Hyde, 1993, p. 103). The reasons are largely monetary—if a family is short of cash for school fees, it will pay boys' fees over girls'—but other factors are involved, such as demands for girls' labor at home, pressures on them to get married, and the risks of sexual harassment at school and of pregnancy. Of girls who finish the secondary course, many go no further, partly because they simply do not think of applying to tertiary institutions. The pressures on girls to think of themselves as filling only traditional, domestic roles are strong, and early marriage followed by frequent pregnancies is the most common career pattern for a woman (Kwesiga, 2002).

The Ugandan authorities are now making strenuous efforts to reduce this gender disparity. With the introduction of universal primary education, many more girls are now enrolled in school, and adult education classes focus especially on women's needs. These policies will in due course reduce female illiteracy rates, but they will not in themselves offer significant amounts of information to women and girls in rural areas. The project described here presents a third and complementary strategy, namely, to provide reading material outside the schooling system to anybody in the community, including those women who have had to leave the system early. In so doing, it offers a new and different model of literacy that does not require the mediation of teachers, is not dictated by any syllabus, and is compatible with the domestic avocations to which most Ugandan girls can expect to devote their lives.

◈ CONTEXT

The project is located near a trading center called Kitengesa, in Masaka District in the central region of Uganda. The trading center is only about 4 miles from Masaka town (the district headquarters), yet it is in a typically rural area: There is no electricity or piped water, and the people earn their living primarily by growing coffee for cash and *matooke* (a kind of plantain) for food. The area was prosperous in the latter days of colonial rule, but the 1970s brought hard times with low coffee prices, war, and general disorder, and now the people perceive themselves as poor. Everyone has enough to eat, but money is hard to come by, and simply keeping a household going requires a good deal of hard work.

Literacy in Kitengesa

The prosperity of the past meant that many people in the area could afford to go to school. Those who achieved a secondary education during colonial times generally work in Kampala (the capital city) or elsewhere, because education in those days was a sure passport to a job and prosperity. Those who dropped out at primary school or who finished secondary school later have not been so fortunate; they have tended to remain in the area, working as peasant farmers like everyone else. Although education has not brought them riches, these people still value it highly and make Herculean efforts to send their own children to school.

The area thus has a substantial literate population. A survey I conducted in 1998 of students at the two secondary schools in the subcounty (one close to the trading center, the other in the parish of Narozali, some 7 miles away) found that nearly all the adults in their families could read. A more recent survey of households in Kitengesa and its neighboring parish Lwannunda identified 1,332 readers—that is, people interested in participating in the library project—distributed over 283 households. Of those readers, 263 were over 20 years old, and 1,069 were adolescents and children. Total population figures for the two parishes were not available, but the probable proportion of the population that these readers represent is suggested by a broader survey done in 2001 for the Ugandan government: Among people over 15 years old in the central region of Uganda, 89.7% of the males and 79.8% of the females were found to be at least minimally literate (Uganda Bureau of Statistics & ORC Macro, 2002, pp. 14–15).

The numbers of young readers are increasing rapidly as a function both of population growth (the rate of which has been 3.3% a year in Uganda since 1991, according to the 2002 census; Wasike, 2002) and of the policy, instituted in 1997, of introducing universal primary education. This policy has more than doubled the number of children in school (from 2.3 million in 1996 to 6.8 million in 2000; Uganda National Commission for UNESCO, 2001, p. 33), and the primary schools around Kitengesa have expanded accordingly. No new schools have been built, but the old ones are bursting at the seams with children. All these children are supposedly learning to read. Thus, in the Kitengesa area, the literate population is fairly large already and is set to expand rapidly over the next few years.

The Role of English

Attendance at primary school implies the acquisition of not only literacy but also English. Uganda is a multilingual country with no universally accepted African lingua franca, so English, the language of the former colonial power, retains a dominant position in the education system and in national life generally (K. Parry, 2000; Schmied, 1991). Children in Kitengesa are taught to read initially in their first language, Luganda, but they start studying English right at the beginning of primary school and are expected to switch to it in the fourth year as the medium of instruction. All the exams that will determine their success are in English, and they know that without it they have no hope of upward social mobility. They also need English if they are to participate in national politics or mediate between government at the national and local levels, because English is the language of all central government business.

Yet in Kitengesa people have little opportunity to use either their literacy or their English. Everyone speaks Luganda when not in school, and the local radio stations broadcast mainly in Luganda. As for reading materials, few are available in either language. Newspapers are not sold in Kitengesa (although they are in Masaka), nor could most people afford to buy them if they were. People have a few books in their households. In the 1998 survey of secondary school students, 52 reported 227 books in their homes, including an assortment of school textbooks in English, a number of Bibles in either English or Luganda, and some popular Luganda story books.

But these figures suggest an average of fewer than five books per household, clearly not enough to sustain a habit of reading, let alone maintain a knowledge of English. Even in the schools, books are few and far between. The primary schools have some but not nearly enough for all the children, and the ones they have are school textbooks; they have no books for general reading. The one secondary school in the neighborhood, which is called Kitengesa Comprehensive Secondary School

(KCSS) even though it is located in Lwannunda, is even worse off: In 1998 it had only a handful of textbooks in the headmaster's office available for the teachers to consult.

KCSS is the location of the project. The school was founded only in 1996 and until 1998 was housed in a couple of ramshackle mud-brick buildings with no proper windows or roof. Its student body was small, with 13 students in 1997 and a staff of only three teachers. Its headmaster, however, is a man of vision. He founded the school with a view to providing an education that would equip young people to make a living locally, and part of his conception was to have a library that should serve not only the school but also the community. In response to this vision, the Kitengesa Community Library Project was developed. The project has grown along with the school, which is now on its own plot of land, with simple but properly roofed classrooms and nearly 100 students.

◈ LANGUAGE AND GENDER

Literacy as a Gendered Issue

Literacy, particularly literacy in a metropolitan language such as English, is undoubtedly a gendered issue. First, in Africa as in much of the rest of the world, literacy is consistently less available to women than it is to men, as is exemplified by the figures quoted in the Context section for the central region of Uganda. Second, once literate, girls and boys have, in various contexts, been shown to read different materials (see, e.g., Boraks, Hoffman, & Bauer, 1997; Davies & Brember, 1993; Langerman, 1990; Simpson, 1996), which suggests that what literacy means personally is not the same for both genders. Third, in a context where boys are encouraged to leave home to seek employment whereas girls are all too often forced into early marriage and domesticity, the practical consequences of literacy are different; for the boy out in the world, it may be a necessary tool for obtaining and maintaining a job, whereas for the girl at home, it may be more important as a means of feeding the imagination and developing her relationship with her children. Literacy, especially English literacy, may also enable some girls to transcend the limitations imposed on them by their gender, as has been demonstrated in Uganda by the remarkable achievements of a small number of highly educated women (Tamale, 1998).

In the case of the Kitengesa Community Library Project, its location in KCSS has meant that it caters more to girls than to boys, simply because the school has more girls than boys among its students. The fact is not a coincidence. The school is new, poor, and locally based, so it is inexpensive on the one hand while lacking prestige on the other. As observed elsewhere in Africa (Weis, 1981, cited in Hyde, 1993, p. 124), parents who can afford it prefer to send their sons to other, better established schools, such as Masaka Government Secondary School in the town or, for those who have less money, St. Martin's at Narozali. For their daughters, on the other hand, the cheaper option is more attractive, and so is the fact that KCSS is nearby. Among the Baganda people, women and girls do not ride bicycles, so transport is more difficult for girls than it is for boys, and parents are concerned for their daughters' safety if they have to travel a long way to school—as, again, has been reported elsewhere (Watkins, 2000, p. 193). By the very fact of working through such a school as KCSS, then, the library project is providing reading opportunities for girls more than for boys.

Girls as Agents for Literacy and Development

In catering more to girls than to boys, the project may well contribute more to local development than would a project based in a more prestigious and less impoverished school. On the one hand, precisely because girls are likely to stop schooling and get married at a younger age than boys, they are less likely to move away to the town. Most will remain in the area, so any knowledge that they have is at least potentially available to the community at large.

On the other hand, women capable of accessing information for themselves through books are likely to become better caregivers and thus improve their families' and therefore their community's well-being (Ballara, 1992). Children whose mothers have attended school are generally healthier and grow up to be better educated than children whose mothers have not; their father's schooling has less strong effects (Watkins, 2000, pp. 29–38). Women's participation in nonformal education programs is similarly beneficial, the mediating variable being, it is argued, empowerment (Moulton, 1997). By coming together in a program and learning to read (or acquiring other skills), women experience an increase in confidence that strengthens their position within their families and in relating to outsiders. The Kitengesa Library Project may have the same effect of empowering the girls who attend the school. They can learn to read for themselves and can continue to do so even if they are forced to drop out before completing the secondary course.

Girls may also be more effective agents than boys for disseminating the material that the library has to offer. According to the headmaster of KCSS and other local informants, girls spend much more time at home than do their brothers. Students, girls and boys alike, usually go home immediately after school to have a meal and change their clothes, and then they fetch the water and firewood for the evening's cooking. After that, the boys' chores are done, and they can go off to the trading center or elsewhere with their friends; they may spend some of their free time reading and talking about books, but there are other distractions, and the circumstances might not be conducive to reading aloud. As for the girls, they must stay at home and peel the *matooke* for supper, a task that takes time but not much concentration. In families with several girls, one might read aloud while the others work—and the younger children and older women may listen in, too. Reading may also be done later, when the supper is cooking, provided that the household has a lamp or candle to read by. In such a domestic environment, reading aloud and talking about books is much easier than in the trading center and is more likely to include the nonliterates in the family. It may also give the girls doing the reading a certain authority that they might not otherwise have.

❧ DESCRIPTION

The Kitengesa Community Library Project began in April 1999 as a simple tin box containing a small collection of books. The collection included 161 titles, most of which were short paperbacks written in simple English, although there were 27 Luganda books as well. Over the following months and years, it was gradually expanded, reaching 182 items in May 1999, 274 at the end of July 2000, 346 in August of the same year, and 456 a year later. A library assistant was appointed to lend the books to the school students each week and to maintain the records. Borrowers could keep a book as long as they liked provided that they returned it before borrowing a new one, and they were encouraged to take the books home to read aloud or lend to people there. For the first 9 months or so they were asked to write a report on each book they borrowed, saying whom they had read or lent it to and what everyone had thought about the book. After this period the reports dried up, but borrowing continued, and the lending patterns were recorded.

At the end of 2000, the United Nations One Percent for Development Fund donated $2,932 for the construction of a library building; this building was completed by the middle of 2002 and was officially opened on June 22, initiating a new phase of the project. The collection was expanded to 783 books, most of which were in English, and because many of the new items were textbooks and other, more expensive publications, they were marked as reference texts, which would not be allowed out of the library building.

At the same time, membership was opened up to people outside the school on payment of a small registration fee. Plans were made to keep the library open all day from Monday to Saturday and for half of the day on Sunday. The library was publicized in various ways, in addition to the survey mentioned above, but at the time of writing it is too early to report on the success of this second phase. The information presented here covers the first 2 years of the project and is based on two sets of data: the students' reports on the books they read between June and December 1999 and the library assistant's records of books borrowed between January and July 2000. I compare the girls' response with the boys' in terms of (a) the number of books borrowed, (b) the number and gender of the people to whom the borrowers read or lent the books, and (c) the kinds of books they chose to borrow.

Books Borrowed

In terms of the number of books borrowed per student, there was no significant difference between boys and girls. Girls borrowed more books than boys between June and December 1999 (an average of 7.1 and 5.9 each, respectively), but the numbers of borrowers—28 girls and 14 boys—were too small to draw any conclusions.

The trend was apparently reversed between January and July 2000, when 54 girls borrowed an average of 4.2 books, and 15 boys, 4.6. As a group, however, the girls borrowed many more books than the boys did, simply because there were so many more of them, and the records show clearly that they were passing the books around among themselves. The library assistant thought that they may often have done this between lending sessions so that the records she made underrepresented the reading that was going on. She heard girls talking to one another in Luganda about the books, so it seems that enough of them were doing enough reading for books to become part of their social life.

People to Whom Books Were Read Aloud or Lent

The students' reports in the early months of the project confirm the impression that reading was becoming something of a social activity, especially for the girls. In these

TABLE 1. LISTENERS AND READERS FOR BOOKS LENT TO KCSS BOYS AND GIRLS

	Loans to boys (n = 87)		Loans to girls (n = 195)		All loans (n = 282)	
	Total	Per loan	Total	Per loan	Total	Per loan
Listeners	187	2.1	541	2.7	728	2.6
Male	116	1.3	163	0.8	278	0.9
Female	71	0.8	371	1.9	442	1.6
Readers	170	2.0	478	2.4	648	2.3
Male	104	1.3	167	0.8	271	1.0
Female	63	0.7	299	1.5	362	1.3
Unspecified	3	0.0	2	0.0	5	—
Total	357	4.1	1,019	5.2	1,376	4.9

reports, the students were asked to indicate for each book that they borrowed those to whom they had read it aloud and those to whom they had lent it to read for themselves along with the age and sex of each of these listeners and readers (see Table 1). The data present problems because the students were not consistent in how they named the individuals in question, making it hard to determine which of the listeners and readers were the same people and to what extent they were the same from one week to another. The totals given in Table 1 are based on a simple count of all individuals listed on each occasion; they are therefore undoubtedly inflated because the same individuals were counted several times. The numbers of listeners and readers per loan, however, give a credible indication of the situation.

The figures in Table 1 suggest that lending books to girls may be a powerful way of getting written information into the community, especially to women and other girls. First, when all listeners and readers are counted, girls who borrowed books seem to have either read them or lent them to more people on average than did the boys (5.2 vs. 4.1 people per loan). Second, the figures for listeners alone suggest that the girls were more likely to read their books aloud to others than were the boys, which means that the books, and the exposure to English that they entailed, could thereby reach people such as young children or illiterate adults, who could not read for themselves. Third, the listeners and readers were clearly divided by gender: Boys read or lent books more to men and boys, girls more to women and girls. The girls also shared their books with a larger proportion of children, reporting that 47% of their listeners and readers were under 15 years old whereas only 32% of the boys' listeners and readers were so young.

Types of Books Borrowed

The third point of comparison between the boys and the girls is the kinds of books that they chose. The books were divided into 12 categories (see Table 2). The initial collection consisted, for the most part, of short texts in simple English, all purchased in Uganda and many produced by local publishers.

Modern stories included both illustrated books written for young children and

TABLE 2. BOOKS BORROWED BY BOYS AND GIRLS, BY CATEGORY, JUNE-DECEMBER 1999

Category	Titles available	Loans to 14 boys		Loans to 28 girls	
		No.	%[a]	No.	%[a]
Modern stories	53	35	40.2	62	31.8
Traditional stories	27	19	21.8	103	52.8
Religion	20	11	12.6	6	3.0
Health	17	7	8.0	13	6.7
Morals	17	4	4.6	8	4.1
Education	11	3	3.4	0	0.0
Biography	9	3	3.4	1	0.5
Society	5	2	2.3	0	0.0
Drama	4	1	1.1	0	0.0
Farming	2	1	1.1	2	1.0
Classics	2	1	1.1	0	0.0
Geography	2	0	0.0	0	0.0
History	1	0	0.0	0	0.0
All books[b]	175	87	100.0	195	100.0

[a] Percentages may not add to 100 because of rounding.
[b] Because of multiple copies of the same title, the number of titles is smaller than the number of books.

adventure stories meant for older ones, often with a strong moral purpose; one example is the most popular book in the modern stories category, *How Busulwa Became a Street Boy* (Najjemba, n.d.), which describes the trials and tribulations of a naughty boy who ran away from home. Traditional stories consisted mainly of African folk tales in English translation, many with animal protagonists; among the most popular in this category, for example, was *How Friends Became Enemies* (Rwakasisi, 1996), a story of Hare and Leopard. Books on religion, health, and morals were also explicitly African, most obtained from Paulines Publishers, a Catholic organization that produces simple readers at low cost to encourage individual and community development; many of these books deal with sex education in both physical and emotional terms. Most books in the biography category were Paulines books, too (belonging to a series on saints' lives), as was one of the two titles on farming.

Drama consisted of plays, mostly in Luganda, and classics was designated for simplified versions of classical European texts. The two texts in question were *The Adventures of Pinocchio* (Collodi, 1881/1985) and *Kidnapped* (Stevenson, 1886/1995); the project consciously decided not to purchase many books of this kind lest the library signal to its users that literature comes mainly from Europe. The other categories were formed from books contributed by the students. The language, geography, and history category consisted of old school textbooks (including a couple of dictionaries without covers); the education category, of prospectuses for educational institutions; and the society category, of political pamphlets.

The most striking point to emerge from this analysis of borrowing patterns is the marked preference shown by the girls for traditional stories, a preference that is not nearly so strong for the boys. The boys seem to have preferred modern stories (which the girls evidently liked, too), but they also tried a wider range of books—including ones in education and classics, which were fairly obviously foreign.

In the following 6 months (January–July 2000), the girls' preference for traditional stories was not so marked (see Table 3), but it was still strong, especially considering that only 27 titles were available as opposed to the 53 modern stories titles. Their liking for modern stories seems to have remained fairly constant. The boys, for their part, were proportionately more interested in modern stories, and they continued to borrow a wider range of other books than did the girls. The girls' range seems to have widened a bit, not surprisingly, perhaps, considering that the number of girls had increased.

These differences in the boys' and girls' choices of books to read may be linked to the social patterns described earlier. The boys, generally, were encouraged to go out and about, and their expectations of going further in education and of eventually getting salaried jobs were probably much higher than the girls' were. Modern stories would have seemed more relevant than traditional ones to people with such expectations, and reading school textbooks and prospectuses might have been a way

TABLE 3. BOOKS BORROWED BY BOYS AND GIRLS, BY CATEGORY, JANUARY–JULY 2000

Category	Titles available	Loans to 15 boys		Loans to 54 girls	
		No.	%[a]	No.	%[a]
Modern stories	53	30	42.3	83	36.6
Traditional stories	27	10	14.1	57	25.1
Religion	20	9	12.7	10	4.4
Health	17	6	8.4	30	13.2
Morals	17	1	1.4	31	13.7
Education	11	4	5.6	3	1.3
Biography	9	2	2.8	4	1.8
Society	5	1	1.4	2	0.9
Drama	4	1	1.4	3	1.3
Farming	2	1	1.4	4	1.8
Classics	2	1	1.4	0	0.0
Geography	2	3	4.2	0	0.0
History	1	2	2.8	0	0.0
All books[b]	170	71	100.0	227	100.0

[a] Percentages may not add to 100 because of rounding.
[b] Because of multiple copies of the same title, the number of titles is smaller than the number of books.

of trying to make their dreams a reality. Another notable point is that the boys' borrowing patterns were closer than the girls' were to those of their teachers, four of whom were men. The teachers borrowed 24 books in the first period and 21 in the second, only one of which was in the traditional stories category. Perhaps the pattern here reflects the modernization of males. The girls, on the other hand, were more confined to the home and probably expected to be so in the future. For them, stories that echoed the themes of those traditionally told by the fireside may still have seemed appropriate, especially for reading to younger brothers and sisters.

Interestingly, in the second period, when interest in traditional stories among the girls was lower, interest in health and morals books was higher, and noticeably higher, especially for books on morals, than it was among the boys. Discussion of such books in the home context, when children may be present, may be a valuable means of encouraging healthy behavior in an area that has been ravaged by AIDS.

Another point about the borrowing patterns is of special interest in consideration of the library as a language teaching project. Most of the books in the collection were, as noted, in English, so most of those borrowed were in English, too; indeed, the teachers informed me that the students "did not want" books in Luganda because one of the major purposes of reading was to improve their English fluency. Interestingly, girls borrowed more English books than boys did. In 1999, 92.6% of the loans to girls were English books versus only 77.2% of the loans to boys. The corresponding figures for 2000 were 91.7% and 63.0%, respectively. These figures should not be overemphasized, as the numbers for the boys, in particular, are small, but such a high incidence of borrowing English books by girls suggests that, through them, the language is reaching into Luganda-speaking homes. People in those homes, then, especially the women, have a better chance of becoming bilingual and hence of gaining access to discourse at the national and global levels.

◈ DISTINGUISHING FEATURES

Rural Focus

The Kitengesa Community Library is an unusual kind of literacy project, being above the level of basic literacy yet being rural in focus. In Uganda, it is not quite alone in serving a rural area— six rural information centers are scattered about the country— but libraries, insofar as they exist, are an overwhelmingly urban phenomenon; all 23 of those administered by the Public Libraries Board, for example, are located in urban centers, most of them in Kampala (Byamugisha, 2001).

Community Outreach

A second distinguishing feature is the library's location in a school. Many secondary schools have libraries—indeed, possession of one is a requirement for recognition as an examination center by the Uganda National Examinations Board—but these libraries are accessible only to the students and teachers of the schools to which they belong. The Kitengesa Community Library is exceptional in being based in a school but attempting to reach out to the community as a whole, first, by encouraging students to take the books home and pass them on to others and, second, by inviting people outside the school to become members.

Provision of Books With No Relationship to the School Syllabi

A third and related feature is the kind of material that the library provides. Naturally, there is a demand for school textbooks, mainly from teachers in the area, and in the latest phase of the library's expansion, the library has supplied these textbooks. The project has made a concerted effort, however, to maintain the emphasis on books that have no direct relationship to school syllabi.

The nonschool books now in the library include not only the storybooks mentioned above but also a number of practical publications that are intended to promote rural development. A number of these directly address issues of gender. *Violence Against Women* (Eastern and Central Africa Women in Development Network, 1997), *Women's Dignity* (Kiura, 1995), *Gender Issues* (Uganda Change Agent Association, n.d.), *Women in Business* (Lochhead, 1990), and *Women Know Your Land Rights* (Uganda Women's Network, 2000) are all among the new titles, the last two in Luganda as well as in English. Also included are a number of new health books: a series of stories about common Ugandan diseases called *Your Companion in the Absence of a Doctor* (2000); a couple of well-known reference books for rural health workers, *Where There Is No Doctor* (Werner, 1979) and *Where Women Have No Doctor* (Burns, Lovich, Maxwell, & Shapiro, 1997); and one or two nutritional guides (the health category now comprises 44 titles, of which 38 are available for circulation).

In addition, the library has acquired a number of books on running small businesses (11 titles) and on farming practices (39 new titles). Not all of these address women's interests—those that are about coffee cultivation and dairy farming, for example, are more likely to be read by men—but many do, and even those that do not may open up new ideas for women's activities. It is a collection of books unlike that of any school library in Uganda, designed to help individuals not only advance within the formal education system but also continue their education and extend their language skills outside it. In this respect, the collection is particularly significant for girls.

◈ PRACTICAL IDEAS

Literacy practices are always embedded in the broader patterns of social life, and these patterns vary from one community to another (Street, 1993). The Kitengesa Community Library Project cannot, then, serve as a model to be applied indiscriminately to other situations. Nor is the work of the project over. The books and the building are now there, but the collection remains small, and the tasks of monitoring and responding to demand continue. More must be done, too, to reach out to the community beyond the school. Four months after the opening of the library building, membership from outside the school remained small and included few women. Yet the girls in the school have shown that the potential for benefiting women is there.

Below I draw from the Kitengesa experience some general guidelines for promoting gender equity through a library project of this kind. These guidelines must be recognized as provisional; there is still much to be learned as the project develops.

Choose a Location Carefully

Locate the library project where there is a substantial literate population, of which a significant proportion is female. Such populations have developed in Africa only within the past generation and are still far from universal (UNESCO, 1995, p. 19). Nonetheless, they will become more widespread as governments and other agencies work toward the goal of Education for All (UNESCO, 1990).

Base the Project on an Established Institution

Base the library project on an institution that is already established in the community. The school at Kitengesa has been an essential starting point for the library, providing its physical location, its core membership, and, through the students and their parents, access to the community at large.

Secure Local Support

In planning a library project, gain the support of at least one locally based person of some social standing who can publicize the project and mobilize local resources. In Kitengesa the headmaster of the school has played this role, and the project has been lent further prestige by one of the diocesan priests, who has served on its organizing committee and preached sermons on its behalf.

Seek Funding and Books From Outside the Community

Work with one or more outside people to raise and administer funds and to organize the purchase of books. Some funds for the Kitengesa Community Library Project have been raised locally, but not nearly enough to launch and sustain the project. Nor can the books be found locally, even in the town of Masaka. They have to be purchased in Kampala, and to expand the collection further, it will probably be necessary to go to Nairobi, in Kenya.

Start Small and Go Slowly

The principle of starting small and proceeding slowly has been dictated by financial constraints, but even without such constraints, it is essential to the project's effectiveness. The box of books that the project began with, the practice of lending them out week by week, and the records collected over the first months enabled the library organizers to gauge and respond to the readers' reactions. Indeed, it was the only way of identifying their interests because before the students had access to books, they could not tell what they would like. This slow approach has also been important for clarifying and developing the project's role in serving the interests of women and girls.

◈ CONCLUSION

The Kitengesa Community Library was conceived initially as a literacy project. The aim was to promote reading beyond the formal education system by capitalizing on the literacy skills and the knowledge of English that local residents had acquired within it. As the project developed, its significance as a means of promoting gender equity emerged: Its location in an impoverished rural school and its strategy of reaching out to people outside that school have resulted in opportunities for reading being provided to girls in particular, offering some small compensation for their systematic marginalization with respect to formal curricula.

Moreover, by focusing on girls, the project is promoting reading all the more effectively. By taking books home and reading them to their family members, the girls of KCSS are conveying a powerful and empowering message: that book learning is not necessarily associated with an alien culture even when it is in a foreign language, nor is it only to be accessed through an overbearing (and male-dominated) authority structure. On the contrary, it can address ordinary village people's interests and may offer valuable ideas for improving the quality of local life.

◈ ACKNOWLEDGMENTS

An earlier version of this chapter was presented at the Women's Worlds Congress held in Kampala, Uganda, July 21–26, 2002. The research on which it is based was funded in part by Professional Staff Congress–City University of New York Research Foundation Award 68517-00-01 in 1997 and a Fulbright Lecturer/Researcher Award in 1998–1999, and it was conducted with the permission of the Uganda National Council for Science and Technology. The database used was set up with the help of Ann Elizabeth Robinson, and the survey of potential readers was conducted by Mansoor Ssewanyana and Deogratias Lwebuga.

◈ CONTRIBUTOR

Kate Parry is a professor in the Department of English at Hunter College of the City University of New York, in the United States, where she teaches courses in linguistics. She spends summers and intersessions in Uganda, where she works on various literacy projects. She has also worked in Nigeria preparing both primary and secondary school teachers and in China, teaching in an in-service program for teachers of College English. Her publications include *From Testing to Assessment: English as an International Language* (with Clifford Hill; Longman, 1994), *Culture, Literacy, and Learning English: Voices From the Chinese Classroom* (with Su Xiaojun; Heinemann, 1998), and *Language and Literacy in Uganda: Towards a Sustainable Reading Culture* (Fountain, 2000).

CHAPTER 8

Creating a Community of Difference: Understanding Gender and Race in a High School ESL Antidiscrimination Camp

Lisa Taylor

◈ INTRODUCTION

What does it mean to understand gender relations as inextricably racialized and as one of the central dynamics in the process of learning English as a second identity? In this chapter, I argue that the practice and theorizing of ESL teaching and learning are incomplete without this perspective. To do so, I draw from a qualitative practitioner study into the learning experiences of 30 high school ESL students in an innovative, Freirean-styled, antidiscrimination leadership program (Taylor, 2003). In this 3-day extracurricular program, public school students of 15 national origins were introduced to critical concepts of social analysis in order to explore their personal experiences of social difference and discrimination playing out in the multiple worlds they inhabit (Cao, Soukamneuth, & Larazin, 1999).

After describing the antidiscrimination leadership program and its genesis, I sketch out the ways TESOL practitioners and researchers might conceptualize gender in relation to the power dynamics of English language learning among immigrant youth in multiracial, multilingual cosmopolitan centers. I then focus on how gender and racial affiliations emerged as central dynamics in participants' processes of translating their sense of identity into the context of Toronto, Canada, and negotiating the meaning of personal experiences from a critical, intercultural and translational perspective. I conclude with suggestions for a pedagogical approach to TESOL informed by the double lens of gender and race.

◈ CONTEXT

The ESL Antidiscrimination Leadership Program

The ESL antidiscrimination leadership program is run within and draws participants from the Toronto District School Board (TDSB), one of the most diverse public school districts in North America. Almost half of the students are nonnative speakers of English, representing more than 70 different language groups; however, visible minority students are overrepresented by families with lower socioeconomic status (63%, vs. 38% among White students; TDSB, 2000).

In this context of increasing diversity, the Toronto School Board (and the amalgamated TDSB after 1997) over the past 20 years has developed a multipronged approach to promoting greater equity among this student population, including staff and curriculum development and extracurricular programs for students such as antidiscrimination conferences, workshops, peer mediator programs, clubs and associations, and leadership training. The school board defines equity as an approach to education that does not presume equality between students in terms of their current positions of social status and access to opportunity and resources, but actively works to achieve this through curriculum and policy (TDSB, 2001). One element of this approach was the Equity Leadership Retreats, offered during their peak period from the late 1980s to the mid-1990s to students from more than 16 secondary schools (in addition to a range of equity programs for junior and intermediate students). Among the specialized camps were the ESL camps.

Explicitly designed as a pedagogical model for individual, social, and institutional change (Equity Studies Office, 2000), the camps combined elements of popular education, critical and feminist pedagogy, and integrative antiracism education. Drawing from popular, critical, and feminist pedagogy, the camp program centered on students' personal experience as the basis of discussion, shared insight, analysis, embodied knowledge construction, and positive identity building (Arnold, Barndt, & Burke, 1985; Barndt, Cristall, & Marino, 1982; Luke & Gore, 1992a) as well as leadership development. Understanding leadership as the capacity to analyze and collectively act on the architectures of power shaping the social and material conditions of learners' immediate worlds, the developers crafted activities designed to elaborate and extrapolate personal understandings and individual interests to a process of building collective commitment and effective alliances around shared values and visions.

Grounded in *integrative* (Dei, 1996) antiracism education, this approach took racism as an analytical starting point but, in implementation, insisted on the interdependence and urgency of all forms of discrimination. Facilitators consistently encouraged participants to see how xenophobia, ethnocentrism (and not only Euro-centrism), linguicism, sexism, classism, and heterosexism played out in different societies and communities and how they intersected and interlocked in everyday interactions (Essed, 1991; Razack, 1998). This emphasis proved crucial to underlining cross-cutting shared values and interest in social change and to ensuring that, for example, male students did not dominate action plans to challenge racism in home schools or that female students of prominent ethnic or class backgrounds did not dominate antisexism projects.

Draconian education funding cuts by the provincial conservative government have effectively eliminated the camps. The camp that participants in my research attended was the only one organized for more than one school in the 1999–2000 academic year, possible only as a 3-day nonresidential program at the University of Toronto and in part facilitated by Ontario Institute for Studies in Education/University of Toronto teacher education candidates.

The Camp Program

By 2000, the design of the 3-day program had evolved to include the following elements:

1. participating in icebreakers, group bonding, and collective identity development games to allow students to establish a positive environment of openness, trust, and play or pleasure with others from their own and up to five other schools (in this camp, one other school). In pair interviews, participants began relating to each other respectfully as individuals.

2. viewing one of a number of videos aimed at illustrating of how linguicism, racism, and xenophobia can marginalize, isolate, and disadvantage ESL students. After the viewing, participants debriefed in small groups by sharing personal experiences or responses to any of the portrayals in the video.

3. in small heterogenous groups, learning specific terminology for analyzing individual, institutional, and societal discrimination of any basis (e.g., stereotypes, prejudice, discrimination). Participants then shared and analyzed examples from personal or immediate experience using these terms (see the Appendix for an excerpt from the *Facilitator's Handbook* [Equity Studies Office, 2000]).

4. in school-based groups, analyzing how antidiscriminatory and welcoming their own school was. Participants brainstormed and presented to the entire group an action plan and time line of specific, collective steps to improve different aspects of their school with the support of attending teachers.

5. making individual written commitments describing individual action plans or resolutions. At a reunion of all participants about a month after the camp, participants were to present progress reports, solve problems, reconnect, and renew momentum.

As elements of an extracurricular program, the activities focused solely on values education without the pressure to cover grade-level subject content. This focus created an atmosphere of support for personal exploration, enhanced through staffing practices: The camp facilitators were not students' subject teachers but board equity program workers, youth workers, and preservice teacher candidates from the University of Toronto. Such an environment was crucial, as the camp activities asked participants to describe negative personal experiences they may have preferred to forget but that represented the necessary basis of a complex understanding of larger societal phenomena as manifest in the participants' lives. This process shifted their position from target to informed analyst.

Participants in the 2000 Camp

Participants were selected for the camps based essentially on expression of interest, with teachers giving permission based on their estimation of students' academic standing and ability to miss time from school. Although school-based ESL teachers had considerable latitude to interpret the selection criterion of leadership potential, program organizers promoted the consideration of both positive and negative leaders (those fitting orthodox measures of the good student and those challenging these measures but displaying social leadership among their peers). The program also stressed gender balance and ethnic diversity in participant selection.

The ESL students selected by their teachers to attend the 2000 camp came from two very different institutional contexts. The first high school, Sunnyfield Collegiate Institute (a pseudonym), an institute focused on academics, had participated regularly in this program for more than a decade: Past camp graduates had built a historical legacy of antiracism activism, including antidiscrimination clubs and programs, although a peak of activism had passed by this point. More than 60% of the student population identified as one ethnolinguistic group (Chinese), of whom more than 75% spoke English as a second language (Taylor, 2003). This category collapses internal distinctions of regional/national dialect, ethnicity, and class as well as immigrant generation. The next largest ethnic group was White Canadian born, with much smaller numbers of South Asian and continental African students.

The second high school, Bonneview High (a pseudonym), had never participated in an antiracism camp before (having belonged to a formerly distinct school board); however, antiracism and minority empowerment were key values promoted by school staff. The number of teachers of color; the Black emphasis of many extracurricular programs (including a steel-drum school band and Caribbean food served in the cafeteria); its combination of teen parenting, adult education, and literacy programs; and a reputation for strong teacher advocacy have tended to attract an ethnically diverse student body, but particularly African and Caribbean Canadian students from the entire metropolitan region. In addition to the 40% of the school population composed of these students, another 15–20% were immigrant students from Africa, Central and Southeast Asia, and Eastern European nations (Taylor, 2003).

The second high school was also in a critical political moment: Under the pressures of drastic budget cuts, the board had announced plans to close a number of schools, including Bonneview. Over a 4-month period (during which time the camp occurred), the students and staff engaged in a passionate and politically articulate struggle to defeat this plan.

◈ LANGUAGE AND GENDER

Gender emerged as a key dynamic in students' learning experiences at the camp, although not in terms of their access to, vocality in, participation in, or reflection on the curriculum. It is not surprising that girls spoke more often and for longer periods in light of the broadly defined antidiscrimination premise of the program. Understanding the role of gender demands different questions: What were girls saying, and what were they able to say and to mean?

My attention to these issues reflects an understanding of the process of learning English as one in which the immigrant youth were not only acquiring new linguistic capacities and resources but were engaged in a high-stakes negotiation of who they (could) become as English learners in this particular English-speaking context. That is, these youth were negotiating the claims they could make in terms of identity (which in its collective dimension includes a sense of community and belonging), knowledge, and authority as speakers to whom others might listen (Canagarajah, 1999; Goldstein, 1994, 2003; Ibrahim, 1999; Leung, Harris, & Rampton, 1997; McKay & Wong, 1996; Norton, 1997, 2000; Norton & Toohey, 2001; Norton Peirce, 1995; Pennycook, 2001; Toohey, 2000). Within this social identity framework, I assume that what one can say, how one might claim through language a legitimate speaking identity with the right to be listened to, how one claims membership in different social groups through language choice and use, and what words mean and what one might claim to mean when using them are sociopolitical dimensions implicit to all second language learning. In the case of the participants in this study, these dimensions clearly reflected competing understandings based in the experience of being a girl or boy of different national or ethnoracial identifications within the cosmopolitan context of a Toronto high school.

Broaching a discussion of the tensions of social identity and difference—including language, gender, and racialized ethnicity—at play and at stake in the experiences, concerns, and challenges participants wrestled with during and after the program requires an understanding of how the relations of difference, identity, and community were staged within the camp curriculum.

Personal, Student-Constructed Understandings of Identity, Difference, and Community

Through the experiential pedagogy, identity, difference, and community were presented not as abstract, academic concepts but as something participants could discover by examining their own lives (see Point 3 of the program outline in the Context section). The personal examples (as opposed to hearsay) provided by participants were referred to as *raw materials* (Equity Studies Office, 2000) of students' apprenticeship in social analysis in an explicit effort to value embodied forms of knowing and to avoid having more linguistically or theoretically adept participants dominate the discussions. This emphasis had the effect of promoting nonacademic forms of knowing and privileging less powerful individuals who, because of their subject position within society, tended to have a greater number of personal experiences of different forms of discrimination to cite (two central practices within feminist pedagogy: see Gore, 1993; Luke & Gore, 1992a; Weiler, 1991).

A Multidimensional, Intersecting Model of Identity and Difference

Participants were encouraged to understand their experience in relation to many intersecting forms of identification and difference, not exclusively those which define and are privileged within the communities they belonged and had belonged to (e.g., nationality, ethnicity, or language). For example, facilitators asked participants for any examples of discrimination, prejudice, or stereotyping they could remember, not strictly examples of linguicism or ethnocentrism (see the Appendix). This practice opened a space for participants to identify themselves according to religion, gender, popular culture, or even class, ability, or sexual orientation, and allowed less powerfully located students' complex examples of multiple marginalization to be heard and examined.

Deliberate, Nonessentialist Identification Within a Community of Difference

A distinctive and powerful aspect of the camp pedagogy is the creation of what I have called a *community of difference* (Taylor, 2003): a gradual, activities-based process designed to foster friendship across distinct as well as common experiences, actively building an explicitly nonessentialist collective identity around shared values and commitment. Participants were encouraged to translate their memories, concepts, and values from their immigration experiences in Canada—and from their home culture and previous country—into present camp discussions.

For most students, this invitation was unprecedented. According to interviews, they had found no space in their lives open to the cultural world view, meanings, or language they had brought with them, except perhaps in their families or same-language peer groups. For many, the severing of these lines of connection felt like a loss (the words *loss* and *lost* appear repeatedly in students' interview transcripts), a nostalgic feeling that encouraged somewhat idealized recollections of the communities of their childhood before immigration. When probed regarding this absence of remembered discrimination or disparity, they gave responses that attested to a naturalized vision of a community that cohered based on commonality and sameness.

Camp activities helped participants purposefully expand this naturalized image of homogeneous, harmonious community into a vision and experience of a community of difference. The students remembered childhood communities united through apparent sameness. While the ethnically or nationally identified communities they may have belonged to in Canada often exaggerated this internal sameness in defense against a sense of nonacceptance by their new host society, camp participants could not fall back on such easy models for community. Indeed, what these ESL students had in common—experiences of dislocation, minoritization, or discrimination based on their positionality as nonnative English speakers, immigrants, and members of minority non-Anglo-Saxon ethnicities—also signaled the differences between them (the group shared neither mother tongue, first culture, ethnoracial affiliation, nor country of origin). As immigrant adolescent ESL learners (unlike EFL learners in their home societies), they could not take for granted the sense of belonging, acceptance, collective identity, and values afforded by community but had to explicitly build it up. Rather than denying their past experiences of community, however, the camp curriculum invited participants to translate these into the deliberate collective construction of a distinctive community sharing no histories save those of the present and future. Within the camp community, therefore, difference and identity were denaturalized and staged as collective relationships that could be questioned or proposed, cobbled and negotiated.

Identity, Difference, and Community Within an Intercultural Frame

Finally, by honoring and including students' current and previous cultural contexts as they remembered and volunteered examples of personal experience for collective analysis, the curriculum opened itself to a process in which participants moved back and forth between the different contexts of their lives to negotiate the meaning of these experiences interculturally. I have elsewhere (Taylor, 2003, in press) theorized this back-and-forth movement of meaning and identification as a process of *double translation* (Mignolo, 2000) and even *transcreation* (de Campos, 1981; Vieira, 1999) in order to better clarify the power dynamics and creative transformations that emerged as students moved between nonequivalent cultural systems to understand who they were becoming in English.

In this space, then, relations of social identity, difference, and community were staged not as abstract or natural absolutes but as deliberate, nonessentialist projects and as something one might come to understand based on the resources of one's personal experience within the many communities of which one is and has been a member. In such a space, many female participants developed the capacity to critically and interculturally analyze the ways sexism and racism were combining in their lives. The two portraits selected for analysis in the Description section reflect this particular combination of discourses of racialized gender shaping the stakes two particular young women faced as immigrant language learners as well as the critical, intercultural understandings they crafted.

◈ DESCRIPTION

The data in this section come from a large, qualitative case study that pursued a complex research agenda (Taylor, 2003). The practitioner study involved participant observation in the camp and schools and 1-hour postprogram, individual, semistructured interviews with 30 adolescent Camp 2000 participants, carried out within 10 months of the program's completion. These data were supplemented by 1-hour individual interviews with four adult graduates of past camps (from 1990–1999), which allowed the refinement of interview questions and the particular insights available through a mature retrospective vision. Here I cite only two participants, Hue and Khatra, in order to offer portraits with sufficient context and descriptive detail to illustrate how issues of gender and race intersected in their negotiation of a critical speaking identity in an anglophone social context.

Although the perspective on gender issues taken in the research reflects an understanding of gender as a relational, performative discursive identification, which plays out in a range of issues of heterosexuality, femininity, and masculinity (Barrett & Whitehead, 2001; Butler, 1993). The selection of these two young, female participants for an in-depth examination allows for the consideration of several key interrelated issues (negotiation of social identity in language learning, racialized gender, linguicism, and the development of a critical, translational perspective).

Hue

Hue graduated from an ESL equity camp as a high school ESL student in the early 1990s. Profoundly impressed by the camp experience, she was one of about a dozen mostly female members of her school's teacher-supported antidiscrimination club, which carried out and presented research to the school board regarding the levels and impact of discrimination among students at four neighboring schools.

Age 22 at the time of the interview in November 2001, she looked back at her childhood struggles for acceptance as a new Canadian before the camp experience. After her family's flight from Vietnam, they were finally accepted and sponsored by the Canadian government as refugees, settling first in Halifax, then Montreal, then Toronto. In the course of the interview, she described the pain of being indelibly marked as different through the lens of a rigid, ethnoracially exclusionary image of gendered beauty that she herself came to internalize:

> Yeah, there was a lot of that, things just associated with Chinese: "your nose flat," "your eyes are—" and all that. It really makes you feel very low about

yourself because first of all you don't speak the language desired, so you can't defend yourself, and then you don't look the same: "Well, you're Chinese, so you look like this—ooh!" So it was pretty bad . . . . Then in Montreal we started high school in Grade 7. So by then I knew that my name was a problem, because people were making fun of it, and that *it was something I could change* [italics added] whereas anything else I could not change . . . . And that was really the reason why because I did not want it to be, my Vietnamese name to be a target, for someone to make fun of. So I changed it. So I gave myself an English name. So in Grade 7, when the teacher called my name, I said I would like to be called as Heather. I still keep Heather now because I identify with Heather . . . for many reasons: like I like it, and it, became who I am, and . . . I guess, like, when I was Heather, I was never made fun of again, right? As Heather, my name was never made fun of. Like [laughing] the thing I get is "It's a beautiful name" now, right! They're like "Heather's a beautiful woman's name!" [laughing].

Hue recognized that the name lovingly given to her by her parents had come to signify ugliness and to function as one more marker of ridicule and rejection, like her eyes or nose, and that *Heather* lent her an air of delicate English beauty. Her analysis of this experience challenges a popular practice of taking English names and proposes, on reflection, a more cross-cultural or translational aesthetic of beauty and femininity:

> I felt kind of ashamed that I had to change names because, that's not my birth name, I wasn't given that name. I chose it, not because I really wanted that name, because I thought it was a beautiful name, but because I did not want to be made fun of. Because *Hue* to me meant that I might potentially be made fun of and be hurt by that name. But, so, as I got older, I'm, like, "By changing my name, it's sort of shameful for my parents because like they think that I don't you know respect the name that they gave me?" I mean, they thought *Hue* was beautiful!

Hue's experience illustrates a complex intersection of gendered, racialized, and linguicist discrimination within the Western image of beauty used to denigrate and exclude her as a new immigrant and language learner. Within discursive relations of racialized gender, Hue was not only particularly hurt and ashamed by the weight of ugliness her Vietnamese name carried in its reminder of other taunts: For her as a girl, beauty also represented a socially exaggerated measure of worth. Furthermore, the racist standards of beauty deployed against her were so essentialist as to foreclose any hope of completely overcoming them: She could never change her physical features; at best, she could assemble certain trappings of White anglophone femininity.

Through the intersectional analysis developed in the camp, then, racialized gender became a critical lens and translational standpoint from which Hue could stake out a powerful speaking position as an antidiscrimination leader (a direction she continued after the program).

Khatra

Relations of racialized gender emerged as particularly prominent in an interview with Khatra, a young Somali camp participant from Bonneview High. An ESL student,

Khatra was a highly articulate, extroverted young woman who participated in and responded enthusiastically to camp activities, although she was less active in the organizing and actions that followed the camp. Among the 30 participants selected and solicited for an interview after the camp (based on the intensity of their apparent engagement with the ideas and analyses that animated the pedagogical curriculum), she agreed to an interview 7 months after the camp.

Khatra had arrived in Canada at age 15 in 1999, only a year before attending the camp. It became clear in her interview that she had left Somalia during the civil war under extremely perilous circumstances. Although her parents had since returned to Somalia to continue her father's legal practice, Khatra lived in Toronto with her older sisters, brother-in-law, and infant nieces in a highly supportive, female-identified family environment.

After considerable trust had been built up in the course of the postprogram, semistructured interview, Khatra recounted what she considered a personal experience of discrimination:

> It was after the March break, this girl just pushed me in the hall, and I was with my Ethiopian friends: "What you looking at fat girl?" It was a Jamaican girl. Then my friends called the principal.

As I encouraged her to explore this example in relation to camp discussions, Khatra recalled more of this interaction:

> And she's like, "You're not African," and I'm, "Dss-k [sucking teeth]. You know, I read in history, slavery is over, it's like, gone! We're like, everyone's free people! What're you tryin' to do, slave me?" and she laughed at me! She laughed and laughed and said, "What're you tryin' to do, slave me?"

This incident has many layers, as does Khatra's shocked reaction. In part, her reaction appears to have stemmed from the experience of losing semantic control of her own body. Whereas she had never questioned who she was and how her body signified certain ethnic, racial, and national identities before immigrating to Canada, she discovered that in her Toronto high school, her body was read in ways she could not control or predict, let alone adequately respond to.

The most powerful culture among many groups in this school was anglophone African Caribbean (based on student and teacher interviews), even though this ethnic group is extremely marginalized in Canadian society (in fact, many teachers consciously and actively work to empower African Caribbean students and support their cultural expression and identifications). In this local context, however, Khatra may not have represented particular dominant images of feminine beauty, either in relation to societally dominant White femininity or to locally powerful Afrocentric images of female beauty with roots in historical contexts of racism, cultural colonization, and the de- or hypersexualization of Black women (hooks, 1992, 1996). In addition to contesting exclusionary gendered aesthetics, however, her body was also read as performing an identity that unsettled dominant notions of Blackness and Africanness in the social context of her peers:

> They say, "Maybe your mother, father is Indian." I say, "My mother is Somali, my father's Somali, so I'm Somali! . . . They say, "You're not African, you're not Somali. You got, like big eyes and your hair is straighter." I say, "'xcuse me, I'm

telling you I'm Somali. My people don't look the same, they're all different! . . . Give me a break! I am Somali, so don't call me that other thing!" [Ethiopian friend interrupts in Dutch, both laugh.] [What did you say?] Oh, my friend says we were like the oldest kings and queens in the world!

At stake in all these interactions were images of African femininity that, within this social context, seemed to depend on hair and skin shade: Khatra recounted conversations with young women who approached her to find out how she straightened her hair and what products they might use to do the same. In these encounters she described, one of the strongest reactions was drawn by Khatra's performance of an authentic Africanness that inflected it with devalued markers— imperfect English, nonidealized femininity, hair and skin that looked Indian—even as it questioned and challenged the anglophone West Indian culture of authentic Blackness in the school. That is, finding herself a translated person expected to perform in mysterious, fluctuating languages of pigmentation, hair consistency, and sometimes shape and height, Khatra asserted a Somali conception of Africanness as a denied knowledge that disrupted the locally dominant image of an essentialist Black African identity (and that she claimed predates it, through her reference to ancient Nubian civilizations).

Khatra's shock had more layers to unpack, however. She was profoundly taken aback by the way this incident forced her to redefine common assumptions about the phenomenon of racism:

> Like in Canada, not in other country I was in, even Kenya, I never saw that, no! It's like, in Africa, we know we are Black, we have different shapes, but the skin is still Black so we never do like that kind of stuff, but, in here, it's like, I saw: They're gonna give you trouble, like "Oh my god, I thought the racism was Like, Black and White! And now I see it's like Black and Black!"

As her narrative exploration continued, Khatra moved back and forth between the here-and-now of Toronto and the there-and-then of Somalia in a personal excavation of why a violent attack by one Black girl on another should be so disturbing to her. Describing her reaction to the film *Amistad* (Spielberg, 1997), she traced the resonance of gendered violence as it cuts across not only diasporic African but also women's history:

> It like gives you a lot of mad, but not for the color. Because you will see a lot of the White people—like, you see the history and you will see a lot of White women getting killed or raped by a White man, so you feel mad, because you're a woman, you're feeling that—how can he do that? He's stronger than her? . . . . So I'm really mad about those women, poor women. But I don't like anyone to hit a woman! I don't like it! I hate a person hitting women! I hate it, it's like, it's like I can't stand it! I say, "It's just a poor woman! Why!"

Going on to trace her repulsion at violence against women back to the violence she witnessed against her own female family members during the war in Somalia, Khatra asked listeners to travel back and forth with her as she wove these disparate moments in a trans-Atlantic history of gendered violence into her position of passionate opposition to its perpetuation. Taking up the language of the U.S. civil rights movement (validated by teachers in her school) in her response—"You know, I read in history, slavery is over, it's like, gone! We're like, everyone's free people!

What're you tryin' to do, slave me?"—Khatra shifted from a position of marginalized victimhood to one of leadership, promoting an antisexist and antiracist vision of solidarity. This vision asserted a common gendered concern across racial and ethnic divides, and she was able to clarify it through a translational exploration of the camp vocabulary.

◈ DISTINGUISHING FEATURES

In interview excerpts examined above, racialized gender emerges as a central dynamic in these young women's struggle to take up legitimate, accepted positions as new English speakers and new Canadians in several ways.

Racialized Images of Femininity

First, racialized gender can be understood as a range of gendered and racialized concepts, images, and markers that work in different cultural contexts to define the limits of recognized performance and acceptable practices of femininity and to naturalize certain identifications and collective affiliations and render others unthinkable (Britzman, 1995). For example, Hue's name and physical features might have been accepted as beautiful within a Vietnamese context, but xenophobia in her Canadian school read them as foreign and ugly, an object of ridicule. Denigration of her cultural values and aesthetics negatively affected even how she might have seen and presented herself as a girl.

These racialized images of femininity can raise the stakes for young women struggling to translate their sense of who they are, who they are becoming, and what community they may claim from what positions as they move between cultural and linguistic contexts in the process of immigration and the learning of English. That is, between nonequivalent ethnolinguistic and national contexts, these concepts can resist translation for female language learners and can act as contradictory arbitrators of belonging and acceptance.

Racialized Gender as a Lens for
Developing a Critical, Intercultural Perspective

At the same time, the discussions quoted above attest that racialized gender can become a powerful lens through which these young women developed critical understandings and identifications between and within different languages and world views in relation to gendered issues of beauty and violence. In this program, young female participants drew from the particular ways social identity, difference, and community were staged in order to demystify, explore, and rework the gendered and racialized issues at stake in their coming to voice in English and taking up leadership roles. Khatra, for example, questioned the ways sexist and racist beliefs shaped who she might claim to be (a young Somali woman), what this looked like (in terms of physical features) and meant (in terms of whether Somalis of mixed heritage were authentically African enough to be recognized as such in her high school context), and what affiliations she might claim (in relation to other women, both of the African diaspora and other ethnicities, who are also subject to a global history of violence against women in which men and women of all ethnicities participate).

Furthermore, in denaturalizing the sexist and racist beliefs in different cultural contexts, Khatra and Hue developed a critical, intercultural perspective on and reworked the particular gendered and racialized concerns—such as beauty and violence—that were at stake in how they might understand and present themselves as individuals through language in their new cultural context. Moreover, they asserted these readings of their own bodies from a position that moved back and forth between local social contexts. This translational standpoint—these new, complex identifications and gendered understandings—reflects a critical confidence in negotiating the meaning of social relations that is invaluable to ESL students and that stands in sharp contrast to disempowering experiences more common to immigration and language learning.

❖ PRACTICAL IDEAS

The camp program referenced in this excerpt from a larger case study is highly particular. The two young women's experiences explored in depth in this chapter can, however, support several suggestions for classroom practice. I offer some here with the intention of opening up a broad discussion of the ways we as TESOL practitioners can attend to the underlying gendered dynamics of students' experiences of language learning and social identity negotiation.

Create Opportunities for Exploration of a Range of Positive and Negative Experiences

Devise opportunities for students to explore—through resources, activities, and discussions—their experiences of being seen or treated as different based on a wide range of categories. The experiences of research participants, including Hue, attest that, in the absence of opportunities to discuss their experiences of discrimination, young ESL learners by default unconsciously lay the blame, shame, and the (impossible) onus to assimilate on themselves.

If, as this study suggests, students' processes of understanding and responding to these experiences are inextricable from language learning, we as teachers might ask ourselves how such discussions might figure in the curriculum:

- What activities could invite students to consider their own and others' different experiences of these, including gender? For example, a class may identify as the same ethnic group. But are there spaces in which students can explore whether this identification means something very different for female members than for male, or for females and males of different ages, social classes, heritages, faiths, or sexual orientations?

- Does learning English open up, demand, or mean different things for students?

- Do different forms of discrimination condition how students can claim this ethnic identity and what comportments favor or disqualify their acceptance?

Plan Activities in Which Students Can Explore Their Complex Identifications

Allow students to explore their complex identifications with a range of communities or categories through discussions, compositions, or projects. Whereas experiences of discrimination can leave students feeling like Khatra—frustrated at being so narrowly pigeonholed in restrictive identity categories—the curriculum may support students in initiating more critical, complex identifications. This suggests several guiding questions:

- Are there a range of complex social identities represented in learning resources that illustrate the intricate ways identity categories intersect?

- When making presentations or discussing fiction, personal experiences, or opinions, how can you encourage students to move beyond seeing identity categories as something one just is to something one does and different stakes or ways of participating in larger collectivities in different contexts? Could you challenge students to prepare presentations about the different communities they belong to or groups they identify with in ways that allow for a range of positions, feelings, and relationships toward these communities?

- Are there examples in film, media, or writing that illustrate or provoke consideration of how these different aspects of students' social identifications are in a state of change, particularly as they carve out speaking positions in English?

Include Opportunities for Critical Insight Into Transcultural, Gendered Themes

In the curriculum, include opportunities for students to develop an understanding of their changing social identity from different, equally valid cultural perspectives. We as TESOL instructors have a responsibility to equip students with the *cultural capital* (Bourdieu, 1986) they need to successfully navigate an anglocentric world by introducing the sociocultural dimensions of English usage. At the same time, if you explicitly value the processes of bidirectional cultural translation students are engaged in, you might seek in your teaching to stage points of translational friction as opportunities for critical insight into the specific conceptual and cultural assumptions embodied in each language.

In English courses, you may be able to identify and stage relevant gendered themes (e.g., body image, morality, career hopes, familial obligations, personal security, in which one's perspective and stakes are influenced by gender relations) that might focus students' exploration and clarification of a developing critical standpoint and intercultural confidence in relation to different languages as well as their own gendered positions within them.

Promote a Community of Difference in the Classroom

Teachers all strive to develop a learning community in their classes. This case suggests that it is worth beginning by asking how you as a teacher understand this process:

- What different conceptions of *community* do you bring to the classroom?

- In these different models of community, what do members need to have in common for a community to be valuable and functional, and what kinds of difference could it encompass?

Through group activities, presentations, and discussions, you can then proactively develop comfort with complex relations of difference between members. The emerging community will be based less in who people are seen to be than in what they value, what insights they can offer from their differences as well as commonalities, and what other projects the group can best accomplish together.

◈ CONCLUSION

There are moments in students' learning that teachers might, within a more conservative, applied linguistics framework, view as merely interlingual difference. That is, teachers may see them as errors that present opportunities for diagnostic analysis and correction. In essence, this chapter makes a case for a feminist and antiracist, anti-imperialist critical curiosity into these moments and the critical intercultural insights and standpoints they inspire. Such an explicit classroom practice can be understood as akin to critical language awareness (Fairclough, 1992). A fairly simple practice once initiated, it works by granting modest intercultural authority to English language learners who are finding themselves at the subordinate (though often resistant) end of a daunting global cultural, epistemic, and linguistic imbalance (Canagarajah, 1999; Maffi, Skutnabb-Kangas, & Andrianarivo, 2000; Pennycook, 1994, 1998, 2001; Phillipson, 1992; Skutnabb-Kangas, 2000b).

This case also urges English language educators to recognize the gendered stakes in first and second language use, encouraging them to take advantage of moments of interlingual friction to map out these gendered, racialized terrains with students. Without taking away from goals of English proficiency, teachers may encourage students to shape critically bilingual concepts within interlingual slips and gaps that might act not as a deterrent but as a feminist postcolonial supplement to their English and first language proficiencies (Derrida, 1967/1998; Willinsky, 1998).

◈ CONTRIBUTOR

Lisa K. Taylor teaches the sociology of education and multicultural and second language education at Bishops University, in Quebec, Canada. As an ESL, EFL, and social justice educator for 17 years, she publishes and conducts research in the fields of multicultural and multilingual education, and critical pedagogy as well as cultural studies, feminist poststructuralist, and postcolonial theory in education.

◈ APPENDIX: POWER ANALYSIS ACTIVITY FROM FACILITATOR'S HANDBOOK (Equity Studies Office, 2000)

DAY TWO

UNDERSTANDING DISCRIMINATION

PURPOSE: To give the students new vocabulary and concepts to organize their experiences.

METHOD: Write the words: Stereotype, Prejudice and Discrimination on the flip chart. Ask the students to define these words as a group. The bottom line of these definitions should be that:

Stereotypes are ideas, generalizations etc.
Prejudices are feelings, attitudes etc.
Discrimination is action.

It will be helpful to have the students give concrete examples of each.

Next, ask the students who can have stereotypes. (Everybody) Who can have prejudice? (Everybody) What does someone need to discriminate? (Power) One needs some sort of power to be able to act. What gives people power in our society? (Authority, size, language, education, money, etc.)

When students are clear on these concepts ask them to fill out the "When I see, hear, fear" forms with a partner. As they report back group the responses under three headings: Dominant ideas, Individual actions and systemic or institutional practices or policies. Don't tell the students what your organizing principle is. Ask them to figure it out.

Ask the students how these areas are connected. . . . . Connections should run both ways from each corner. Ask them what it feels like to be in the centre of all this and on the receiving end of such ideas and actions.

Finally ask them what kinds of activities are necessary to change this cycle at each corner, i.e., ideas are changed through education, individual actions are changed by rules and consequences, systemic practices are changed by political action.

Note. From Equity Studies Office, 2000, *ESL Equity Leadership Camp: Facilitator's Handbook*, n.p. Toronto, Ontario, Canada: Toronto District School Board. Reproduced with permission of Toronto Board of Education.

CHAPTER 9

Explorations of Language and Gender in a Graduate Technology Course

Sarah Rilling and Rebecca Biles

◈ INTRODUCTION

The backdrop for this case is a graduate-level TESL course on computer technologies in language teaching. In the course, we, the instructor and a graduate student participant, collaborated to highlight issues related specifically to gender in the electronic language classroom. We felt that a technology course was an ideal site for students to learn how gender can affect teacher-student and student-student interactions. Graduate students in the course could experience firsthand what the effects of technology were on their abilities to communicate with each other and examine what role gender plays in those communications. Through a series of discussions and activities involving computer technologies, students in the course learned how gender can affect classroom interactions in the traditional and the computer-mediated classroom.

This case describes activities that we designed to highlight issues of gender in the language classroom and the ways the technologies used in the course supported the goals of learning about gender and computer technology. We overview the technologies used and describe the activities and tasks that students used to explore gender in the traditional and online classroom. In both sections, one of us (Rebecca) comments on the efficacy of the materials and tasks from a graduate student perspective. By presenting the activities and the technologies involved in the course and by including this commentary, we hope that other teacher educators can similarly explore gender in the (online) classroom and the role of the teacher in mediating effective and egalitarian classroom interactions.

◈ CONTEXT

The Course

The course on technology in language teaching described in this case is an elective course in an MA TESL/TEFL program at a midsized public university in the western United States. Even though the course is not required, approximately 90% of recent graduate students in the program have taken it. In addition, graduate students in education and modern languages have enrolled in the course. Because many recent language teaching job announcements indicate a preference for candidates with computer expertise, many students feel that taking the course will increase their chances of gaining successful employment on completing the MA.

In spring 2002, the class met twice a week over the course of a 15-week semester in a computerized classroom. In the course, we explored pedagogical applications of computers through both traditional and computerized means—that is, we met both face-to-face (FTF) and through computer media for discussion and presentation. Because the course was a workshop, it included hands-on practice of a variety of skills needed in integrating technology into the language classroom. These skills included evaluation and production of support materials for native and nonnative speaker software, focused and critical use of the Internet for research, the use of computer-mediated communication (CMC) (e.g., multiuser domains, object oriented [MOOs]; chat rooms; conference use and management) in language teaching, and corpus linguistics in language materials development (for an extended case description of the course, see Rilling, 2000). Individuals experimented with different technologies and later reported interesting technical findings to the class. In class, exploration was encouraged, and professional sharing provided a wealth of technological resources and presentation opportunities to all participants.

The Participants

One of us (Sarah) was the instructor. She had a good rapport with her students, which helped them feel confident about becoming involved in class discussion, both in traditional and CMC modes, especially when it came to introspective subjects such as gender and personal language use. The other (Rebecca) was working on her thesis on language and gender in the online classroom to complete degree requirements and was therefore instrumental in furthering the topic of language and gender as she assisted in planning lessons and implementing the activities described here. The other students in the class were all graduate students preparing to be language teachers.

The majority of students were female (11 women and 4 men); Sarah, a female faculty member, made a total of 12 women in the group. Six countries were represented (France, Saudi Arabia, Taiwan, Turkey, the United States, and Venezuela). Most students were in their mid-20s and from the United States; 2 men and 1 woman were over 40. Age as well as gender and cultural background seemed to play a role in how participants, including the faculty member, interacted in the classroom, both in traditional and online sessions.

The students with the most computer literacy were typically those from the United States in their mid-20s. This is not surprising, as computers have been available in higher education and to individuals at relatively low costs in the United States over the past few decades. Many of these students had been using computers extensively throughout adolescence, and the course encouraged them to consider professional teaching applications. One man in his mid-50s had previously worked as a computer programmer and had more technical knowledge about the workings of computers and associated technologies than anyone else in the course, including the faculty member. International students typically had had less exposure to computer technologies than their U.S. counterparts, but they were nonetheless inquisitive and eager to learn, especially in the areas of CMC and corpus linguistics. Having students with a range of previous technology experiences worked well for both inexperienced and more experienced computer users as a natural mentoring relationship developed among classmates and the faculty member.

In terms of previous gender and language studies, two students in the course had formally studied language in relation to gender, one in a sociolinguistics course and the other through interdisciplinary course work. Other participants had a vague awareness of gendered language, ranging from the notion of grammatical gender (remaining in the English pronoun system) to popularized lore on male/female interactional styles.

◈ LANGUAGE AND GENDER

MA TESL programs often incorporate analyses of language and gender into courses such as sociolinguistics and classroom-based or second language acquisition research. We feel that it is important to include overt discussions about gender and other awareness-raising activities into language teacher education for several reasons. First, although the TESOL community does not typically think of gender as being a cultural influence on how students and teachers interact, linguistic research has shown that gender can influence linguistic choices—from word choices to turn-taking strategies in conversation. Many language teacher education programs have courses on culture and cross-cultural communication issues but may overlook gender as a cultural phenomenon.

Second, students in language teacher education programs may be only marginally aware of how their own behavior in the classroom affects students' participation in class. For example, teachers may inadvertently give more attention to certain individuals in a class (e.g., one cultural group or gender) while slighting others. Making developing teachers aware that their behavior in the classroom can affect the interactions of all participants can assist teachers in modifying their own behavior so as to treat all students more equitably.

Students in language teacher education programs usually enjoy the challenges inherent in considering their own behavior as gendered. By using action research techniques, teachers can explore their own teaching behavior. If these principles are incorporated into language teacher education, developing teachers can become critically aware of how the teacher's behavior affects the interactions in the classrooms and the learning that takes place there. Finally, the implicit anonymity of interacting with and through computers online may create an environment where intolerance of different cultures and genders produces an unsafe learning situation for many students. By exploring issues of acceptable-use policies in computerized classrooms, developing teachers gain experience in maintaining online classrooms that are productive places for students to participate equally and without undue harassment.

In our MA program, students may not be exposed to studies of language and gender or to research on classroom or language learning behaviors related to gender because research and sociolinguistics courses are often elective components of the program. The computer and language teaching course incorporates activities related to gender and possible influences on classroom language and interactional patterns, focusing especially on the online classroom. In addition, students read from the variety of articles available on gender and computers as part of a required annotated bibliography assignment (see Appendix A for a sample entry). In this way, graduate students in the program had additional opportunities to explore the role of gender in classroom language and interactions.

◈ DESCRIPTION

The technology class met in a university computer lab with approximately 20 computers placed against the outer walls and a conference table in the middle of the room. Class time was often devoted to online discussions and activities (see the descriptions below), and transcripts from all online discussions were available for class analysis. Class time was additionally used for FTF discussions and presentations. We often gathered around the conference table to listen to technology presentations given by Sarah or a classmate, focusing on a variety of aspects of computers in language teaching. The presentations enabled everyone to highlight useful technology for language teaching while providing students with practice in teaching about technology. The presentations focused on software or Web sites (for students, teachers, or both), networking systems with associated hardware (e.g., real-time conferencing utilizing Webcams and chat technologies), or electronic teaching environments useful to the language teacher (e.g., SyllaBase, 2001).

A service learning project required students to provide computer support to university or community agencies involved in second or foreign language teaching. In these service assignments, the students often presented available technologies to agency staff, highlighting the usefulness of the computer support to the agency's goals (e.g., classroom use, individualized language learning support, teacher resource). Overall computer presentations and service projects supported students in their development as technology-enabled language teaching professionals.

Below we describe the technologies used in the course. Following each description, one of us (Rebecca) comments on the use of this technology from a student participant perspective.

SyllaBase

Overview

SyllaBase (2001) is a proprietary, Web-based teaching environment with many features (e.g., a homework manager, bulletin board, and grade keeper). Although we mainly used SyllaBase for its discussion forum, students fully illustrated its other pedagogical features in presentations.

SyllaBase's discussion forum is a non-real-time, threaded discussion space where students designated by the teacher can interact. Sarah often posted introductory information on a particular topic followed by a prompt or questions. Students then replied to her posting with a paragraph or two. After this, classmates could read each others' postings and respond directly to each other. The discussion forum could be viewed through an index function showing the hierarchical structure of the threads of discussion (e.g., who responded to whom, who posted when, how often each message had been read). Also, the postings could be archived and viewed online as one contiguous text, which could be printed or processed through a concordance program.

Rebecca's Comments

Many students liked the discussion forum because it allowed us to express an idea fully without the interruptions that we encountered in FTF discussions. On the other hand, the SyllaBase discussion forum was a bit problematic because we often had time only to type out our own postings, and we did not have time in class to read and reply to others' postings. We could express our ideas but not interact as much with each other's ideas as we would have liked.

e_Chat

Overview

e_Chat (Bagneski, 1999) is an electronic chat program for the Web that allows participants to interact by writing in real time. Participants each provide a user name and can choose a color for their text. Sarah linked e_Chat to her Web site and invited groups of three or four people to participate in separate electronic chat groups.

In order to allow all participants to recognize each other, Sarah requested that students use their own names—not pseudonyms—in the electronic chats. This issue was one among many issues related to acceptable use that Sarah introduced to the class as a way to discourage the off-topic or abusive interactions that may occur online when full anonymity is assured (e.g., through the use of pseudonyms).

Rebecca's Comments

The electronic chat format was more interactive than the SyllaBase discussion forum. Our statements in the electronic chats were short, perhaps because we could see the entire conversation unfolding in a single screen rather than clicking from screen to screen as in the discussion forum. When we chatted via a campus computer, our postings loaded almost instantaneously, so we could read the messages as they were posted. However, because of the time it took for us to type, our postings would often appear after the rest of the group had already moved on to a new topic. Many of us became frustrated with this synchronous form of CMC because of the confusion it could cause: Who was responding to whom? What was the topic of the discussion? Why is so-and-so talking about candy? Although we had fun with the online chats, we found it a little difficult to remain on one or two particular threads.

Despite the difficulties of the electronic chat medium, classmates felt that chats allowed us to communicate with classmates we may not have otherwise communicated with because of differences in culture, gender, or simply geography (i.e., where we sat in the room). We felt that this form of CMC has great potential for leveling the playing field in ESL/EFL classrooms; it is just a matter of determining how best to facilitate productive CMC discussions. Some ideas we generated included assigning group roles to chat participants and keeping discussion topics simple. In addition, we found that later analysis of chat transcripts provided lots of language for grammatical and lexical analyses and for using conversation analysis techniques to investigate, for example, issues of turn taking and topic development.

Tapped In

Overview

Tapped In (http://www.tappedin.sri.org/), a MOO developed for educational exchange, is a virtual space in which participants engage in collaborative activities with colleagues and students. Members can occupy virtual office spaces and hold office hours, meeting online with students in real time. Other public discussion areas at *Tapped In* provide spaces for pair or group discussion. *Tapped In* also provides tools such as virtual white boards, shareable text documents, Web page projection, and personal tape recorders. The tape recorders produce a record—a kind of transcript— of all verbal and nonverbal encounters that a member has when visiting *Tapped In*. These transcripts are e-mailed to the member shortly after he or she logs out, providing a written record of the member's encounters.

Four student volunteers, including Rebecca, became members of *Tapped In* before the class was assigned to meet in the virtual space. The four could obtain a personal office or locate a suitable meeting space, and a personal recorder was then generated for each to document class discussions. We worked together to prepare the discussion activities for *Tapped In,* and the four volunteers led the discussions with small groups that joined them in the MOO. After discussing the questions Sarah had posed, students had opportunities to explore the MOO further in order to see what other resources and language learning opportunities it enabled.

Rebecca's Comments

Compared with the other public MOOs we had tried for online discussions, several of the features at *Tapped In* (whispering to just one individual in a group, paging someone, and incorporating nonverbal messages such as *Rebecca nods*) were especially useful for language learning because we could incorporate verbal and nonverbal messages. As for our discussions, most of us felt *Tapped In* was similar to the electronic chat function but with added features, such as a white board and a person on duty at the help desk to consult if we had problems.

MonoConc Pro

Overview

With MonoConc Pro (2000), a computer concordancer, users can conduct lexical and simple grammatical searches on large bodies of electronic texts. We used MonoConc Pro to search the transcripts we had produced in the CMC discussions for specific lexical and grammatical markers of gendered language. By archiving our CMC discussions from all the media described above into text files, we could process the discussions extremely efficiently in our explorations of specific lexical or simple grammatical features we were interested in. MonoConc Pro not only provides key-word-in-context and simple frequency output but also has collocational and other advanced search capabilities useful in the analysis of patterns of language use.

Rebecca's Comments

The concordance program made us more aware of how our language use reflects our individuality. I was interested in the concepts of corpus linguistics and concordancing, so as part of my research for the course, I discovered the *Michigan Corpus of Spoken*

Academic English (MICASE; Simpson, Briggs, Ovens, & Swales, 1999) and its concordancing features. MICASE is a collection of almost 2 million words of spoken academic English. It can be searched with its own concordancing tools and browsed by speaker characteristic (e.g., age, gender, first language status) and speech event (e.g., lectures, meetings, graduate defenses). Because the corpus can be sorted in this way, linguistic exploration is efficient and interesting.

Face-to-Face Discussions

Overview

FTF discussion occupied a very small part of our class time because the course was mainly a workshop; hands-on activities and presentations with and on technology for classroom teaching consumed most of the class time. When we had time for FTF discussion, one or two people in the room often dominated, leaving most of the students less involved.

Rebecca's Comments

FTF communications among classmates were most productive when we were in small groups exploring some new computer technology (e.g., voice recognition software) or when we had conversations before or after class. For this particular group of classmates, CMC seemed essential if more than a few voices were to be heard.

◈ DISTINGUISHING FEATURES

Through the computer technologies described above, class members reflected on personal experiences with gender issues in traditional classrooms and how these experiences might transfer to teaching and learning with technology. Sarah used the sample prompts below to enable the exploration of technology through the topic of gender and language in the classroom. Rebecca's comments following each prompt reflect her developing-teacher perspective on the ensuing discussions and activities.

Awareness of the Teacher's Power in CMC

Prompt for FTF Minilecture and Discussion

The Teacher's Role and Control in CMC

In the literature on computers in composition, many have held utopian views of computer mediated communication—or CMC—because cues as to gender, disability, and race are said to be reduced or eliminated (Mason, Duin, & Lammers, 1994). Some have claimed that the teacher's role is diminished as it was for Faigley (1992), who felt like a student in the electronic class he was teaching. Others have found that teacher control may in fact be increased (e.g., Gruber, 1995). Janangelo (1991), for example, talks in terms of *technoppression* and equates the CMC classroom to Foucault's Panopticon with the teacher as ultimate jailer.

FTF Question: Should the teacher see all and control all in classroom-based discussions? What should the teacher's role be in using CMC in the classroom?

Rebecca's Comments

We had not considered how much more power teachers might have with CMC: They can literally monitor every word in a classroom. My small group had a lively discussion on the ethics involved with a lot of teacher control and with diminished teacher control. We also discussed how much work was involved in closely monitoring an online class.

Suitability of CMC for a Given Interaction

Prompt for SyllaBase and e_Chat Discussion

Gender and Technology, Equity Issues

The literature on computers in language teaching is full of research pointing to inequities in access to technology for girls (e.g., Hesse-Biber & Gilbert, 1994), and although the playing field is leveling, there may remain inequalities in the classroom even as opportunities and access for girls and women increase. In terms of participation, women may not interact freely due to power differentials in society (Markley, 1998). Discuss these questions in a small electronic chat group:

1.   In your experience, have boys and girls/men and women had equal access to computer technology in the home and at school?

2.   Some cultures segregate children and adults in education. Have you experienced this style of education before, or do you anticipate an EFL career in which you will? What might some of the challenges and benefits of teaching in such a system be? How might technology be used to enhance education in segregated contexts?

3.   What are some of the potential challenges and benefits of teaching in a system that integrates males and females? How might technology be used to eliminate any challenges and enhance any benefits of integrated education?

4.   Did you enjoy using e_Chat to discuss these questions?

Rebecca's Comments

In this electronic chat, we examined our own gendered experience in education and learned about others' gendered experiences. However, the chat function of CMC seemed to make our topics somewhat disjointed, leaving many issues unaddressed.

   My group focused on Question 2 by barraging a Saudi male classmate with questions about gender in his society. He answered our questions with insightful comments about his culture. One female classmate felt that the chat was not the place to discuss such an involved topic. A classmate in another group supported this position; he felt the group's discussion of gender was too weighty without FTF contact. However, this man often dominated FTF discussions. As a result, many female students in class privately commented that some form of CMC was a better medium for creating a more egalitarian discussion space.

Awareness of the Teacher's Role in Controlling Online Behavior

Prompt for SyllaBase Forum and Discussion

Gender in CMC

In some studies, men have been found to dominate public discussions through CMC (e.g., e-mail discussion lists as described by Herring, Johnson, & DiBenedetto, 1995), but other studies have shown that women participate more in CMC classrooms than in traditional FTF language classrooms (e.g., Meunier, 1997). CMC has been described as a space where prowess at verbal dueling can be demonstrated (Cameron, 1997a)—a supposedly male characteristic in oral interactions.

In my dissertation research on language in traditional and CMC contexts of freshman composition, I found that these students produced more language in CMC than in the traditional context. In the electronic forum context, students produced a lot of academic talk, but the forum was not used very interactively by any of the teachers. The electronic chat function generally produced off-topic language, with men producing significantly more *gaming and flaming* language (language behaviors ranging from playing around to being outright hostile and malicious; Daisley, 1994; Holcomb, 1997) than women in that context. Social and academic exchange may become blurred in CMC (Barrett & Lally, 1999) as it did in the classes in my study, and CMC spaces may be used both as playground and as classroom resource (J. L. Wolfe, 1999). Perhaps it is the informality of the chat function that encourages purely phatic communication (Talbot, 1998).

Questions for Discussion:

1. How might you define *gaming and flaming*?

2. Have you experienced or used gaming and flaming in your CMC interactions? In what context? To what effect? In your experience, do women or men game and flame more? How might you empirically study this question?

3. What should the teacher's role regarding gaming and flaming be in the online language classroom?

Rebecca's Comments

As graduate students, we had all had experiences with gaming and flaming in different forms of CMC. We felt that gaming was inevitable in all forms of CMC, and although the teacher may be monitoring or even participating in the computer-mediated class discussions, the computerized space still seemed a bit more private than FTF interactions in the classroom. We decided that flaming, on the other hand, could be quite detrimental to the safe space of the CMC classroom because it hindered students from expressing themselves. Therefore, some of us felt teachers needed to police flaming and establish with their students acceptable-use policy statements for appropriate online behavior.

Awareness of Virtual Rape
Prompt for FTF Lecture and Tapped In Discussion

Going Too Far: CMC Attacks on Women

Harassment of women in CMC (see Herring, 1999, for a discussion of gender-related harassment in Internet Relay Chats) and even online rapes have been reported (Dibbell, 1993; Stone, 1995). In many anonymous CMC spaces, CMC participants use forenames (Pagnucci & Mauriello, 1999) and age and gender checks—asking recently joined participants to identify age and sex (Soukup, 1999)—as indicators of participants' physical selves. So much for a utopian disembodied space for sharing ideas!

Questions:

1. How do the findings of these studies of public CMC spaces affect conduct in private, classroom CMC spaces? For example, do you think that students will transfer behaviors learned from past CMC experiences in public spaces to the private space of the classroom?

2. How does this affect the role of teachers and students?

Rebecca's Comments

When we were experimenting with the MOO, *Tapped In,* I became so excited when I got my own personal office in the *Tapped In* office building that I e-mailed my classmates telling them about it: the hardwood floor, tons of plants, and a virtual boxer puppy. On doing this, I became aware of how real my excitement about my office felt, yet it did not really exist beyond zeros, ones, and the minds of my potential students and me. This experience compelled me to reconsider Sarah's minilecture about online rape. The virtual world is something between reality and imagination. The interaction with an imagined reality and the ability of others to interact with this imagined reality bring forth emotions that are real.

In our discussions of virtual rape, we considered student use of CMC and the creation of a safe virtual world. What happens in online public discussion spaces threatens to enter the private realm of the classroom. My classmates all seemed to agree that it is the teacher's job to create a safe space in computerized classrooms by adopting practices like the creation of acceptable-use policy statements and the overt discussion of issues like *netiquette* (etiquette for the Internet) with the class.

Awareness of Gendered Language Behavior
Prompt for SyllaBase Forum and Discussion

The Performative Nature of Gendered Language and
Potentials for Online Discourse

Consider the following two propositions:

1. We gender ourselves through our language behavior. [Sociolinguists argue that we construct our own identity through our language choices, both conscious and unconscious. In other words, we perform or construct our identity, including our gendered identity, through the verbal choices we make (Ehrlich, 1997; Livia & Hall, 1997).]

2. CMC can be dissociating in a personal sense, enabling the development of one's own persona online. [CMC has been called depersonalized (J. L. Wolfe, 2000) and deindividuated (Andrianson, 2001).]

If we consider these propositions together, where does that leave us in terms of classroom language teaching? Do we want to encourage the development of alternate personae for online class discussions? Will the use of pseudonyms, for example, assist or hinder class discussions? Do the answers to the above questions vary if our class also meets in a traditional classroom or if our CMC communications are our only class contacts—as in some forms of distance learning?

Rebecca's Comments

In this discussion we examined how we personally identified with technology and explored what identities we perform through CMC. Classmates commented that this discussion facilitated reflection on previously unexplored areas of technology use. For some, it was the first time they had considered technology as a medium in which people communicate (or hide) who they are, including their gender.

Classmates noticed that the use of pseudonyms in CMC could be distracting to students; yet the decision to use or not to use pseudonyms may depend on class dynamics, the goal of the activity, or other factors. We also found it interesting that our FTF persona could be, at times, very different from our CMC identity. Simply stated, in CMC we had a space to express our identity; in our FTF interactions, many of us voiced our identity only nonverbally.

The development of online persona also applies to ESL. In a language learning classroom, self-expression is important because it allows teachers and students to learn from their classmates' experiences and ideas. Self-expression raises critical questions and highlights commonalities in human experience. Creating different types of spaces for ESL learners to discuss issues and explore language could motivate a variety of students. These spaces might be used for authentic discussion, role play, and simulations—spaces where students could explore both their own and alternate personae.

Awareness of Women's Language

Prompt for SyllaBase Discussion and Concordancing Task

Women's Language

Here are some features identified as women's language by Lakoff (1975).

- hedges: *sort of, kind of, I guess, it seems, it might*
- polite forms: *I'd appreciate it if you, would you please*
- tag questions: *He's nice, isn't he? It doesn't rain much here, does it?*
- emphatic words: *That dress is so beautiful.*
- hypercorrect grammar
- question intonation with declarative sentences

Empirically based research has refuted many of Lakoff's claims. For example, O'Barr and Atkins (1998), in an analysis of the language of men and women of unequal standing in the court system, found many of the features identified by Lakoff to be linguistic markers of power rather than of gender.

Just for fun, however, and to have some concrete linguistic concepts to search on, choose one or two of Lakoff's linguistic features, and operationalize them into a list of search items (partial words, whole words, or multiword units). For example, for polite forms, the search items could be *would* and *'d*.

Load transcripts of the various discussions we have had through CMC into MonoConc Pro concordancing software. Then run your search queries. Be aware that the computer may return sentences where your target search item functions differently than the function you are seeking. For example, your search on *would* as a politeness marker will also return any interrogative use of *would*.

Rebecca's Comments

Using a concordance program, we discovered the power of corpus linguistics in the analysis of language patterns. I discovered that in several of the transcripts of discussions I participated in, I often gave my opinion in the form of questions instead of asserting it as a statement. By analyzing a transcript of only their own contributions in the class discussions through the concordance program, women in the class found that they sometimes hedged with words such as *sort of* and *kind of* and the use of various modals. Men seemed to use this linguistic feature less.

We all agreed that in a language classroom, small- and whole-group analyses of CMC transcriptions are vital as language teaching tools. Teachers can use such analyses as sources for error analysis activities, to prepare vocabulary and grammar minilessons, to present other effective discourse features (e.g., strategies for getting the floor in an electronic chat), to reinforce ideas generated by the students themselves, and as prewriting materials.

Discussion of the Use of CMC to Solve Teaching Problems

Prompt for FTF and e_Chat Discussion

Implications of Language and Gender in CMC Classrooms

Students can show dissent in the classroom as a form of resistance to reproductive pedagogies (Pennycook, 2001) and CMC may not be as liberating for all, as predicted (J. L. Wolfe, 2000). However, through analyses of transcripts from online classes, students can make discoveries about language use and teachers can explore appropriate pedagogies for online literacy instruction. Potentially, as teachers, we can raise awareness in ourselves while encouraging our students' identity development online. We can also critically address human fears—such as xenophobia, racism, homophobia, and sexism—that may hinder effective classroom communications (Gruber, 1999).

Discussion: How might you use CMC to solve language teaching problems like resistance? How might you use the transcripts of classroom CMC interactions?

Rebecca's Comments

In our discussion, we developed ideas about the importance of students' examining their own language and comparing it with the language of others, especially by analyzing classroom transcripts. We know that we will encounter instances of student resistance, but we hope that we can diminish it by providing students in our future classes with multiple opportunities to interact and explore language through a variety of traditional and computerized class-based activities. We feel that concordancing software gives students hands-on opportunities to analyze surface-level patterns in language. Analysis of class transcriptions also gives us, as teachers, a chance to look at our own language use. For example, we consider it beneficial to look at which students' statements we responded to and which we ignored.

◈ PRACTICAL IDEAS

We have generated several practical ideas that might be useful to others interested in incorporating CMC into classroom discussions and the pedagogical scrutiny of gender in the (online) language classroom.

CMC and Concordancing in Language Teaching

Use More Than One Form of CMC

Different forms of CMC have the potential to involve different language production and processing strategies. Consider carefully, however, the best use of each CMC medium to meet the goals of your lessons and to ensure that you create a safe learning environment for your students.

Analyze Transcripts From Students' CMC Sessions

Use transcripts from students' CMC sessions for self-reflection and classroom analysis. For example, you might explore the transcripts for clues to effective class management.

Students produce an abundance of language in CMC discussions, and this language should be exploited for student learning. You might use the transcripts to highlight issues of vocabulary and grammar use, interactional patterns, and interactional strategies. In addition, you might use ideas generated in the transcripts in preparing other tasks involving reading or writing.

Use Concordancing Output From Transcripts of Online Discussions

Prepare language learning activities using concordancing output from the transcripts of the students' online discussions. Have students do some simple analyses on the concordancer to find lexical and simple grammatical patterns of use.

Gender, Language Awareness, and the Developing Teacher

Extend Students' Awareness

Include activities that assist students in reflecting on the role of gender in language teaching across the TESL curriculum. Do not limit these activities to research and sociolinguistics courses.

Draw on Students' Personal Experiences

In encouraging classroom discussion, draw on students' personal experiences with language and gender. Provide a safe space for discussion by allowing students to select from the prompts and topic discussion questions what to share with the class.

Do Not Shy Away From Controversial Topics

Do not be afraid to push students' comfort levels by introducing controversial topics, as we did with online rape. Have students consider how behaviors outside the language classroom may shape behaviors inside the classroom.

Develop an Acceptable-Use Policy Statement

Develop a policy statement that spells out acceptable use in your class discussions (FTF and CMC). Stating the policy explicitly will provide a safe space for discussion of all topics, academic and personal.

◈ CONCLUSION

The topic of gender in this technology course enabled us to explore how a variety of CMC and other software applications facilitated class discussion and language analysis. We found our discussions on gender to be interesting and motivating for students in the course, who benefited both by increasing their computer skills and by considering gender issues from a pedagogical perspective. We look forward to finding other such opportunities to feminize the curriculum—creating through our classroom discussions and language analysis activities awareness of gender and other human interaction issues that influence language use.

◈ CONTRIBUTORS

Sarah Rilling is an assistant professor at Kent State University, in the United States, where she teaches graduate and undergraduate courses in applied linguistics. Her research interests include corpus-based approaches to analyzing language in context and discipline-based writing and the nonnative speaker. She regularly uses computers in teaching and research.

Rebecca Biles teaches in the Intensive English Program at Colorado State University, in the United States. Her research interests include gender dynamics in the ESL classroom, critical language analysis, and feminist pedagogy.

◈ APPENDIX: SAMPLE ENTRY FROM ANNOTATED BIBLIOGRAPHY ON GENDER IN THE ONLINE CLASSROOM

Takayoshi, P. (2000). Complicated women: Examining methodologies for understanding the uses of technology. *Computers and Composition, 17,* 123–138.

In this article, Takayoshi calls for more holistic research on women's experience with technology. Past research has been mainly student-based-teacher-told, and the stories reported have left the reader with *either/or* inferences: Either "Technology is conducive to women's empowerment" or "Technology is detrimental to the empowerment of women." Takayoshi argues that in order for one to understand the complicated relationship women have with technology researchers need to become more involved in the feelings and motivations of the research, possibly by including multiple narratives in future studies.

PART 4

Insights
From Japan

CHAPTER 10

Transforming Emerging Feminist Identities: A Course on Gender and Language Issues

Andrea Simon-Maeda

◈ INTRODUCTION

This chapter describes a gender and language issues program that I initiated in 1997 at an all-women's junior college in central Japan. The incentive to include a feminist course in the academic curriculum derived from a serious concern over the absence of an EFL course that incorporated students' lived experiences into their English language studies. A 2-year critical ethnographic investigation of students' attitudes toward their education (Simon-Maeda, 2002) revealed that normative curricular policies were not enabling learners to reach their full academic and personal potential.

The larger study's constructivist approach to interpreting participants' under-standings of local contexts highlights how identities and meaning-making processes are constituted through ongoing social interactions in and outside school. In this chapter, excerpts from narratives in student journals illustrate how macro- and microlevel sociocultural factors affect the gendered identities of young Japanese women struggling to resist hegemonic ideologies. The women's entries suggest that when learners are given the opportunity to negotiate the meaning of gender and language issues that affect their lives, they can begin to imagine alternative life trajectories. I also discuss from a poststructuralist feminist perspective the issues of positionality and reflexivity in a pedagogical context involving a teacher and students from different sociocultural backgrounds.

◈ CONTEXT

The Program

The gender and language issues (GALI) program (see Appendix A for a course outline) is an interdepartmental elective course for first-year students in the junior college where I have worked since 1993. GALI is the only *kougi* (lecture-type) course in our EFL curriculum that is taught by a *gaikokujin koushi* (foreign instructor) from the United States. In my institution, as well as in most educational contexts in Japan, foreign EFL instructors are usually assigned only *jisshuu* (practicum-type) courses aimed at developing students' English language skills. However, the junior college administration and English department faculty, recognizing my Japanese language proficiency and knowledge of a particular area of studies (gender and language), decided that I was qualified to conduct a lecture-type course.

My academic interest in gender and language issues began with my participation in a Temple University Japan special seminar with feminist sociolinguist Janet Holmes, who inspired me to consider how this important topic could be incorporated into an EFL program in a tertiary-level situation in Japan. The data reported on below are representative entries from 60 students' journals that were part of the requirements for the GALI course in 1999.

Power Relations in the Classroom

Positionality, as it is understood in poststructuralist feminist pedagogical theories and practices (Ellsworth, 1992; Gore, 1992; Lather, 1991; Orner, 1992), is not a static social situation that naturally exists between a teacher and students. Instead, when the teacher's privileged position in the classroom is reflexively examined, the very essence of the pedagogical relationship itself and its inherent claims to empowerment begin to shift and erode.

What, then, are the different types of power relations that are operating in my classroom? I hold power simply by virtue of my position as a professor in the junior college hierarchy—a person who possesses different types of coercion and reward power in the classroom and who is valued as an expert in the subject area and directly involved in ways that students cannot be in shaping the school's academic agenda. As a *gaijin no sensei* (foreign teacher) from the United States, I am also accorded a considerable amount of cultural power. My powerful role is thus defined by the junior college institution and by students who expect me to act as the dispenser of knowledge in the classroom. This situation would seem to defy a feminist educator's goal of altering the latent *banking system* (Freire, 1970, pp. 52–67) or paternalism in a pedagogical situation in order to allow students to become empowered.

Poststructuralist feminists suggest that a workable solution to the dilemma above may lie in a shift in focus rather than in a complete abandonment of liberatory aims. That is, pedagogy is viewed as a process of knowledge construction, or what Gitlin and Thompson (1995) call "reconstructed knowledge [that] takes power in relationship as the very basis of inquiry . . . in a way that changes what will count as knowledge" (p. 133). Or, in more practical terms, as Lather (1991) suggests, instruction should be viewed as "a site not for working through more effective transmission strategies but for helping us learn to analyze the discourses available to us, which ones we are invested in, [and] how we are inscribed by the dominant [discourses]" (p. 143).

Lather's (1991) deconstructive approach to pedagogy helped me unlearn my own traditional teacher background and recover a sense of the complex and political nature of education. By focusing on the specific contexts of how the students and I constructed knowledge in the feminist course, I attempted to maintain what Lather describes as the core component of praxis-oriented research/pedagogy—"an empirical stance which is open-ended, dialogically reciprocal, grounded in respect to human capacity and, yet, profoundly skeptical of appearances and 'common sense'" (p. 65). As I followed the pedagogical procedures outlined in the Description section, my position as *the teacher* became decentered (for a while at least) through students' collaborative control of the class time, students' ability to use their own knowledge sources gained some legitimacy, and a co-constructed (by teacher and student) knowledge base became integrated into a cross-cultural understanding of how sexist language sustains the subordinate position of women in society.

The importance of choosing topics that students are able or willing to engage with cannot be overemphasized here. By monitoring the level of on-task activity during group discussions, checking the worksheets, and reading individual journal entries, I can check students' interest in or knowledge of certain topics and issues.

◈ LANGUAGE AND GENDER

As Vandrick (2000) admonished TESOL practitioners, "attention must be paid to the needs and learning styles of females as well as to the problems of sexual harassment and stereotyping that harm female students" (pp. 19–20). The Japan Association for Language Teaching devoted two special issues of *The Language Teacher* (Fujimura-Fanselow & Vaughn, 1991; Smith & Yamashiro, 1998) to feminist issues in order to encourage language educators in Japan to develop a more critical pedagogical perspective on gender inequality in society as a whole and within educational institutions in particular.

In line with this aim, my praxis-oriented research and teaching practices follow recent analyses of language and gender (Eckert & McConnell-Ginet, 1999; Ehrlich, 1997; Freeman & McElhinny, 1996) and poststructuralist feminist (Davies, 1989; Lather, 1991; Luke, 1992; Weiler, 1988) interpretations of the gendered construction of academic identities. That is, I am concerned with the ways that female learners' gendered, multiple subjectivities operate within an intricate network of *power relations* (Foucault, 1980) that either deny or allow access to particular discourses, which in turn influence educational and future life choices. For example, in educational contexts, the degree of legitimacy attached to students' and teachers' right to speak is intimately implicated in the types of knowledge that are given credence. In a hegemonic classroom situation, then, the teacher's belief system, actualized through classroom discourses and practices, impinges on students' right to use their own knowledge systems to make different statements about the course content. A feminist gender and language course that actively attempts to create space for the multiplicity of voices in the classroom therefore provides the perfect opportunity to explore with students how language reflects and maintains power inequities, such as sexism, in everyday social interactions.

Young women in Japan face many obstacles in their attempts to move beyond established societal norms that define them "primarily by their relationship to domesticity, reproduction and the family" (Liddle & Nakajima, 2000, p. 317). Although guaranteed equal access to the educational credentials needed for professional occupations, female learners still make up only 35% of the total 4-year university population and an even smaller number (6.5%) of graduate students (Ministry of Education, 1999). Against this oppressive backdrop, gender and language issues become crucial in the lives of women who are trying to renegotiate traditional notions that constrain rather than expand their academic and life options.

◈ DESCRIPTION

GALI (the name for the course as it is listed in the English department curriculum handbook) meets for 90 minutes, once a week for a 15-week semester. During the first 60 minutes, I introduce a certain topic related to the linguistic aspects of gender inequality with examples from English and Japanese by using handouts, showing a video, or inviting a guest speaker to conduct a special session on, for example, the sociolinguistic aspects of domestic violence. Students then get into groups of four or five people for about 15 minutes and complete a worksheet (see Appendix B for an example) that contains questions or points for discussion concerning the lecture content.

The remaining 15 minutes of class time are reserved for journal writing. I regularly collect the journals and make a few comments (in English) in each journal before giving them back to the students. In this way, I can assess how students are engaging with the course material at the same time that I show my interest in their thoughts on the course lecture.

S. Parry (1996) describes the different kinds of journal writing commonly used in feminist classrooms:

1. Personalizing theory—students write about their own personal experiences in relation to a certain theoretical notion, prejudice, for example.

2. Reflection—students reflect on the implications of certain experiences in their lives.

3. Reading responses—students write their opinions about assigned readings. (pp. 48–49)

The worksheet assignment for the GALI course is designed to be a somewhat structured activity, like No. 3 above, whereas the journal-writing requirement is intended to be more like Nos. 1 and 2.

Topic Introduction

My overall plan for the topic sequencing is to begin from microlevel examples of gender-based differences in language use (e.g., conversational patterns, titles and forms of address, sexist proverbs, gender bias in textbooks) to broader examples of gendered linguistic and nonlinguistic disparities as found in popular cultural material, such as advertisements, newspapers, television, and movies. Studies on male/female linguistic differences (Holmes, 1984, 1997), Sunderland's (1994) collection on gender and language issues specific to English language education, investigations of male/female conversational patterns (Tannen, 1990), and more recent research on the interaction of gender and social practices (Bucholtz, 1999; Cameron, 1998; Eckert & McConnell-Ginet, 1999) are just a few of the rich sources from which I select topics and adapt them to my particular context.

The point I stress in each class session is that language both reflects and perpetuates gender divisions and power asymmetries in society (Japanese and North American). For example, I introduce samples from (outdated) English dictionaries that give demeaning examples of the use of the words *emotional, virgin,* or *womanish* in sentences such as *Women are often said to be more emotional than men, She's 40 and still a virgin,* and *That fellow is a bit womanish for my liking!* (McArthur, 1981). I then provide examples from my stock of sexist word usage in Japanese—*hako iri musume* (a girl brought up with tender care who knows nothing of the world), *urenokori* (literally, unsold merchandise; an unmarried older woman) (Cherry, 1987), and so on.

In addition to showing videos or inviting guest speakers (e.g., the director of a women's shelter) as different ways of introducing a topic for discussion, I try to model, as much as possible, the personal and the intellectual by giving examples from my own experiences with, in one case, sexual harassment. Usually rather noisy students become very silent and attentive when I start to tell them about my encounters with perverts on trains and subways or about how I am sometimes addressed in an unflattering way as *yankii babaa* (old Yankee lady) by Japanese men who think that I do not understand what they are saying.

I also relate an incident in which I chased a *shitagi dorobou* (underwear robber) whom I caught in the middle of his attempt to steal some of my underwear off the clothesline in the backyard of my house. The students chuckle at the thought of their U.S. teacher chasing a Japanese man down the street, but I tell them that this kind of crime is no laughing matter; especially because when I called the police to report the incident, they too chuckled and did not pursue the case.

The point here is to let students know that, as women, we share the same kind of dehumanizing experiences even though our circumstances (e.g., ethnicity, social class, age) may differ. This modeling technique is in line with hooks' (1994) concept of *engaged pedagogy*, which centralizes the notion of power/empowerment in educational contexts—the point of departure for my feminist course and something that I have had to reflexively account for in my pedagogical practices.

Worksheet

After introducing the topic, I pass out a worksheet that asks the students to think of more examples of sexist language that they feel are related to the topic that I have introduced. It does not take very long for students to come up with Japanese words or phrases that fit the categories of demeaning language used in reference to women. Examples are *busu* (ugly woman; a term with no masculine equivalent), *hisuterii* (hysterical; primarily used in reference to a woman), and *obatarian* (a popular derogatory term used to refer specifically to middle-aged women).

Then, using a classification scheme often used in feminist sociolinguistic learning tasks, I ask students to fit some English examples that I provide, and afterwards some Japanese examples that they come up with on their own, into different categories, as shown below:

Animal	Food	Thing
chick	peach	dish
pussy	honey	skirt
hato mune (pigeon breast, large bust)	*daikon ashi* (radish legs)	*sentaku ita* (washboard, flat-chested)

The point of this exercise is to impress on students the way women are dehumanized through a host of descriptive terms that often have no masculine equivalents. I then elicit comments from students about what they noted on their worksheets or discussed in their groups, add my own comments, and finally ask students to think about why sexist language exists, how changes in word usage come about, and what relevance this may have to their own situations.

Journal Writing

Students have the remaining class time to reflect individually on the relationship between the lecture topics and their personal experiences. All the journal entries reproduced here were originally written in Japanese, translated by me, and checked for accuracy by the participants.

The Link Between Language and Ideology

Even after 6 years of English language education beginning in junior high school, many students learn for the first time in the GALI course that many proverbs in English—and Japanese as well—contain sexist folk-linguistic views of women. An example is *Many women, many words; many geese, many turds* (English proverb, as cited in Coates, 1993, p. 33) and its Japanese equivalent, *Onna san nin yoreba kashimashii* (When three women get together, it's noisy) (Arai, 1992).

One student's journal entry for this class session follows.

> There are so many bad proverbs about women. For example, I can under-stand the proverb about a group of talking women being noisy, but couldn't the same be said about men as well? Isn't it because there are these negative proverbs that negative images of women increase? But in order for positive proverbs to increase I think it's also important for women to always try to be better. (Meg, journal, 10/21/99)

Notwithstanding Meg's failure to problematize the fact that it is usually women who are expected to "be better" to fit the norms for appropriate behavior, she demon-strates here an awareness of the link between language and ideology.

Gender and Language Issues in Students' Lives

By writing about gender and language issues as experienced in their daily lives, students develop an awareness of the social construction of gender, language, and knowledge; acquire a sense of voice; and begin to consider alternative ways of being in their social worlds. Herein lies the challenge of this type of program. As mentioned in the Language and Gender section, Japanese women's academic and career choices are severely limited within an endemic *phallocentric discourse* (Luke & Gore, 1992b) in society in general and educational contexts in particular. Through my larger ethnographic project, I became aware of how overt sexist schooling practices in Japan are sustained by innumerable sociocultural factors, such as parents' giving academic (financial) preference to sons, who are expected to be the main wage earners in their future families.

If they were asked, the students I work with would certainly not describe themselves as feminists, and most of them, as one would expect in a society that relegates them to subordinate positions, adhere to a *domestic code* (Weis, 1988)—a socialization process in which women consider marriage and child rearing to be the top or sole priorities in their lives without a serious consideration of alternative default options. Although the author of the following journal entry critically reflects on caretakers' influence on children's gendered (linguistic/social) lives, it is danger-ously naive to think that students will suddenly undergo a radical transformation in their attitudes toward deeply entrenched hegemonic societal and educational systems:

> In Japan, there are many little girls who say they want to become brides. When I was small, I thought that doctors or pilots were jobs for boys. This is definitely due to the influence of teachers and parents. When I become a parent, I want to give my children, even my daughters, many chances to realize their dreams. (Na, journal, 11/11/99)

To illustrate how female students react to sexism in their daily lives, I present first a student's contribution to her group's discussion on the topic of the linguistic manifestations of sexual harassment and then her journal entry, written after the discussion.

Many students have part-time jobs after school, and their stories of their work experiences contain shocking accounts of verbal and physical sexual harassment from their (usually male) superiors:

> The man's [male boss] mouth, words, saying my breasts are small, as a kind of joke. Not really one who fools around, but talking as if he were, saying things like, he wants to go to a [love] hotel or asking about my boyfriend. It's [sexual banter] subtle. Almost touching my buttocks. He's perverted. Playfighting, coming closer and closer. I hate this. It's not funny at all, but I laugh. (Kei, discussion, 12/9/99)

Kei's laughter here reverberates with the many other ways that women may participate, however unwillingly, in facilitating their own subordination by enacting an appropriate female way of responding to (unwanted) sexual advances. Although most of the students are familiar with the loan word *sekuhara* (sexual harassment) in Japanese, they are not completely attuned to how sexual banter and play, as in Kei's quote above, come under the heading of sexual harassment.

To begin the class session during which the above in-class discussion took place, I explained how words are coined or changed in response to feminist social movements. Terms such as *sexual harassment, domestic violence,* and *gender awareness,* and gender-inclusive titles such as *chairperson, homemaker,* and *salesperson,* have become part of society's vocabularies and therefore shape perceptions of the shifting social positions of women and men. Equivalent Japanese examples are *kangoshi* (male or female nurse), *hofu* (male nursery school teacher), and *hoikushi* (male or female nursery school teacher).

As a way of demonstrating how the term *sexual harassment* encompasses a broader range of meanings, in North American contexts at least, than what students may commonly associate with the word *sekuhara,* I first showed the video *The Mosaic: Men and Women Working Together* (Marofsky & Grote, 1991), which dramatizes, through short scenarios based on real-life cases, the different types of sexual harassment that women and men encounter in their workplaces and shows how to bring charges against abusive superiors. I then asked students to talk in their groups about their own experiences with sexual harassment and to make a list of sexual harassment guidelines (not yet in existence at the time) for our school based on guidelines in North American college handbooks. I felt that the video presentation helped stimulate an awareness that subtle types of sexual harassment in everyday life are just as damaging as the more overt types that are reported on with increasing occurrence in the media. I hoped that students would remember the full gamut of the meaning of the term *sexual harassment* and ways to deal with the problem when it occurred at school or in their jobs after graduation.

Kei's journal entry below indicates that, in addition to making a self-reflexive connection with the above topic, she projected into the future what action she would take in an oppressive work situation:

> I thought it was wrong that I left it as a joke when I was sexually harassed. When I think now about what happened at my part-time job, I should have said something to that person. When I become a full-time employee if my superior does something like that to me, I will face the situation and demand that the person be dismissed. I felt disgusted just watching the video. (Kei, journal, 12/9/99)

Another journal entry for the same class session demonstrates not only an awareness of the seriousness of sexual harassment but also the *yuuki* (courage) that is needed to stand up to an abusive superior:

> I was sexually harassed at my part-time job. After becoming friendly with everyone, I was touched [by a male coworker]. He was a year older than me and would suddenly hug or touch me. At first I let it go as a joke but now I hate it. Because I told him that I didn't like it, he stopped, so I thought that saying this was necessary, but I think it's because he was like a friend and only one year older than me. However, if a superior harassed me I don't think I could say anything. This is a really difficult problem. (Eko, journal, 12/9/99)

Criticism of Textbook Material

Despite students' progressively oriented engagement with the course material, as observed in their journal entries, the literature on critical/feminist pedagogy (in Western contexts, see, e.g., Bell, Morrow, & Tastsoglou, 1999; Luke & Gore, 1992b; and in Japanese higher education contexts, see, e.g., Dyer, 1998; Fujimura-Fanselow, 1996) reports that the best liberatory educational intentions do not automatically result in students' positive responses to the course. Mixed reactions to feminist topics are the logical outcomes of a pedagogical environment in which students' varied meaning-making processes and value systems are legitimated. That is to say, in the poststructuralist spirit of recognizing and working with the *multiplicity of knowledges* (Ellsworth, 1992) that students bring to the classroom, it makes sense that conflicting inter- and intrapersonal understandings of feminist issues surface during class discussions or in reflexive journal writing, as each student's individual knowledge base has been forged from a particular set of sociocultural factors. I am not concerned with either acceptance or rejection of my feminist intentions, but rather with whether or not students demonstrate an understanding of why they hold a certain opinion about a particular issue. The following example is from the journal of a student who was reacting in a somewhat negative way to the topic of gender bias and stereotypes in EFL textbooks:

> In every [GALI] class I'm always made to think about stereotypes. But there are many different kinds of people and it doesn't matter what is said to a

person if that person does not think it's bad. In today's class my group made two texts [dialogues] but I thought that the bad text was how people generally speak. As for myself, I think that the bad text is natural and that if I were spoken to in that way I wouldn't mind. (Yuka, journal, 11/4/99)

The dialogue that this student is referring to is from a class session on sexism in EFL textbooks. Examples of sexist stereotyping (women depicted primarily in domestic or subordinate roles) can be found throughout O'Neill's *Kernel Lessons Intermediate* (1970), and I felt that because students' English language learning experiences spanned at least 6 years of instruction, they would have a lot to say about this topic. Below is a dialogue from *Kernel Lessons Intermediate* that was distributed to students for a discussion and exercise on how a "bad" dialogue could be rewritten to make it less sexist:

Husband: Don't you want me to get that promotion? Don't you want my shirts to be whiter than anybody else's?

Wife: (With a tear running down her cheek) Of course I do, darling. Please don't shout at me! It isn't my fault I can't get your shirts any whiter!

(Wife is talking later to another woman at the laundromat.)

Woman: I'd advise you to use GLEAM. It's so much better than ordinary washing powders.

(Husband comes home from work the next day.)

Husband: I got that promotion yesterday, darling, and all because of you!

Wife (thinks): No, darling. All because of new MIRACLE GLEAM. (p. 88)

Most of the students recognized that negative or stereotypical portrayals of women in educational materials do not serve the interests of those women who are struggling to break out of confining roles in society, and they expressed their thoughts accordingly:

I thought that male/female discrimination even in textbooks was wrong, but didn't notice. I wouldn't have known if Andy [the name the students call me] hadn't explained what discrimination was. They say that society will be gender equal now, and when I get married I don't want to be like the women in the textbooks. (Nori, journal, 11/4/99)

The group exercise for this session was to create original dialogues in English with sexist stereotyping similar to the *Kernel Lessons* example and then rewrite it in a "good" style that they thought would be more gender balanced.

Bad
Tom: I'm hungry, Kathy. Prepare a meal!!
Kathy: Ok, wait a moment.
Tom: I've been working so hard at the office all day and want to eat dinner right now!!

Good
Tom: I'm back.
Kathy: I'm preparing a meal now.
Tom: I help you.
Kathy: Thanks!! (class, 11/4/99)

The majority of the students' "bad" dialogues and their revised versions still depicted mothers and fathers in traditional domestic and work roles that are the mainstay of Japanese society. After further discussion on commonsense norms for the roles of husband and wives or same-gender partners, however, some students displayed an awareness that gender equality does not simply mean reversing the roles for men and women but rather involves a more encompassing shift in consciousness, as Ka wrote in her journal:

> It is taken for granted that women take care of the home. But in my home my father makes the breakfast. I don't think it should be decided that housework is for women or that it's strange for my father to make miso soup. In a homosexual relationship, male/female roles do not matter. Men and women are separated in society, but I think it will be a good thing if ways of thinking about this change. (Ka, journal, 11/4/99)

For this same class session, I explained to the students during the discussion that because of pressure from feminist groups, there are now publishing guidelines for avoiding sexist stereotyping in textbooks (Sunderland, 1994), and two students responded to this point in their journals:

> I think that it's good that things [textbooks] have changed because it changes stereotypical views about men and women. Textbooks are things that we always use when we study and so their influencing powers are great. I think that from now on things like stereotypes have to change. (Ka, journal, 11/4/99)

> That women should be silent and just follow men, or the idea that housework is a woman's job are still prevalent notions. Also, the idea that a man should be strong exists because this is the image that all of society has of men. If textbooks or television change, then equality would become common sense and society would be perfect. (Eko, journal, 11/4/99)

Involving students in a critique of sexism in textbook material helped them make a connection to the point that societal views both shape and are shaped by sexist textual material, and, more importantly, that feminist social movements can interrupt this process.

◈ DISTINGUISHING FEATURES

Recognition and Integration of Students' Distinctive Histories

I recognize that each student comes to school with her own personal history and knowledge base, which become legitimated through incorporation into the syllabus. The transformative potential of my feminist course is maximized through microlevel transactions between our (the teacher and the students') knowledge and value systems during the group discussions and projects. Integrating learners' experiences into the curriculum challenges the normative transfer and validation of knowledge not only in school but also, as an extension, in society at large.

Acceptance of Politically Incorrect Reactions

I constantly remind students during the semester that politically correct responses to the course content serve no purpose. Entries like the one above from the student who saw nothing wrong with the sexist dialogue helped reassure me that students understood that I was interested in hearing what they really felt about the topics and not what they thought would be an appropriate response. Imagining that every student will uncritically or passively accept the feminist notions that I promote exacerbates the oppressive situations for women that I claim to be concerned about.

Educators interested in social change should realize that individual students' reactions to oppressive forces are a complex combination of ongoing resistance and accommodation—processes that both constitute and are constituted by gendered identities emerging from lived experiences. Through participation in group projects that promote a reexamination of a *shikata ga nai* (it cannot be helped) attitude toward hegemonic ideologies and practices, students may develop an awareness, on their own terms, of how women have come to be positioned in certain ways (linguistically, academically, professionally, socially) and how the limits of these positionings can be expanded. These transformations in emerging feminist identities may be neither all-inclusive nor immediate, but at least students will have the exploratory tools they need to imagine how they might change inequitable conditions that are not of their own making.

I attempt to gauge the effectiveness of my pedagogical agenda for social change by reading students' reflective comments in their journals while remembering to continually check the ethics of espousing my feminist (White, liberal, North American) stance on certain issues or assuming "to know what the politically correct end points of liberation are for others" (Luke, 1992, p. 48). This last concept is crucial in feminist pedagogy aimed at the empowerment of students by educators who unproblematically assume that they are in a privileged position with a "what *we* can do for *you*" attitude (Gore, 1992). In other words, Western feminists involved in research or pedagogical endeavors in non-Western contexts must maintain a reflexive accounting of how colonialist tendencies (Spivak, 1988) compromise a truly collaborative effort with students to transform unjust conditions.

⬦ PRACTICAL IDEAS

For personalized learning to occur, the classroom activities (e.g., rewriting of dialogues, journal writing, group projects), topics for the different sessions, and classroom management procedures must all be in line with the poststructuralist interpretation of knowledge construction outlined in the Context section. That is, learners must be encouraged to use their own social and intellectual resources, together with those of their classmates and teacher, to challenge discourses that would inscribe them as other than the imaginative, dynamic individuals that they are.

Involve Students in Interpreting Gender and Language Issues

I have found the following activities to be particularly effective ways of involving junior college students in a collaborative, co-constructed interpretation of gender and language issues.

- Supplement lectures on the course topics by using videos or inviting guest speakers. Most major cities in Japan have a women's center with a video library and contact information for local experts who are willing to speak at schools about women's issues.

- Have students reflect on the course topics through group discussion and individual journal writing. Especially relevant topics for junior college women are sexual harassment at school and in the workplace, domestic violence, sexist portrayals in textbooks and the media, and sexuality.

- Assign various hands-on activities for groups, such as rewriting textbook dialogues, making sexual harassment guidelines, visiting the local women's center, and searching for examples of sexist advertising in magazines and newspapers.

Use Interactive Forms of Assessment

For assessment purposes, have students do a final group project on one of the lecture topics or a topic that they think is related to the course material. Whereas traditional, quantitative testing measures (multiple-choice, true or false, fill-in-the-blanks) can provide valuable information on what is learned in a course, feminist assessment follows a more interactive route in finding out how students got where they are in terms of their own learning and whether their worksheets, journals, and final projects show that they took the time to seriously reflect on the course material.

Kenway and Modra (1992) discuss the issue of traditional assessment, which is seen as a "problem for [feminist] educators who see part of their mission to be the complete transformation of androcentric education systems, which are hierarchical and based on competition and credentialing" (p. 154). I would not characterize my evaluation strategies in such radical terms and instead follow assessment procedures that I feel are appropriate to the overall goals of the course.

As part of the GALI course requirements, students must choose one of the course topics for further investigation using either the school library, the Internet, or other research resources (e.g., magazines, newspaper articles, personal information). Students submit a group project, but each member must include her own individual comments on the researched material.

The first sample project below is what I considered to be well-thought-out comments on the topic of demeaning terms of address and proverbs concerning women. There is evidence of serious engagement with the topic and a rational extension, based on personal or collaboratively constructed knowledge forged from group work, to the implications in terms of gender (in)equality. Unfortunately, I failed to instruct students in the correct way of citing sources and thus only have the name of what appears to be a poem that, according to a member of the group, came from a U.S. bestseller:

> In this way, while researching terms that discriminate against women, I found that there was an endless amount of items. On the first page [of the final project] is something from *Let's Get Rid of "the Girl,"* an American best-selling book. Likewise, in Japan, for example, in a company, I thought how [female employees] are called *girls*. A friend of mine who is working told me, "I'm always called *girl;* no one remembers my name." Male superiors group all the

female [employees] under the title *girl*. Because the value and importance of life are the same for both men and women, I thought that the way that this [discrimination] is taken for granted is definitely wrong. During the summer vacation, I felt again how difficult it is to do away with discrimination. (GALI projects, 1999)

Proverbs have been passed down for generations, and we can get a sense right away of how women were viewed in the past. There are many proverbs that do not fit with modern Japanese society. But among the proverbs, the most numerous are those that show a prejudice or bias against women. The proverb that made the biggest impression on me was *A wise woman will hurt the sale of cows* [i.e., a woman's intelligence is not considered an asset in business deals]. The explanation that was written for this proverb says that women are thought not to be able to think things through clearly and will ultimately ruin business deals. This implies that women are completely unsuited to doing any kind of work—something that really upsets me. There were many more examples, but all in all, it's a reality that women are positioned after and below men. This is inexcusable. By taking this course, I could renew my thinking about sexual discrimination. I'm really glad that I took this course. (GALI projects, 1999)

◈ CONCLUSION

Although all women in Japan face challenging situations in their school, work, and home situations, most junior college female learners are marginalized because of the devalued status of their educational background. As in most North American academic contexts, junior or community college graduates are in a subordinate position to their 4-year-college counterparts (male and female) in the educational and employment hierarchy.

The students are well aware of their inequitable lot in life, are dubious of the school's meritocratic ideology, have little confidence in themselves, and as a result often become disengaged from their studies, which they do not believe are related to their real-life circumstances after graduation. As a result of Japan's current economic recession, junior college female graduates are being passed over in favor of university graduates, who, companies assume, have already acquired at school the skills necessary for becoming the next generation of corporate warriors.

The overall junior college EFL curriculum, and especially feminist courses purportedly aimed at empowering students, should therefore prepare students to assert their power in whatever career path they follow after graduation. I am not advocating an overemphasis on vocationalism in the curriculum solely for the purpose of improving students' employability clout in the labor market. Rather, an educational program that recognizes and values learners' divergent experiences and the knowledge systems that learners bring to school will go a long way in helping students develop "voices that speak in opposition to the local and global discourses that limit and produce the possibilities that frame their lives" (Pennycook, 1997, p. 48).

I can only hope that students' renewed attitudes toward gender and language issues, as expressed in their journals and final projects, will lead to a lasting awareness that even a small change in one's own emerging feminist identity is the first step in the transformation of inequitable social conditions for all women.

◈ CONTRIBUTOR

Andrea Simon-Maeda is an associate professor in the Department of Communication Studies, Nagoya Keizai University, Junior College Division, in Inuyama, Japan. She has taught tertiary-level EFL to female learners for the past 28 years. Her interests include poststructuralist feminism and critical ethnographic research in education.

◈ APPENDIX A: COURSE OUTLINE

Course Description

This course investigates current issues of gender and language and how these issues are related to society's structures of power and authority. The following questions will form the focus of the course:

- How does language reveal and perpetuate sexist attitudes?
- What role does language play in the empowerment and marginalization of women trying to achieve gender equality?

By examining the relationship of gender and language in Japanese and North American society, the teacher and students will become involved in a collaborative learning process that will hopefully lead to the development of a deeper awareness of gender inequality.

Course Requirements

Students are required to complete a project on a lecture topic of their choice. In addition to the project, students will be required to read handouts and write in their journals during the course. As the topics are closely related to our daily lives, your questions, comments, and personal experiences will play an important part in the course.

Course Plan

1. Introduction	Explanation of requirements
2. Gender/sexuality	Definition of terms, video
3. Status and Power	Occupational titles, forms of address
4. Discourse analysis	Examples of hedges, tag questions
5. Politeness and gender	Analysis of politeness forms
6. Prescriptive grammar	Generic and prescriptive pronouns
7. Patriarchy in language and proverbs	Investigate sexism in dictionaries and proverbs
8. Gender portrayals in EFL texts	Analyze students' textbooks
9. Extralinguistic construction of gender	Body postures, gestures, etc.
10. Children's speech	How are gender differences learned?

11. Fairy tales	Watch Snow White and rethink from a feminist perspective
12. Gender portrayals in newspapers	Japanese/English newspaper headlines
13. Media: sexism/violence	Video, *Killing Us Softly* (Kilbourn, 1979)
14. Guest speaker	Domestic violence
15. Consolidation	Discuss projects

◈ APPENDIX B: WORKSHEET

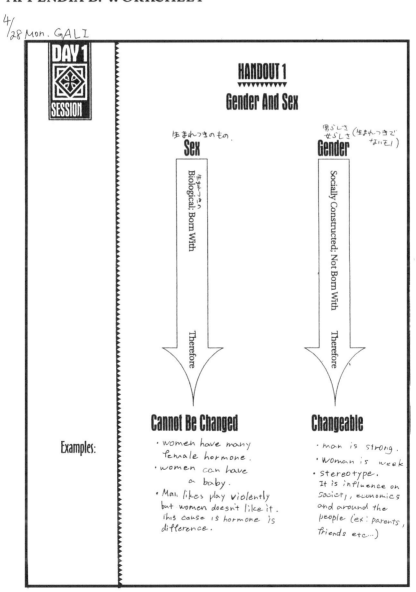

CHAPTER 11

Promoting Critical Reflection About Gender in EFL Classes at a Japanese University

Scott Saft and Yumiko Ohara

◈ INTRODUCTION

Teachers of English in EFL contexts often endeavor to prepare students for travel to and survival in cultural contexts that are unfamiliar to them. At the same time, however, EFL teachers undoubtedly remain aware that students are active, daily participants in their own cultures. Teachers who are concerned about various social issues might therefore want to adopt pedagogical procedures that enable students to think critically about certain aspects of their sociocultural environments. For example, teachers concerned about the position of women may be able to use the EFL classroom to work with students to encourage critical reflection on gender as it is situated in the students' own culture.

In this chapter, we describe our attempts to use freshman EFL classes at a large Japanese national university to promote critical reflection about gender in Japanese society. Specifically, we hoped to: (a) encourage students to appreciate the complex and dynamic character of gender and (b) challenge them to explicitly reflect on expectations and attitudes toward women and men in Japanese society. We also discuss the institutional and cultural constraints that influenced the classroom procedures we ultimately decided to adopt. As we note, these constraints led us to limit the amount of class time devoted to gender.

The specific critical perspective we follow is that of critical pedagogy, an educational philosophy developed by Freire (1970) and more recently applied to second and foreign language instruction (Auerbach, 1992; Crawford-Lange, 1981; Norton & Toohey, 2004; Ohara, Saft, & Crookes, 2001). Critical pedagogy takes the position that education can never be a neutral endeavor; it can foster critical reflection on the world and thereby support human beings' efforts to improve their life conditions, or it can be a vehicle for encouraging people to merely accept the world as it is (Crawford-Lange, 1981; Freire, 1970).

Feminist writers have criticized Freire for ignoring or downplaying the position of women (Vandrick, 1994; Weiler, 1991), but we believe that critical pedagogy, with its fundamental goal of aiding oppressed people, is consistent with many of the basic concerns of feminism. In Freire's critical pedagogy, the key to promoting critical consciousness is dialogue among students and teachers. Dialogue allows both students and teachers to learn from each other and to strive to bring about the social changes that will enhance the quality of their lives.

◈ CONTEXT

Setting

This study took place in the EFL program at the University of Northeast Tokyo (UNET; a pseudonym), a large national university. Like most universities in Japan, UNET requires students to take English classes during their freshman year. At UNET, this requirement consists of three different English classes: one devoted to reading, one to communication, and one to listening. At the time of the study, one of us (Scott) was teaching English communication classes at UNET. In three of those classes during the 2001–2002 school year, we implemented procedures intended to facilitate dialogue about gender.

Participants

The three classes had a total of 116 students, 52 women and 64 men. All were between the ages of 18 and 21, and all had been born and raised in Japan. Although most freshmen in Japanese universities are 18 or 19 years old, 5 upperclass students in the classes, the oldest of whom was 21, were retaking freshman English because they had failed to earn credit for the class previously. Schools in Japan begin formal English instruction during the first year of junior high school, which meant that, as members of a class intended for freshmen, the students had had at least 6 years of English study.

Based on a placement test given at the beginning of the freshman year, students were divided into classes according to their perceived English level. The three English classes included one high-level, one intermediate-level, and one low-level class. Although we were somewhat concerned about our ability to promote dialogue about gender in the low-level class, we decided to use the same procedures in all three classes. UNET is regarded as a relatively top-level university in Japan, and thus we felt that even students in the low-level class would be capable, to at least a certain degree, of engaging in class discussion.

At the time of the classes reported on here, one of us (Scott) was in his second year of teaching EFL at UNET and in his seventh year of teaching English in Japan. Born and raised in the United States, he was employed as a full-time teacher at the university and had a 5-year contract with the possibility of renewal. (Some full-time, non-Japanese teachers at universities in Japan serve as fully tenured faculty, but many more work under a contract that limits their employment period. Some may renew their contracts, but many are expected to leave the position after their contracts expire. In contrast, full-time Japanese faculty are generally granted tenure from the time they accept their positions.)

The other of us (Yumiko), who was born and grew up in Japan, was not involved in teaching the classes. Both of us had been engaged in research on the teaching of gender in second/foreign language settings for quite some time (e.g., Ohara, Saft, & Crookes, 2001), and we devised the teaching procedures described below and analyzed the data together.

Curricular Concerns

No standardized syllabi exist for any of the freshman classes, but teachers are expected to spend time in the class on a range of materials rather than limit their focus to one topic. For example, in communication classes, teachers are generally expected to focus on basic speaking skills in various contexts, such as business situations, travel, and public speaking, and, depending on the students' level, to cover topics that might include politics, current events, sports, and entertainment. In fact, on being hired, Scott was told to be careful because there had been complaints in the past against teachers who had tried to spend an entire year on one topic.

Accordingly, despite our desire to spend the whole academic year on gender, we felt considerable pressure to do so only for a small part of the class. Especially because Scott was only in the second year of his 5-year contract, we concluded (on the advice of a tenured Japanese faculty member) that any attempt to devote more class time to discussion of one topic might harm future attempts to extend his employment at the university. In light of Scott's position, we limited our study to a module on the topic of gender that involved four regular class meetings in succession. This research falls into the type of small-scale, local explorations advocated by Crookes (1993).

Freshman English classes at UNET meet once a week for 75 minutes and continue for a 33-week span across three semesters. Our module was implemented during the third semester, for Weeks 25–28 of the class. In accordance with institutional expectations, before the beginning of the module Scott had covered a variety of materials in class. In choosing the materials and in teaching the class, he had tried to follow Freire's (1970) educational philosophy and create a class that revolved around dialogue. In order to do so, he chose topics, including the relationship between politics and language, bioethics, war, and globalization, that he felt would be conducive to class discussion.

Cultural Concerns

Although the module was to revolve around dialogue in the classroom, some writers and teachers have noted that engaging students in dialogue in the Japanese EFL classroom can be very difficult (Ellis, 1991; Law, 1995). In particular, they have pointed out that in the Japanese educational system, an emphasis on the rote learning of facts and cultural influences that place a priority on group dynamics often leave students reluctant to speak out in class in front of their peers even when they know the answer to a question (see Anderson, 1993, for an extensive discussion of the relationship between the Japanese culture and students' lack of active participation in the classroom).

Based on our own experiences working and teaching in Japan, we were aware of how difficult it can be for students to voluntarily speak out and exchange opinions, and accordingly we adopted techniques that we thought would make it easier for students to speak out in class (see the Description section).

◈ LANGUAGE AND GENDER

Gender (In)equality

Although the majority of the faculty members were male, because UNET was a coeducational institute, female and male students were generally assumed to have equal access to English and other foreign language classes. This was indeed the case at UNET because freshman English was a required course. However, we wanted to focus our class on gender partly because of a social structure in Japan that often denies women access to public domains. A number of studies have been critical of women's unequal access to many social institutions, including business (Kawashima, 1995; Roberts, 1994), education (Fujimura-Fanselow, 1995; McVeigh, 1996), politics (Kubo & Gelb, 1994), and the media (Suzuki, 1995; Tanaka, 1993).

Feminist Influences in Japan

The existence of a literature that has been critical of the treatment of women in Japan indicates a need to adopt feminist perspectives in an attempt to encourage social change, but some analysts have claimed that the feminist movement in Japan has had little or no impact on the structure of Japanese society (Ide & McGloin, 1990). As Ide and McGloin have noted, "It must be remembered that among highly industrialized countries Japan is unique in that feminism has not revolutionized people's way of thinking and living" (1990, p. i). Our own experiences living and working in Japan basically support Ide and McGloin's observations.

But even though the influences of feminism are still not very noticeable in everyday Japanese society, some researchers and teachers have endeavored to use English as a means for promoting critical thinking about gender (e.g., Fujimura-Fanselow, 1996; McMahill, 1997, 2001; Smith & Yamashiro, 1998). For example, McMahill (1997, 2001), noting that the study of English can present women with opportunities to enhance their lives, has described her involvement in developing grassroots feminist English classes that were attended primarily by adults. Although a Japanese university context undoubtedly differs from privately organized adult classes, by designing our module to promote feminist concerns, we were attempting to follow the example set by McMahill and other researchers and teachers in Japan.

Language

Because it has been a source of feminist thinking in the United States and Europe (e.g., Cameron, 1990, 1995; Talbot, 1998), the study of language would seem to be a possible avenue for thinking critically about gender in Japan. Yet, as Reynolds (1993) has pointed out, relatively few scholars have taken a feminist perspective on the relationship between gender and language in Japanese. But although sociolinguistic research on gender in Japan has often not taken a critical perspective, it has emphasized the complexity of gender. Some studies have stressed Japanese women's ability to use language in innovative ways and to create a diverse range of gendered identities for themselves (Matsumoto, 1996; Okamoto, 1995). Moreover, this research has demonstrated that it is impossible to understand women's speech only by examining gender as a social variable. Okamoto (1995; Okamoto & Sato, 1992), for example, has shown that women's speech styles diverge according to age and social situation, a finding that suggests a need to view gender as a dynamic aspect of society that changes over time and according to context.

Indeed, in developing procedures to reflect on gender and language in the EFL classroom, we saw a need to encourage students to realize that gendered identities vary across ages and social situations. At the same time, based on our experiences living and working in Japan, we believed that it was important to reflect on the attitudes toward and inequalities facing women in Japanese society. We devised our classroom procedures in an attempt to deal with both of these concerns.

❖ DESCRIPTION

The instructional sequence for the 4-day module on gender was designed as follows:

- Day 1: Introduce the topic of gender, compare gender words in Japan and the United States, begin discussion, and assign reading homework.

- Day 2: Discuss gender roles in Japan based on the reading (first in groups and then as a class).

- Day 3: Discuss gender and language in Japanese (first in groups and then as a class).

- Day 4: Wrap up, discuss the module in general, and have students complete a questionnaire.

All of the classes were audiotaped with the students' knowledge, and they gave their consent to use both the audiotapes and their responses to the questionnaire as part of this research.

Because the purpose of the first day was to introduce the students to the topic, we began by comparing gender terms in English and Japanese. Scott first presented students with genderless words in English, such as *police officer, fire fighter, mail carrier,* and *waitperson.* Next, he presented Japanese words with overt gender prefixes, which are common in the Japanese language. The terms chosen included *joshidaisei* (female university study), *joi* (female doctor), and *bijin anaunsaa* (beautiful [female] TV reporter).

For the reading homework on Day 1, we chose two pages from a short book about gender in Japan entitled *Looking Inward, Looking Outward* (Birat, 1988). We selected this reading because of its easy-to-understand style and its critical perspective on the position of women in Japan. Within the two pages were criticisms of society for not allowing women to make advancements in the business world and of the expectation that women would stay at home and take care of the children and the household. We hoped the critical tone of Birat's writing would elicit reactions from the students on Day 2 of the module. In addition, we felt that, because the book had been published 14 years before, students would compare Birat's arguments with their own experiences. In particular, we hoped to use the reading to prompt students to recognize a relationship between age (or generation) and gender on Day 2.

In focusing the class on language and gender on Day 3, Scott told students about the debate surrounding so-called Japanese women's language. He informed them, on the one hand, about the tradition of expecting women to use an *onna rashii hanashikata* (a womanly way of speaking) and, on the other, about more recent studies showing that women, especially younger women, use various speech forms, including vulgar forms, once thought to be used by men only. Scott then asked the students about their experiences and opinions concerning the language used by women and men in Japan. On the final day of the module, Scott asked students for their impressions about studying gender in an EFL class and administered a questionnaire concerning the module.

As noted, we were aware that cultural influences would bear on the students' ability to participate in dialogue. Accordingly, instead of expecting students to immediately express opinions, we relied on written questions and group discussions throughout the module. Typically, after hearing an explanation of the topic of the day (in English), the students received a set of printed questions to discuss, first in groups and then with the teacher and all the students. Students were allowed to use their written responses as the basis for the discussion. As we describe below, although such procedures meant that students were not expressing their ideas spontaneously, at least at the beginning of the discussion, the procedures promoted the students' ability to engage in dialogue about gender.

◈ DISTINGUISHING FEATURES

The data from the audiotapes and the questionnaire responses revealed significant results of the module in three areas: classroom participation, awareness of gender dynamics, and critical consciousness.

The Emergence of Dialogue About Gender

In a significant amount of the classroom discussion, Scott asked questions, and the students responded, but it became apparent on the first day that students were willing to voice their own opinions and engage in dialogue about gender with Scott and their classmates. Excerpt 1 is from the first day of the module in the low-level class, when Scott asked students whether they felt there was a need to create genderless words in Japanese.

1.	1	Scott:	Uh, how about you, Koji, do you think people in Japan should try to use genderless words?
	2	Koji:	I think there is no need because Japan is different from America.
	3	Scott:	Okay, does anyone—yes, Midori.
	4	Midori:	I don't think saying *joshigakusei* or *bijin annaunsaa* is fair to women. We should not have to emphasize gender with words. I think Japan should change.

In Turn 3 of this excerpt, as Scott was about to ask if anyone wanted to respond to Koji's statement, Midori, a female student, raised her hand, prompting Scott to stop what he was saying and call on her. As the excerpt shows, Midori contradicted Koji, a male student, by stating that Japanese people should not use gender terms because they are not fair to women.

As indicated by this excerpt, much of the discussion was filtered through Scott. The students rarely responded directly to each other without first receiving permission from the teacher. Nonetheless, we were pleased to see students expressing their opinions and sometimes responding by opposing or challenging statements made by their classmates. Particularly, we were encouraged, as in Excerpt 1, to see female students willing to challenge the assertions of their male classmates.

In addition to selecting students to talk, Scott took advantage of his role as facilitator of the discussion by sometimes attempting to provoke students. Excerpt 2, from Day 2 in the intermediate-level class, shows how a male student resists Scott's attempt to lead the discussion in a certain direction.

2.	1	Scott:	So like I told you, I want to ask you whether you agree with the writer's opinion about gender in Japan. Tetsuya, how about you?
	2	Tetsuya:	We think that maybe a long time before it was true, but the situation is different now.

3	Scott:	So how about now, is there gender discrimination in Japan?
4	Tetsuya:	Uh [silence for about 4 seconds].
5	Scott:	But there is still gender discrimination against women, don't you think?
6	Sho:	I don't think there is much discrimination against women. Women can go to university the same as men and get a good job if they try.

After Tetsuya, a male student, failed to respond in Turn 4, Scott followed with a stronger statement in Turn 5, asserting that there is still discrimination against women and ending his statement with a tag question. Another male student, Sho, who was sitting near Tetsuya and was part of Tetsuya's discussion group, responded in Turn 6 by stating that he did not think there was much discrimination against women and that women were equally free to engage in the same endeavors as men.

As Excerpts 1 and 2 suggest, one pattern that developed over the 4-day module was that very few of the male students perceived problems in gender relations in Japan. In contrast, as the module continued, female students became more vocal in expressing their experiences and opinions. This pattern can be seen in Excerpts 3 and 4, presented in the next subsection.

Dialogue About the Dynamic Character of Gender

As is apparent in the comments by Tetsuya and Sho above, many students strongly believed that the younger generation's views toward gender were very different from those of older Japanese people. Excerpt 3 comes from Day 2 of the high-level class.

3.	1	Yukiko:	My mother has always been a housewife, but my sister and me can have more choices. We can go to the university, and we will search for careers.
	2	Scott:	Yes, Tomoko.
	3	Tomoko:	I agree Yuki-chan, these days women can do many things in Japan.
	4	Scott:	Many things? Like what?
	5	Tomoko:	Like finding a job and going to foreign countries.
	6	Scott:	So, Tomoko, do you want to go to another country?
	7	Tomoko:	Yes, I want to go to England.
	8	Scott:	Oh, that's great.
	9	Tomoko:	Yes, but my mother does not want me to go. She thinks I should stay in Japan so she can take care of me. She is an old Japanese.
	10	Scott:	Oh, that is a problem.
	11	Tomoko:	Yes, she does not understand that a woman should be free to do many activities.

In this excerpt, Yukiko and Tomoko, both women, stress the differences between themselves and their mothers. Tomoko, by relating the disagreement with her mother about studying abroad, shows how these different generational views of gender can cause problems. According to Tomoko in Turns 9 and 11, an "old Japanese" like her mother does not understand that women should also be free to do things like travel abroad.

As the module progressed, it became apparent that many of the female students were conscious of this fluid sense of gender. On Day 4 in the high-level class, during the general discussion of the module, one woman formulated this dynamic sense of gender in terms of different identities.

4. 1 Makiko: I am very surprised by my mother. She can be very strict with me and sometimes she uses rough language with my father too. But she is very polite and *onna rashii* [woman-like] when she goes to work. She can change her attitude very quick. She is like different people.
   2 Scott: It is like she has different identities.
   3 Makiko: Yes, yes.
   4 Scott: Is that because she is a woman?
   5 Makiko: Yes, yes, because she has to be *onna rashii* at her work. She has to wear beautiful clothes and a nice skirt. At my home, she just has regular clothes.

With the statement that her mother is like different people (Turn 1), Makiko shows an appreciation of the fact that women have to change their actions and language according to the situation. The family represents one particular context of language use, and Makiko's mother, by using "rough" language to keep her daughter and even her husband in line, is carrying out her role in this context. At her job, Makiko's mother must participate in a different context, one where is she expected to be *onna rashii*.

Displays of Critical Consciousness

Many of the women in the classes were aware of the dynamic quality of being a woman in Japan. As a part of this awareness, they displayed an ability to be critical of Japanese society. That students were capable of being critical about the material they were covering was apparent from the beginning of the module. In Excerpt 1 above, for example, a female student criticized the use of gender terms and stated a desire for change on the first day of the module. In addition, many students expressed a critical perspective in response to the reading assignment on Day 2.

Excerpt 5 occurred in the high-level class after Scott, in expressing agreement with the opinion of the book's author, told the students how surprised he was on first coming to Japan to find that one of women's tasks in schools and companies was to serve tea to their male colleagues and to customers. The excerpt begins as a male student, Masato, states that he would be willing to make tea for himself as well as prepare it for women.

5. 1 Masato: If I work in the company, I would not expect women to serve me tea. If I had free time, I would make myself and give to women, too.
   2 Scott: Okay, that would be—yes, Asami, what do you think?
   3 Asami: I think it is so bad that only women have to serve tea. My sister is an OL [*ofisu redii,* or office lady], and she always has to make tea for men. Women want to work, too, they don't just want to be the servant at the company. The company must treat women as equals. They will find that women can do very good work.

Asami, a woman, asserts that women are not servants. Explaining that her sister always serves tea as an OL, Asami criticizes companies for not treating women as equals.

Although students made critical comments during the class discussions, perhaps the place where students displayed the greatest ability to be reflective was the questionnaire administered at the end of the module. As in the dialogues, in the questionnaires many students criticized the treatment of women in Japan but showed a capacity to think about the complex nature of being a woman in Japanese society. Excerpt 6 comes from a intermediate-level female student's answer to an item on the questionnaire that asked for students' feelings about women pursuing careers in Japan.

6. I am woman, and I will keep working after I get married and have children. I have thought about this since I was a high school student. I think it is not fair for women to have pressure to quit working just because she is a woman. But I wonder will it be good for my children? I know a man whose mother is a very good teacher, but when he was a child, he couldn't meet his mother long time and he felt loneliness. I don't want my children to feel loneliness. The best way is to find a partner to help me keep working and take good care of my children, but I am not sure if he can do that.

This student is critical of the pressures on women to give up their careers after they have a family. She says that it is not fair and indicates that she has actually been thinking of this issue since she was in high school. Yet she expresses concern about the children she might have. Not wanting her children to feel lonely, she states her desire to find a partner who will make it possible for her to care for her children and have a career at the same time. There is, however, a sense of despair apparent in the final sentence. She is doubtful about whether she will be able to find such a partner. This same sense of despair can be found in Excerpt 7, a response by a woman in the high-level class to the same question.

7. The problem is that Japanese fathers have no time to care about his children. They are too busy now. Even in their holiday, they often have *tsukiai* [business-related socializing] and have to play the golf. If their tasks are diminished more and they can give priority to their family, then the situation will be improved. I want to keep working even after I get married, but it will only be possible if my partner helps me. I hope he can do that, but I don't know if I can find such a person.

Here, the student is critical of the fact that Japanese fathers lack the time to help care for their children. She does not blame men directly but seems to place the blame on society for not diminishing the tasks men have to do. She also recognizes the effects this lack of assistance from men will have on her life. She states that she wants to keep working even after getting married, but she realizes that it will be possible only if she has a partner who can help her. Like the author of Excerpt 6, the student can only hope to find a partner who will allow her to take care of her family and pursue her career at the same time.

As these two passages indicate, many young women are aware that their gender might prevent them from being able to pursue careers in Japanese society. Moreover,

Excerpts 1–5 show that the students, especially the women, were aware of the fluid sense of gender and capable of expressing critical ideas about gender in Japanese society.

◈ PRACTICAL IDEAS

Based on our module, the ideas below center on two concerns: ways of dealing with institutional constraints and means for fostering dialogue in classrooms where students may not be accustomed to expressing themselves.

Dealing With Institutional Constraints

Use a Module Approach

Especially if your status does not make it possible to exert much influence on the curriculum, the module approach offers a way of working within institutional boundaries to promote critical thinking about various social issues. In our case, the 4-day module allowed us to develop a coherent set of procedures that gave students a chance to think about gender. Without jeopardizing Scott's tenuous position at the university, we could try different techniques in the classroom that encouraged students to reflect on an issue of relevance to their own lives.

Use Qualitative Research Methods

By using audiotapes and questionnaires, you can review the procedures you employ in class; think about and revise your instructional methods; and, after securing permission from students, present your data and findings to colleagues, including colleagues who might have more power to initiate changes in the curriculum.

Based on our experience with the 4-day module presented here, we made efforts to improve our critical teaching techniques. In addition, we showed some of our data to tenured faculty at UNET, who encouraged us to devote more time to gender in future EFL classes there.

Fostering Dialogue About Gender

Give Students Printed Questions Before Engaging Them in Dialogue

Eliciting opinions from students with little or no background in discussion-oriented classes can be difficult. If students receive a set of printed questions and are allowed to discuss those questions among themselves, they may feel less inhibited about speaking in front of their teacher and their peers. In our module, many of the students responded to Scott's questions by reading the answers they had prepared with the help of their friends, and they grew more and more comfortable expressing their views about gender.

We know from our experiences teaching in Japan that students' collective silence can be very frustrating, but we nonetheless see a great need to continue searching for means of encouraging students to express themselves in class, particularly concerning social issues, such as gender, that are pertinent to their own lives.

Give Students Concrete Materials to Work With

Instead of presenting gender to students as a general topic and using abstract terminology such as *gender roles* or *gender identities,* work with concrete materials that students are either familiar with or can read or see for themselves. We presented students first with a written set of gendered and genderless terms in English and Japanese; second, with a short reading assignment; and then with a concept, namely, *onna rashii* (womanlike), that students already knew. The incorporation of these items into the module made it easier for students to formulate and express opinions because they could respond to specific aspects of gender and relate them to their own lives rather than approach gender as an abstract concept.

◈ CONCLUSION

In constructing a 4-day module devoted to gender, we set out to see whether we could use an EFL class to prompt Japanese university students to consider the dynamic quality of gender and think critically about the position of women in Japanese society. In many ways, our findings greatly exceeded our expectations.

Students, especially the women, showed that, when given the chance to express their opinions and relate their experiences to the material they were studying, they could appreciate the complexities involved in being a gendered individual. This finding not only indicates the possibility of using the EFL classroom to emphasize gender as a complex social variable but also suggests a need for research on gender and language to continue approaching gender as a fluid aspect of society.

In addition, the students, again particularly the women, demonstrated an ability to voice criticisms about certain aspects of society. In doing so, they sometimes took advantage of the dialogue to disagree with male classmates' opinions. Feminist writers have been critical of women's lack of access to public domains in Japan, but when the female students were given a chance to think critically in the classroom, they could use the university, one important public domain, as a context to voice their experiences and express their opinions and desires.

Although most of the critical voices in our module were women's, the study also indicates how important it is to promote critical reflection about gender among young men in Japan. Though pleased that our module enabled many women to voice their feelings relatively freely, we were disappointed that more male students did not use the module as a chance to explore in more depth their feelings about gender. As exhibited in Excerpts 1 and 2, many male students resisted the idea that change in gendered relationships in Japan was necessary. This resistance is, of course, a legitimate feeling, and we did not want to be dictatorial. Nonetheless, because men still hold the majority of the powerful positions in Japan, any change in the gendered hierarchy of Japanese society will ultimately require the cooperation of both women and men. Men, like women, are affected by gender attitudes in Japan, and we are therefore planning to make more efforts in our future classes to enhance men's capacity to reflect on gender.

As our study made apparent, even in a 4-day module, teachers can use the EFL classroom in Japan to engage in critical reflection about gender. We hope that our experience will encourage other teachers and researchers to develop procedures that will allow them to work within institutional constraints and promote both women's and men's ability to think about the relevance of gender to their lives.

◈ CONTRIBUTORS

Scott Saft has taught English in Japan and Japanese in the United States. He has published in the areas of conversation analysis and critical pedagogy. In addition to studying the relationship between gender and language pedagogy, he is currently pursuing research on social interaction in institutional settings, including news broadcasts, university faculty meetings, and medical consultations.

Yumiko Ohara teaches gender and ethnic studies at Hawai'i Tokai International College, in the United States. She has taught at various institutions in Mexico, Japan, and the United States and has published in the areas of critical discourse analysis and critical pedagogy, with a particular interest in the way gender is represented and socially constructed in Japanese society.

CHAPTER 12

Critical Feminist Engagement in the EFL Classroom: From Supplement to Staple

Tamarah Cohen

❧ INTRODUCTION

In this chapter I describe an advanced EFL undergraduate course within the Intensive English Studies (IES) Program at a private language university in the Kansai area of Japan. Entitled Academic Preparation and Linguistic Theories and Advanced Reading/Listening Comprehension (hereafter Linguistics), the intensive, 6-hour per week, year-long sophomore course is designed to verify in praxis my commitment to the development of an explicit critical feminist pedagogy. Included is a sampling of course materials derived from both student-generated and non-EFL-specific academic texts. These materials are designed to foster intellectual inquiry, critical reflection, and cultural critique as well as to draw out and celebrate differences of position and voice among students.

❧ CONTEXT

In 1993, the university where I teach introduced the IES Program to its undergraduate students. The purpose of the program, states the *Faculty Manual and Class Roster,* "is to help students develop communicative language competence and skills through English education." Participants, the majority of whom are working toward BAs in English or international communication, are selected primarily on the basis of scores on the Test of English as a Foreign Language (TOEFL).

Throughout the first 2 years, program participants are privileged to relatively small IES-exclusive, exclusively English-medium classes of roughly 25. First-year students attend courses that are skills based and essentially modality specific, for example, Reading and Writing Strategies and Vocabulary Building. Second-year students—my domain—attend courses that are more content based, such as Linguistics. Third- and fourth-year students, who are expected to have mastered basic grammatical and academic skills, are deemed ready to engage in what is called *autonomous learning.* This means one of two things: Attending capacious Japanese-medium seminars, such as English Seminar, along with non-EFL students or, if they have managed to jump through the myriad hoops that render them qualified, studying overseas for up to 2 years in one of hundreds of highly competitive study-abroad programs worldwide.

An examination of IES curricula, including syllabi with associated textbooks, shows a very limited effort at gender balance, even if only "as an add-on category or compensatory gesture" (Luke & Gore, 1992b, p. 7). Across the board, female and male students are conflated into a singular human model. In other words, women are "construed on the model of the masculine, whether in terms of sameness/identity, opposition/distinction, or complementarity" (Grosz, as cited in Luke & Gore, 1992c, p. 207). This "abstracting, universalising and generalising of masculine attributes"—known also as *phallocentricism*—represents the death of women's "concrete specificity and potential for autonomous definition" (Grosz, as cited in Luke & Gore, p. 207).

This phallocentric state of affairs is never more obvious than when examining IES course textbooks, few of which demonstrate any but the lamest attempts at breaking down the stereotypes that help maintain destructive gender relations. Course reading lists reflect a similar pattern, featuring mostly nonfeminist and non-female-authored works. The same can be said of the university library collection, which contains almost no works by scholars who work to one side of the *malestream* (O'Brien, 1981) in their fields and almost none that are explicitly feminist, postmodernist, or left leaning. No courses focus on women per se, gender, or issues of particular concern to women, nor are there any university-sponsored gender-based clubs or circles, that is, extracurricular groups. Men are vastly overrepresented in the faculty and administration. What makes this overrepresentation all the more astonishing is that more than three quarters of the student body is female: 74% in the regular and 79% in the IES Program.

❧ LANGUAGE AND GENDER

English, like most languages of the modern world, partakes of the male-is-norm ideology. It therefore reflects and helps constitute sexual inequality. Consider, for instance, pseudogeneric masculine word forms, such as *he, man, freshman, guy, gay, fraternize,* and *patronize,* which contribute to "the framing of human experience in terms of males' experience and the concomitant neglect of women's" (Gibbon, 1999, p. 42). Because these word forms turn females, but not males, into potential nonreferents, in their presence girls and women tend to experience alienation whereas boys and men do not. Specifically, when females encounter pseudogeneric word forms, they have difficulty, relative to males, identifying with those referred to. This lack of identification obligates girls and women to develop additional processing strategies—strategies involving the suppression of male imagery—in order to cope with the underlying alienation caused by such words (Silveira, 1979).

In response to these enduring patterns, a growing number of feminist linguists have begun developing compensatory strategies for combating masculine gender normativity. Cameron (1994), for example, has proposed the use of female generics, explaining that

> rather than actually excluding or marginalising men, [using *she* generically] draws attention to the way women are excluded and marginalised by the traditional convention; by undermining our normal expectations as readers and listeners, it forces us to ask why we take those expectations as natural and therefore to acknowledge sexism for what it is . . . . If a time ever comes when feminine generics do not violate anyone's sense of what is natural, normal and

right, that will be the time to abandon the visibility strategy as outdated. (p. 31)

Pseudogeneric masculine word forms constitute only one aspect of the problem. Recent feminist theoretical discussions among linguists, sociologists, social psychologists, historians, literary critics, philosophers, and geographers have in fact moved away from an emphasis on isolated words and sentences to more extended samples of language in use, that is, from decontextualized items constituting what is commonly known as *sexist language* (including pseudogenerics) to the role of discourse in the reproduction of sexism. The relationship between gender, language, and discourse in current theoretical debates is thus a central concern across disciplines.

◈ DESCRIPTION

In writing the syllabus for Linguistics, I opted to aim explicitly for gender inclusion or, as Kenway and Modra (1992) put it, *gender expansion,* with respect to framework. I applied the notion that

> curricula should include and value the range of experiences of women [and men], while at the same time recognizing that the definitions of femininity and masculinity which are formed and promoted in school curricula should encompass a wide range of possibilities which make women [and men] not only "equally human" (Blackburn, 1982) but equally free in the public and the private sphere. (p. 142)

Textbooks

To that end, I selected textbooks shaped by a feminist problematic of gender. Each emphasizes themes that are primary to feminist engagement, namely, the politics of knowledge, language, individual differences, and identity, such as *Language: The Social Mirror* (Chaika, 1994), *Linguistic Genocide in Education—or Worldwide Diversity and Human Rights?* (Skutnabb-Kangas, 2000a), *Womansword: What Japanese Words Say about Women* (Cherry, 1987), *Living Language* (Nilsen, 1999), and *The Woman's Encyclopedia of Myths and Secrets* (Walker, 1983).

I also included *The English Language* (Barber, 1997), which assumes a patriarchal and Eurocentric frame of reference in that it obviously targets a readership with a privileged relation to cultures of European origin and virtually no interest in the cultural contributions of women, as these excerpts show:

> We know little of their history in this turbulent period of migration and expansion, but we do know that, towards the end of these centuries of flux, *our Germanic ancestors* [italics added] settled in England. (p. 100)

> *The Germans* [italics added] dislike peace, for it is only in war that renown and booty can be won. In peacetime, the warriors idle about at home, eating, drinking, and gambling, and leaving the work of the house and of the fields to women, weaklings, and slaves. They are extremely hospitable, to strangers as well as to acquaintances, but their love of drinking often leads to quarrels. They are monogamous, and *their women* [italics added] . . . . (p. 82)

This text contrasts to a great, albeit varying, degree with the others in terms of both rhetorical purpose and context (see Appendix A).

I also decided to include an analysis (in English) of the norms of Japanese linguistic behavior, as indices of, among other areas, gender and ethnic identity and power relations. I developed an array of assignments that tap materials drawn from (or at least related to) both high and popular Japanese culture—some written, others visual; some in Japanese, others in English. These materials include academic journal and newspaper articles, television news magazines, advertisements, Web sites, music videos, song lyrics, and *manga* (comics). *Womansword: What Japanese Words Say About Women* (Cherry, 1987) served as the starting point for this portion of the course and has proven to be a particularly provocative and rewarding resource, as it gently encourages students to denaturalize their mother tongue, that is, to understand that Japanese, too, comprises institutionalized constraints within which students must learn to negotiate their meanings.

Texts in hand, students explore such issues as voice audibility and the role that writers assume with regard to their own voice and audience, that is, who is writing to whom. In reading between the lines, the students begin to assert themselves against the power of text, discovering that meaning lies not in text itself but in the social relations in which it is embedded. Thus, rather than simply focusing on form for form's sake, they are actually adducing evidence for text-based ideological positioning—including, of course, their own.

Teaching Sequences

Below are two fairly representative teaching sequences from Linguistics. Each verifies in praxis the fundamentals of engaging dialogically with text (i.e., constructing embodied knowledge using both subjective and objective methods) as a means of developing individual awareness of linguistic agency.

Sequence 1

As a class, we watch a 20-minute, English-medium video excerpt from *World Reports,* a Japanese TV news magazine composed of special-interest reports produced by non-Japanese news media—typically BBC, CNN, and ABC. The topic of this week's film segment (and thus this sequence) is "I Want to Become an American: Changing Race Through Cosmetic Surgery" (1998). I selected the excerpt for its accessibility with respect to formal linguistic features, propositional content or plain sense meaning, ideological positioning, and timeliness (at this point in the term, the class is focusing on the cumulative and interactive character of racial and gender oppression as expressed through language).

In keeping with the TV program's standard format, the segment is followed by a brief dialogue between a demure young woman and an extremely self-assured, much older man. The discourse could, however, be more appropriately described as a monologue, with the female interlocutor's contribution amounting to nothing other than sustained conversational support. I replay this Japanese dialogue as many times as requested (usually three), inviting those who are interested to interpret and transliterate the exchange and then to send me their work via e-mail. I make clear that this is an exercise in straight aural-to-text interpretation, as in translation, and not a vehicle for personal expression.

In this particular instance, four students send in transliterations. I compile the submissions, making no corrections for grammar; remove names; apply a few by-now familiar before- and after-reading questions related to rhetorical purpose; and print out the results in handout form (see Appendix B, Part 1).

In the next class, we begin by discussing the before- and after-reading questions. Students then form small groups. I back off, giving them roughly 30 minutes to analyze the various submissions for language choices that they feel reveal ideological assumptions and presuppositions. Group members are asked to find at least one point that they are confident their peers will find illuminating and to describe it in abbreviated form on the chalkboard. (Students whose transliterations are being examined are asked not to reveal their identity.) Once the board is full, a group representative comes to the front to explain the group's findings. These mini-presentations are viewed as practice in developing, among other things, audience awareness and the ability to communicate spontaneously in a formal register.

Students are then given the transcript of the follow-up dialogue (see Appendix B, Part 2) and asked to replace terms that I consider to be sociopolitically problematic with those that state the speakers' intended message in direct and disambiguated terms. Finally, students are invited to participate in one final follow-up, extra-credit opportunity: "Respond in approximately two typed pages to at least one of the after-reading questions on the handout." These submissions, too, are regularly trans-formed into critical analytical exercises (see Appendix C, Part 3).

The principal challenge of this exercise is to see the (video) text as an intersection of language codes and in the process tease apart ownership of the various manifestations of bias. Could, for example, what some groups identified as evidence of racist sentiments on the part of one or both of the Japanese TV commentators actually be attributed to the (surgically altered) individuals featured in the clip or to the student interpreters themselves? Could the students convincingly support their claims? And, finally, what accounts for the failure of two of the four student interpreters to acknowledge the very presence of the female commentator? These issues are explored in follow-up work both in and outside the classroom.

Sequence 2

Students are asked to coin new words by experimenting with English affixes and nouns (see Appendix C, Part 1). Their coinages are submitted to me via e-mail. During the following class I distribute a compilation of student-generated neolo-gisms (see Appendix C, Part 2), plus some of my favorites from *Websters' First New Intergalactic Wickedary of the English Language* (Daly, 1988).

Students then compose a short dramatic statement or story using as many of the words from the list as they can. They are instructed to establish the meaning of each neologism by way of context or text-embedded definition. Again, they submit their work to me via e-mail. I compile the students' stories and transform the grammar problems into *and/or* exercises to be completed collaboratively (see Appendix C, Part 3). In small groups, they create titles for those entries that have none. The class ends with each group listing on the chalkboard what they think the objectives of the exercise were.

At the beginning of the final class of this sequence, students display their favorite titles, written during the previous class, on the chalkboard. As the students read their own work, the class corrects the exercise item by item. The writer-narrator of each story ends by choosing a favorite title(s) from those listed on the chalkboard. For homework, students address an extra-credit opportunity (see Appendix C, Part 3).

Of course, Teaching Sequence 2 is rigged. My choices with respect to word parts (e.g., *ex-, hyper-, bi- trans-, sexual, woman, masculinity*; see Appendix C, Part 1) nearly guarantee written responses that relate to sexual role play, identity, and orientation. So, in addition to encouraging students to exercise their oral, interpretive, and word- and text-attack skills—and their imaginations—this sequence promotes expression and awareness of the gendered dimensions of experience in a nonjudgmental and student-centered (albeit carefully monitored) multivocal framework.

◈ DISTINGUISHING FEATURES

Development of Interpretive Skills

Concern for administrative reprisal does not appear to factor significantly in the quietism about the gender imbalance that pervades the university's curricula (as described in the Context section), although rumors of official censorship or, in any case, censure occasionally circulate. My course syllabi, published annually along with everyone else's, reflect an unabashedly feminist orientation, as do the books that fill my portion of the library's reserve section.

But what most distinguishes my course from others within the IES Program is that, instead of prioritizing the reproduction of normative—that is, andro- and ethnocentric—cultural values and knowledge that promises closure, the course is designed to privilege the development of interpretive skills: the skills required to negotiate the intersecting cultural narratives of class, gender, sexuality, ethnicity, and national identity.

Such a methodology has as its primary goal learner awareness of and appreciation for *positionality*—where one stands in relation to what one says—and *multivocality*—the reality "formed by the interaction of several consciousnesses, none of which entirely becomes an object for the other" (Bakhtin, 1984, p. 18). When exploited, these two interrelated concepts can emancipate students, prompting them to think critically: to de- and reconstruct the ground rules of language and the ideological premises on which they are based.

Use of Course Evaluations

Because of the unconventional nature of my goals as a teacher, I am accustomed to encountering an initial measure of disorientation from students. For this reason, I begin each course with an exercise, the body of which comprises unedited but abbreviated student-generated course evaluations collected from the previous year.

This exercise functions as a preview of some of the more probable hurdles and rewards as well as some of the key terms and concepts, including *feminist*,[1] *critical awareness, connotation, bias, power relations, rhetorical purpose,* and *linguistic sexism,*

---

[1] Japanese has borrowed *feminist* from English (hence *feminisuto*), but the term has undergone semantic distortion, or as Takashi Wilkerson (1998) would say, "semantic confusion" (p. 616). As she explains, when asked what they visualize when they hear the word *feminist,* most college-educated Japanese describe "a man who is kind, such as those who practice Western-style gallantry" (p. 615).

that students can expect to encounter as they proceed through the course (see Appendix D).

◈ PRACTICAL IDEAS

Below are recommendations for developing critical feminist engagement in the classroom.

Choose Texts With Conflicting Biases

Select thematically related texts that display a range of conflicting biases. Then exploit the biases as a means to developing critical awareness in students.

Encourage Dialogic Engagement With Text

Model active reading. Then provide materials that facilitate dialogic engagement with (aural or written) text. Such materials should incorporate such features as before-, while-, and after-reading and discussion questions related to rhetorical purpose and context (see, e.g., Appendix B, Parts 1 and 2).

Ask and Elicit Many Types of Questions

Explore the many kinds of questions that can be asked, going beyond simply demanding the identification of significant textual propositions. Then gradually move away from questions that elicit fixed or singularly correct answers. Instead, offer (and encourage the generation of) questions that invite a multiplicity of defensible interpretations, questions that focus on buried ideological investment and competing schemata, and the ways both affect meaning.

Raise Awareness of Pseudogenerics

Demonstrate how pseudogenerics lead to ambiguity of reference and female invisibility. Then model both female and male generics in equal numbers. Also demonstrate how gender-neutral terms, such as *doctor, homosexual,* and *person,* perpetuate the invisibility of women in positions outside traditionally defined roles. Model explicit and consistent gender marking, such as *female doctor/male doctor, female homosexual/male homosexual,* and *woman/man.* (Note: it has never been the Japanese who have enjoyed lifetime employment; rather, it has been Japanese men.)

Have Students Question Prescriptive Grammar Rules

Encourage students to challenge the prescriptive rules of language. Ask why, for example, most male referents precede female referents, as in *men and women.* Then invite students to consciously violate the rules.

Use Etymology to Sensitize Students to Sexism in the Lexicon

Incorporate etymology into vocabulary development as a means of sensitizing students to the phenomena of semantic derogation and linguistic asymmetry, such as *girl* versus *boy, female* versus *male,* or *bachelor* versus *spinster.* Then invite students to coin words of their own to compensate for perceived gaps in the lexicon.

Explore Markedness

Explain the patterns of markedness, as in *How tall are you? Is he a male prostitute? Is she seeing a woman doctor? Are they non-White?* Then encourage students to critically manipulate the patterns as a means of deconstructing the natural.

❖ CONCLUSION

Because the student body is predominantly female and the curriculum language arts oriented, the university where I currently teach is an ideal—though by no means the only appropriate—environment within which to take into account the gendered dimensions of experience (i.e., to make central the experience of women) in a linguistic framework that by definition demands the recognition of social and political context. The course described above is the fruit of this observation.

The course represents a commitment to the development of critical feminist methodology that takes into account the "cognitive significance and social ramifications of . . . linguistic choices" (Penelope, 1990, p. xxxii). Accordingly, it exploits a range of ways of drawing attention to and prioritizing the exploration of ideological positions, assumptions, and preconceptions, as revealed in textual features such as passive nominals, suppressed experiencers, euphemisms, markedness, false deixis, and truncated (agentless) passives. By capitalizing on the metalingual resources (Wallace, 1992) and contrapuntal vision (Said, 1984) of second language learners within a multivocal framework, the course helps students come to recognize that all interpretive work (i.e., the construction of knowledge) is "a matter of overlapping and contested terrains" and not a "search for a sacred originating point" (Gunew, 1994, p. 38). It is, in other words, a context-dependent endeavor that is profoundly influenced by social forces and that can best be understood in the context of power relations, both within the classroom and beyond.

My course guides learners through an exploration of the discursive processes by which gender, among a variety of intersecting cultural narratives, is constructed. The methodology I use relies on textual analysis to draw learners, as interpretive agents, back into the process of knowing. Instead of aiming for deference to my interpretive strategies—be they normative or otherwise—I believe I am serving the students better by offering them a sustained opportunity to acquire the emotional and cognitive tools required, as outsiders, to unpack the unmarked cultural narratives of gender, sexuality, ethnicity, class, and national identity (Wallace, 1992) and thereby prepare themselves for increasingly complex acts of critical feminist engagement.

❖ ACKNOWLEDGMENTS

I thank Erika Helene, Kerstan Cohen, and Elizabeth Lokon for their insightful comments; the IES students, whose words form the substance of my work; and Aki Kajimoto for interpretation and translation in Appendix B.

◈ CONTRIBUTOR

Tamarah Cohen is an instructor in language studies at a language arts university in the Kansai area of Japan. She is currently at work on a book tentatively titled *What's a "Womyn" That a "Woman" Can't Be? Erosion of the Link Between Etymology and Meaning.*

◈ APPENDIX A: SAMPLE TEXTBOOK EXERCISES

"Woman and Man, Black and White"
(Skutnabb-Kangas, 2000a, pp. 144–150)

Note: There may be more than one valid answer for multiple-choice items.

1. *Rights of Man, you guys,* and *mankind* (when used to include both males and females) are examples of
   a) pseudogeneric forms in English.
   b) pseudocyesis among men.
   c) male forms used inclusively.

2. The unmarked form of *doctor/woman doctor* is *doctor. Marked* must mean:

   _____

   _____

3. Think of at least four more marked/unmarked pairs in English:

   _____

   _____

4. In Info Box 3.3,[2] Skutnabb-Kangas (2000a, p. 145) shows that
   a) Pseudogenerics account exclusively for female linguistic invisibility.
   b) Males get more dictionary space than females in all categories.
   c) Females get more space than males in only one category (the maternal).

5. On page 146, Paragraph 2, Skutnabb-Kangas makes use of the feminine pronoun *she* to refer to the reader because
   a) She believes/hopes all her readers are female.
   b) She appears to have adopted a compensatory strategy with respect to genericity in an attempt to promote women's visibility.
   c) She wants to draw attention to the way women are excluded and marginalized by the traditional convention.
   d) She is trying to undermine our normal expectations as readers.

---

[2] Info Box 3.3 reads, "Women get less space in [Swedish and Finnish] dictionaries than men—except as mothers," and continues, "Space in column centimeters given to females and males in four big dictionaries **woman** 55.3 cm; **man** 124.3 cm; **girl** 29.6 cm; **boy** 70.5 cm; **sister** 20.2 cm; **brother** 45.2 cm; but **father** 32.8 cm; **mother** 47.1 cm" (Skutnabb-Kangas, 2000a, p. 145).

"Gender and Persuasiveness" (Chaika, 1994, pp. 382–383)

TRUE or FALSE or MAYBE—If you choose MAYBE (M), a clear and concise explanation is due, reverse side.

1. One's gender has a lot to do with one's persuasiveness. T/F/M

2. Women should not be assertive and direct around men if they wish to have their views taken seriously. T/F/M

3. Many women and men remain unaware of gender disparity in language and interaction. T/F/M

4. Even professionals are frequently unaware of sexist language. T/F/M

5. Imprisonment in our respective language systems is unavoidable. T/F/M

6. The vocabulary of a language is a mirror of its speakers' attitudes and ideas. T/F/M

7. Mirrors, like languages, reflect; they do not determine. T/F/M

Extra-Credit Opportunity

Find the pseudogeneric reference(s) in the paragraph below. Describe the resulting problem (i.e., which population of people is made to be invisible).

> One is inevitably reminded of African Americans before advances in their civil rights when they spoke of "shucking" and "jiving" to the white man in order to be at all effective in their demands. That is, they had to dissemble and pretend to an exaggerated humility in order to hope to get any advantages from whites. One certainly hopes this is not still the case, although, considering the wrath that bluntly speaking African Americans like Spike Lee call on themselves, one suspects that this pretense is still as advantageous to African American males as it is to women. (Chaika, 1994, p. 383)

◈ APPENDIX B: CRITICAL ANALYSIS EXERCISE

Part 1: Exercise Based on World Reports

"I Want to Become an American: Changing Race Through Cosmetic Surgery" (1998): Four IES Students' Interpretive Transliterations

An Exercise in Critical Analysis

BEFORE READING: Do you expect to find meaningful differences among the four submissions (below)? Why/Why not?

WHILE READING: Ask yourself

- What do the students' word choices—personal pronouns, nouns, adjectives, adverbs and verbs—tell you about their attitudes towards the material? How do their choices affect your attitude?

Student A's Interpretation

Woman: There are various reasons and purposes for taking surgery and serious problems. It depends on the person.

Man: Yes. Some Japanese-Brazilians are looking for clear-cut features. Also, some foreigners come to Japan with faces that are surgically altered to resemble Japanese faces. 20% of them are men. Besides, their ages account for 17 to 22. 17–18% of the people in Japan who take cosmetic surgery are foreigners living in Japan now. I think it is significant to respect unvarnished self.

Student B's Interpretation

Woman: The purpose of the cosmetic surgery depends on the patients. But in Brazil, some Japanese Brazilians have cosmetic surgery to be advantageous when they get a job.

Man: One plastic surgery hospital in Tokyo has three thousands patients through the year. Some Asians go there to be made to look Japanese. The age range of Japanese patients is from 11th grade to roughly 22. And 20% of them are men. Also around 17% to 18% are foreigners, including those who live in Japan.

Man: Everyone has a reason for changing their appearances, but I would like them to take things as they are.

Woman: Hope they can have confidence.

Student C's Interpretation

Man: Those who wish to have plastic surgery do so for various reasons. In Brazil most of them tend to have plastic surgery because they come to get their jobs easier. In Tokyo three million people come to hospital to get the surgery; about 18% of them are foreigners living in Japan, and they wish to look Japanese. And also we find that many young people—from the second year of high school to 20 years old—wish to have plastic surgery. Most are female: males account for only 20%. Lastly we should be confident about what we are now without having plastic surgery.

Student D's Interpretation

Man: It seems to them (those who are going to experience the cosmetic surgery) that their worries about their appearance are serious. I heard that some Brazilian Japanese underwent the cosmetic surgery of clear-cut features in order to pass job interviews. There is a hospital that has 30,000 patients of cosmetic surgery. Asians in Japan go there in order to look Japanese. The age of patients varies from 17 to 22 years old. 20% of all the patients are men and 17% are foreigners living in Japan. The reasons why they take cosmetic surgery are different. However why don't they think of the importance of living as they originally are?

AFTER READING: Ask yourself these questions:

- Why do you imagine two of the four contributors didn't think to include the words of the female commentator (or in any case didn't attribute those words to her)?

- What questions do you have for the interpreters?

- What have you learned from this exercise?

Part 2: Exercise on Follow-Up Dialogue

The [*sic:* _____] Exercise

Below is a transcript of the follow-up dialogue from "I Want to Become an American: Changing Race Through Cosmetic Surgery" (1998). Replace the italicized words with those that state the speakers' intended message in direct and disambiguated terms. Remember, [*sic:*] indicates that a quoted passage, especially one containing an error, is precisely reproduced. (For an example, see No. 1 below.)

Woman: Those who undergo cosmetic surgery seem to have serious problems. In Brazil, Japanese-Brazilians who can be identified as (1) *Japanese* [*sic:* Asian] have cosmetic surgery to obtain (2) *clear-cut features* [*sic:* _____] in order to avoid disadvantages in job interviews. I think the purposes of cosmetic surgery are varied.

Man: Yes. There is a cosmetic surgery hospital in Tokyo that accepts thirty thousand people a year. Even in Japan, some (3) *Asian foreigners* [*sic:* _____] wish to have (4) *Japanese features* [*sic:* _____] and so have cosmetic surgery. [Pause. Returning to the topic of the cosmetic surgery hospital in Tokyo . . . .] Well, Japanese patients are from about 17 to 22 years old. 20% of them are men. 17% to 18% of them are (5) *foreigners* [*sic:* _____]. And the latter number includes (6) *zainichi gaikokujinn* [*sic:* _____]. Although each person who wishes to change her/himself has her/his own reasons, I think, I would like them to think about the importance of living as they (7) *naturally are* [*sic:* _____].

Woman: I hope that they can develop confidence in their appearance.

◈ APPENDIX C: EXERCISES ON NEOLOGISMS

Part 1: Coining Neologisms

In this exercise, you will coin words (neologisms) by experimenting with prefixes and suffixes. Look at the following lists.

Prefixes	Nouns	Suffixes
mini-	cow	*-able*
tri-	bird	*-less*
contre-	city	*-ness*
ex-	woman	*-ment*
fore-	activist	*-ous*
meta-	student	*-ly*
hyper-	cell phone	*-ary*
neo-	slave	*-hood*
para-	masculinity	*-ship*

ultra-	violence	*-ance*
trans-	artist	*-ency*
retro-	consumerism	*-sion*
sub-	sexual	*-tion*
sym-	body	*-ity*
post-	pencil	*-th*
proto-	toilet	*-en*
counter-	cosmetics	*-ize*
ambi-	hatred	*-ical*
cata-	dating	*-ive*
bi-	noodle	*-like*
vice-	death	*-y*

Now coin three words of your own and define them.

1. _____ : _____
2. _____ : _____
3. _____ : _____

Part 2: A Few of Your Neologisms [Excerpt]

discosmetics (n.): cosmetics which make those who use them ugly. Good for the traveling female loner.

ex-man (n.): a man who has undergone a sex change operation.

minimom (n.): a neglectful mother (antonym: *maximom*).

paracellphonism (n.): a condition in which one is addicted to emailing and calling by cell phone.

pencilize (v.): diet excessively.

pretoilethood (n.): the state of being a person still in diapers.

semibushhood (n.): the time when an adolescent girl's bush has not grown enough.

tridate (v.): the act of dating three people simultaneously.

trisexual (adj.): driven to think about sex, speak about sex, and do sexual things.

Now use some of the above neologisms in a short dramatic statement (or story), making sure the meaning of each is established by way of context or definition (embedded directly in your statement). Don't be timid: Use your imagination. Have some fun!

Part 3: Neologism Stories [Excerpt]

In small groups, choose the best answer for each item (1–50) among the bolded options. Also give each story a (catchy!) title, if it doesn't already have one.

A. Strange family

There is a woman who is famous for eccentric behavior in this town. Her name is Mary. Mary grew into a very eccentric woman because of her strange father and *minimom*. In her *pretoilethood*, Mary was left behind in her house alone everyday because her mother was *trisexual* and often *tridated*. Moreover, her bald father was an enthusiastic supporter of baldness and participated in **1. the 'Anti-hairhood party'/anti-hairhood parties** everyday. He **2. thought/ was thinking** only about polishing his glistening head. Like this, Mary wasn't given any affection by her parents in her *pretoilethood*. Because of her **3. parent's abandonment of child care/ parents' neglect,** Mary grew into an eccentric woman. In fact, Mary is a *hyperslave* and chases her *ultramonkeyful* boyfriend all the time. Of course, Mary's boyfriend is also weird. He has an excessive longing for slim fashion models and always tries to *pencilize* his body. People in this town call them a grotesque family. (Chiaki)

B. Title: _____

I still can't believe this. I rather don't want to believe it. The other day, I found out the woman, who I have always believed was my mother, is actually an *ex-man*!!! She (or he) has been an extreme *paracellphonist* recently. The person she talked to and emailed was her secret lover!! Not an ordinary man, but an *ex-woman*!!! I happened to hear her (Mum, I mean) talking about operations they had each gone through. She (or he) said she couldn't hide the truth anymore and she'd be happier with him (or her). **4. What made me so shocked/What shocked me so much** was not that she has a lover, but that she used to be a man. What's all this? How could I **5. have been/be born**? Whose child am I?? Somebody, help me!! (Asami)

Extra-Credit Opportunity

"Dear Tamarah," wrote one of you by e-mail, "I have finished writing a story. I didn't mean to insult 'ex-men,' 'ex-women' or gay or lesbian people, but if my story sounds discriminatory or unsuitable, please do not put mine on the list (of stories). [For various reasons] I am kind of too sensitive to this kind of issue . . . honestly, I don't know why I wrote a story using these terms though . . . ."

So, class, what do you think? Are there any insulting/discriminatory stories included in this collection? Are there any stories that rely on stereotype or caricature? If so, tell me about it by e-mail.

◈ APPENDIX D: COMMENTS BY FORMER IES STUDENTS [EXCERPT]

In small groups, read your assigned excerpt carefully. Then

1. Summarize (in a sentence or two) what the student is saying.

2. Explain (in a sentence or two) why you think I chose such an excerpt. In other words, explain what you think your new teacher wants you to conclude from reading your assigned item.

Comment 1

You gave us a lot of opportunities to practice close reading and critical thinking and I strongly believe that these practices have helped us step one stage up from students who can think in English and who have good command of English. I think this course has caused a kind of revolution in me which has changed the way of looking around the world and has given me confidence. (Masami)

Comment 2

How a word is perceived depends on each person or each group of people. Though a word is thought to be neutral or at least not offensive by one group of people, another group of people might find the word offensive or of negative connotation. (Junko)

Comment 3

Well, honestly, truly, I have learned a lot from you. Especially, the technique of thinking critically, and the importance of "aiming for specificity" whenever I say something or write something. By thinking critically about, for example, an article in the newspaper, various kinds of questions pop up in my head, and then I start concentrating on thinking about the issue from many different angles. I used to see things from only one direction and was satisfied with having only one answer, but you have totally changed my attitude towards looking at something. And I like that. (Chizuru)

Comment 4

Every time I read a book (English or Japanese), I find myself doing "critical reading," which Tamarah taught us in this class. At first I couldn't understand, but I learned it through the class without notice. Critical reading has made my horizon broad, because it requires my own questions: searching and finding some answers to my own asking, and fresh knowledge is born inside me. I will continue to read books with critical thinking even if I become 80 years old! (Hikari)

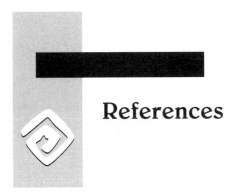

References

Abadzi, H. (1994). *What we know about acquisition of adult literacy: Is there hope?* Washington, DC: World Bank.

Adelman, C. (Ed.). (1981). *Uttering, muttering: Collecting, using and reporting talk for social and educational research.* London: Grant McIntyre.

Alexander, M. (1996). *The shock of arrival: Reflections on postcolonial experience.* Boston: South End Press.

Amin, N. (1999). Minority women teachers of ESL: Negotiating White English. In G. Braine (Ed.), *Non-native educators in English language teaching* (pp. 93–104). Mahwah, NJ: Erlbaum.

Anderson, F. (1993). The enigma of the college classroom: Nails that don't stick up. In P. Wadden (Ed.), *A handbook for teaching English at Japanese colleges and universities* (pp. 101–110). Oxford: Oxford University Press.

Andrianson, L. (2001). Gender and computer-mediated communication: Group processes in problem solving. *Computers in Human Behavior, 17,* 71–94.

Angelo, M. (1997). *The Sikh diaspora: Tradition and change in an immigrant community.* New York: Garland.

Anzaldúa, G. (1999). *Borderlands/la frontera: The new mestiza* (2nd ed.). San Francisco: Aunt Lute Books.

Arai, S. (Ed.). (1992). *Koji kotowaza kanyouku* [Traditional proverbial expressions]. Tokyo: Obunsha.

Aries, E. (1997). Women and men talking: Are they worlds apart? In M. R. Walsh (Ed.), *Women, men and gender* (pp. 82–90). New Haven, CT: Yale University Press.

Arnold, R., Barndt, D., & Burke, B. (1985). *A new weave: Popular education in Canada and Central America.* Toronto, Ontario, Canada: OISE Press.

Auerbach, E. (1992). *Making meaning, making change: Participatory curriculum development for adult ESL literacy.* McHenry, IL: Delta Systems.

Bagneski, M. (1999). e_Chat [Computer software and manual]. e_Scripts Software. Available from http://www.e-scripts.com/echat/

Bains, C. (2003, November 30). Case of second accused terrorist in Air India trial to begin. *CNews.* Retrieved December 8, 2003, from http://www.canoe.com/CNEWS/Law/2003/11/30/273220-cp.html

Bakhtin, M. (1984). *Problems of Dostoevsky's poetics* (C. Emerson, Trans.). Minneapolis: University of Minnesota Press.

Ballara, M. (1992). *Women and literacy.* London: Zed Books.

Bannerji, H. (1993). Popular images of South Asian women. In H. Bannerji (Ed.), *Returning the gaze: Essays on racism, feminism, and politics* (pp. 176–186). Toronto, Ontario, Canada: Sister Vision Press.

Bannerji, H. (2000). The paradox of diversity: The construction of a multicultural Canada and "women of colour." *Women's Studies International Forum, 23,* 537–560.

Barber, C. (1997). *The English language: A historical introduction.* Cambridge: Cambridge University Press.

Barndt, D., Cristall, F., & Marino, D. (1982). *Getting there.* Toronto, Ontario, Canada: Between the Lines.

Barrett, E., & Lally, V. (1999). Gender differences in an on-line learning environment. *Journal of Computer Assisted Learning, 15,* 48–60.

Barrett, F. J., & Whitehead, S. (Eds.). (2001). *The masculinities reader.* London: Blackwell.

Bean, J. (1999). Feminine discourse in the university: The writing center conference as a site of linguistic resistance. In J. Addison & S. J. McGee (Eds.), *Feminist empirical research: Emerging perspectives on qualitative and teacher research* (pp. 127–144). Portsmouth, NH: Heinemann.

Bell, S., Morrow, M., & Tastsoglou, E. (1999). Teaching in environments of resistance: Toward a critical, feminist, and antiracist pedagogy. In M. Mayberry & E. Cronan Rose (Eds.), *Meeting the challenge: Innovative feminist pedagogies in action* (pp. 23–48). New York: Routledge.

Benesch, S. (1999). Thinking critically, thinking dialogically. *TESOL Quarterly, 33,* 573–580.

Benesch, S. (2001). *Critical English for academic purposes: Theory, politics, and practice.* Mahwah, NJ: Erlbaum.

Bernstein, B. (1971). On the classification and framing of educational knowledge. In M. F. D. Young (Ed.), *Knowledge and control* (pp. 47–69). London: Collier Macmillan.

Bhopal, K. (1997). *Gender, "race" and patriarchy: A study of South Asian women.* Aldershot, England: Ashgate.

Bing, J., & Bergvall, V. (1996). The question of questions: Beyond binary thinking. In V. Bergvall, J. Bing, & A. Freed (Eds.), *Rethinking language and gender research: Theory and practice* (pp. 1–30). New York: Longman.

Birat, K. (1988). *Looking inward, looking outward: Japanese women today.* Tokyo: Sanshusha.

Bizzell, P., Herzberg, B., & Reynolds, N. (2000). *The Bedford bibliography for teachers of writing* (5th ed.). Boston: Bedford/St. Martin's.

Bonvillain, N. (1995). *Women and men: Cultural constructs of gender.* Englewood Cliffs, NJ: Prentice Hall.

Boraks, N., Hoffman, A., & Bauer, D. (1997). Children's book preferences: Patterns, particulars, and possible implications. *Reading Psychology, 18,* 309–341.

Bourdieu, P. (1986). The forms of capital. In J. G. Richardson (Ed.), *Handbook of theory and research for the sociology of education* (pp. 241–258). Westport, CT: Greenwood Press.

Bourdieu, P. (1991). *Language and symbolic power* (G. Raymond & M. Adamson, Trans.). Cambridge: Polity Press. (Original work published 1982)

Boxer, D. (1993). Complaining and commiserating: Exploring gender issues. *Text, 13,* 371–395.

Boxer, D., & Tyler, A. (1996). A cross-linguistic view of harassment. In N. Warner, J. Ahlers, L. Bilmes, M. Oliver, S. Wertheim, & M. Chen (Eds.), *Gender and belief systems: Proceedings of the Fourth Berkeley Women and Language Conference* (pp. 85–97). Berkeley, CA: Berkeley Women and Language Group.

Brah, A. (1987). Women of South Asian origin in Britain: Issues and concerns. *South Asia Research, 1*(1), 39–54.

Brah, A., & Minhas, R. (1985). Structural racism or cultural difference: Schooling for Asian girls. In G. Weiner (Ed.), *Just a bunch of girls: Feminist approaches to schooling* (pp. 14–25). Milton Keyes, England: Open University Press.

Britzman, D. P. (1995). Is there a queer pedagogy? Or, stop reading straight. *Educational Theory, 45,* 151–165.

Brooke, J. (2001). *Sikhs in British Columbia.* Retrieved December 8, 2003, from http://www .sikhreview.org/march2001/dynamics.htm

Brush, S. G. (1991). Women in science and engineering. *American Scientist, 79,* 404–418.

Bucholtz, M. (1999). "Why be normal?": Language and identity practices in a community of nerd girls. *Language in Society, 28,* 203–224.

Burns, A. A., Lovich, R., Maxwell, J., & Shapiro, K. (1997). *Where women have no doctor: A health guide for women.* London: Macmillan.

Butler, J. (1993). *Bodies that matter: On the discursive limits of "sex."* New York: Routledge.

Byamugisha, H. (with Okello-Obura, C., Akiteng, F., & Batambuze, C.). (2001). *Community libraries: Strengthening decentralisation through universal access to information. A concept paper.* Unpublished manuscript, Makerere University Library, Kampala, Uganda.

Cameron, D. (1990). *The feminist critique of language.* London: Routledge.

Cameron, D. (1992). *Feminism and linguistic theory* (2nd ed.). New York: St. Martin's Press.

Cameron, D. (1994). Problems of sexist and non-sexist language. In J. Sunderland (Ed.), *Exploring gender: Questions and implications for English language education* (pp. 26–33). London: Prentice Hall International.

Cameron, D. (1995). *Verbal hygiene.* London: Routledge.

Cameron, D. (1997a). Performing gender identity: Young men's talk and the construction of heterosexual masculinity. In S. Johnson & U. H. Meinhof (Eds.), *Language and masculinity* (pp. 47–64). Cambridge, MA: Blackwell.

Cameron, D. (1997b). Theoretical debates in feminist linguistics: Questions of sex and gender. In R. Wodak (Ed.), *Gender and discourse* (pp. 21–36). London: Sage.

Cameron, D. (Ed.). (1998). *The feminist critique of language: A reader* (2nd ed.). London: Routledge.

Cameron, D. (2001). *Working with spoken discourse.* London: Sage.

Campo-Flores, A. (2002, July 15). "Macho" or "sweetness." *Newsweek,* 52.

Canagarajah, S. (1999). *Resisting linguistic imperialism in English teaching.* Oxford: Oxford University Press.

Canale, M., & Swain, M. (1980). Theoretical bases of communicative approaches to second language teaching and testing. *Applied Linguistics, 1,* 1–47.

Candlin, C. N. (1989). Language, culture and curriculum. In C. N. Candlin & T. F. McNamara (Eds.), *Language, learning and community* (pp. 1–24). Sydney, Australia: Macquarie University, National Centre for English Language Teaching and Research.

Cao, Y., Soukamneuth, H. S., & Larazin, M. (1999, April). *Navigating the ethnic and racial borders of multiple peer worlds.* Paper presented at the meeting of the American Educational Research Association, Montreal, Quebec, Canada.

Casanave, C. P., & Yamashiro, A. (Eds.). (1996). *Gender issues in language education.* Tokyo: Keio University, Shonan Fujisawa Campus.

Chaika, E. (1994). *Language: The social mirror.* Boston: Heinle & Heinle.

Cherry, K. (1987). *Womansword: What Japanese words say about women.* Tokyo: Kodansha International.

Clarke, M. A., Dobson, B. K., & Silberstein, S. (1996). *Choice readings.* Ann Arbor: University of Michigan Press.

Coates, J. (1993). *Women, men, and language: A sociolinguistic account of gender differences in language* (2nd ed.). London: Longman.

Cochran, E. P. (1996). Gender and the ESL classroom. *TESOL Quarterly, 30,* 159–162.

College assistance migrant program. (1999). Retrieved September 27, 2002, from http:// www.clubs.psu.edu/LULAC/camp.htm

Collodi, C. (1985). *The adventures of Pinocchio.* Bombay, India: Better Yourself Books. (Original work published 1881)

Corson, D. (1993). *Language, minority education and gender: Linking social justice and power.* Clevedon, England: Multilingual Matters.

Corson, D. (2001). *Language, diversity, and education*. Mahwah, NJ: Erlbaum.

Crawford-Lange, L. (1981). Redirecting foreign language curricula: Paulo Freire's contribution. *Foreign Language Annals, 14,* 257–273.

Crookes, G. (1993). Action research for second language teachers: Going beyond teacher research. *Applied Linguistics, 14,* 130–144.

Cumming, A., & Gill, J. (1992). Motivation or accessibility? Factors permitting Indo-Canadian women to pursue ESL literacy instruction. In B. Burnaby & A. Cumming (Eds.), *Socio-political aspects of ESL* (pp. 241–252). Toronto, Ontario, Canada: OISE Press.

Daisley, M. (1994). The game of literacy: The meaning of play in computer-mediated communication. *Computers and Composition, 11,* 109–119.

Daly, M. (1988). *Websters' first new intergalactic wickedary of the English language*. London: The Woman's Press.

David, M. K. (2000). Status and role of English in Malaysia: Ramifications for English language teaching. *English Australia, 18*(1), 41–50.

Davies, B. (1989). The discursive production of the male/female dualism in school settings. *Oxford Review of Education, 15,* 229–241.

Davies, J., & Brember, I. (1993). Comics or stories? Differences in the reading attitudes and habits of girls and boys in Years 2, 4, and 6. *Gender and Education, 5,* 305–320.

de Campos, H. (1981). *Deus e o diablo no* Fausto *de Goethe* [God and the devil in Goethe's *Faust*]. Sao Paolo, Brazil: Perspectiva.

Dei, G. J. S. (1996). *Anti-racism education: Theory and practice*. Halifax, Nova Scotia, Canada: Fernwood.

Delpit, L. (1988). The silenced dialogue: Power and pedagogy in educating other people's children. *Harvard Educational Review, 58,* 280–298.

Derrida, J. (1998). *Of grammatology* (G. C. Spivak, Trans.). Baltimore: The Johns Hopkins University Press. (Original work published 1967)

Dibbell, J. (1993, December 23). Rape in cyberspace: How an evil clown, a Haitian trickster spirit, two wizards, and a cast of dozens turned a database into a society. *The Village Voice,* 36–42.

Dyer, B. (1998). Reflective teaching practice in cross-cultural contexts: Teaching women's studies in Japan. *Women's Studies Quarterly, 26,* 152–166.

Dziech, B., & Weiner, L. (1984). *The lecherous professor: Sexual harassment on campus*. Boston: Beacon Press.

Eastern and Central Africa Women in Development Network. (1997). *Violence against women: Trainers manual*. Nairobi, Kenya: Paulines.

Eckert, P., & McConnell-Ginet, S. (1999). New generalizations and explanations in language and gender research. *Language in Society, 28,* 185–201.

Ehrlich, S. (1997). Gender as social practice: Implications for second language acquisition. *Studies in Second Language Acquisition, 19,* 421–446.

Ehrlich, S. (2001). Gendering the "learner": Sexual harassment and second language acquisition. In A. Pavlenko, A. Blackledge, I. Piller, & M. Teutsch-Dwyer (Eds.), *Multilingualism, second language learning, and gender* (pp. 103–129). Berlin: Mouton de Gruyter.

Ellis, R. (1991). Communicative competence and the Japanese learner. *JALT Journal, 13,* 103–128.

Ellsworth, E. (1992). Why doesn't this feel empowering? Working through the repressive myths of critical pedagogy. In C. Luke & J. Gore (Eds.), *Feminisms and critical pedagogy* (pp. 90–119). London: Routledge.

Equity Studies Office. (2000). *ESL Equity Leadership Camp: Facilitator's handbook*. Toronto, Ontario, Canada: Toronto District School Board.

Essed, P. (1991). *Understanding everyday racism: An interdisciplinary theory*. Newbury Park, CA: Sage.

Fader, S. (1990, February). Targeting companies that promote women. *Graduating Engineer* [Women's issue], 101–109.

Faigley, L. (1992). *Fragments of rationality: Postmodernity and the subject of composition.* Pittsburgh, PA: University of Pittsburgh Press.

Fairclough, N. (Ed.). (1992). *Critical language awareness.* London: Longman.

Fitzgerald, L. F. (1992). *Sexual harassment in higher education: Concepts & issues.* Washington, DC: National Education Association.

Flyvbjerg, B. (2001). *Making social science matter.* Cambridge: Cambridge University Press.

Foote, C. (2000). I know what I know: A study of gender differences in item specific confidence. *Education Research Quarterly, 23*(3), 35–44.

Foss, K. A., Foss, S. K., & Griffin, C. L. (1999). *Feminist rhetorical theories.* Thousand Oaks, CA: Sage.

Foster, P. (2001). Rules and routines: A consideration of their role in the task-based language production of native and non-native speakers. In M. Bygate, P. Skehan, & M. Swain (Eds.), *Researching pedagogic tasks* (pp. 75–97). Harlow, England: Longman.

Foucault, M. (1980). Truth and power. In C. Gordon (Ed.), *Power/knowledge: Selected interviews and other writings 1972–1977.* New York: Pantheon Books.

Fox, W., & Gay, G. (1994). Functions and effects of international teaching assistants. *Review of Higher Education, 18,* 1–24.

Freeman, R., & McElhinny, B. (1996). Language and gender. In S. McKay & N. Hornberger (Eds.), *Sociolinguistics and language teaching* (pp. 218–282). Cambridge: Cambridge University Press.

Freire, P. (1970). *Pedagogy of the oppressed.* New York: Continuum.

Frye, D. (1999). Participatory education as a critical framework for an immigrant women's ESL class. *TESOL Quarterly, 33,* 501–513.

Fujimura-Fanselow, K. (1995). College women today: Options and dilemmas. In K. Fujimura-Fanselow & A. Kameda (Eds.), *Japanese women: New feminist perspectives on the past, present, and future* (pp. 124–154). New York: The Feminist Press.

Fujimura-Fanselow, K. (1996). Transforming teaching: Strategies for engaging female learners. In C. P. Casanave & A. Yamashiro (Eds.), *Gender issues in language education* (pp. 31–46). Tokyo: Keio University, Shonan Fujisawa Campus.

Fujimura-Fanselow, K., & Vaughn, D. (Eds.). (1991). Feminist issues in language teaching [Special issue]. *The Language Teacher, 15*(7).

Gal, S. (1991). Between speech and silence: The problematics of research on language and gender. *Papers in Pragmatics, 3*(1), 1–38.

Geertz, C. (1973). *The interpretation of cultures: Selected essays.* New York: Basic Books.

Ghuman, P. A. S. (1994). *Coping with two cultures: British Asian and Indo-Canadian adolescents.* Clevedon, England: Multilingual Matters.

Gibbon, M. (1999). *Feminist perspectives on language.* New York: Pearson Education.

Gitlin, A., & Thompson, A. (1995). Creating spaces for reconstructing knowledge in feminist pedagogy. *Educational Theory, 45,* 125–150.

Goldberger, N. (1997). Ways of knowing: Does gender matter? In M. R. Walsh (Ed.), *Women, men, and gender* (pp. 252–260). London: Yale University Press.

Goldstein, T. (1994). "We are all sisters, so we don't have to be polite": Language choice and English language training in the multilingual workplace. *TESL Canada Journal, 11*(2), 30–45.

Goldstein, T. (1995). "Nobody is talking bad": Creating community and claiming power on the production lines. In K. Hall & M. Bucholtz (Eds.), *Gender articulated: Language and the socially constructed self* (pp. 375–400). New York: Routledge.

Goldstein, T. (2001). Researching women's language practices in multilingual workplaces. In A. Pavlenko, A. Blackledge, I. Piller, & M. Teutsch-Dwyer (Eds.), *Multilingualism, second language learning, and gender* (pp. 77–101). Berlin: Mouton de Gruyter.

Goldstein, T. (2003). *Teaching and learning in a multilingual school: Choices, risks and dilemmas.* Mahwah, NJ: Erlbaum.

Gore, J. (1992). What we can do for you! What *can* "we" do for "you"?: Struggling over empowerment in critical and feminist pedagogy. In C. Luke & J. Gore (Eds.), *Feminisms and critical pedagogy* (pp. 54–73). New York: Routledge.

Gore, J. (1993). *The struggle for pedagogies: Critical and feminist discourses as regimes of truth.* New York: Routledge.

Govindasamy, S., Mohamed, I., & Zain, A. (2000). *Gender-based interaction in the ESL classroom: A case study of Malay students in IIUM.* Paper presented at the International Islamic University Malaysia Colloquim, Kuala Lumpur.

Graddol, P., & Swann, J. (1989). *Gender voices.* Oxford: Blackwell.

Gruber, S. (1995). Re: Ways we contribute: Students, instructors, and pedagogies in the computer-mediated writing class. *Computers and Composition, 12*(1), 61–78.

Gruber, S. (1999). Communication gone wired: Working toward a "practiced" cyberfeminism. *The Information Society, 15,* 199–208.

Gumperz, J. J. (1982). *Discourse strategies.* New York: Cambridge University Press.

Gunew, S. (1994). *Framing marginality: Multicultural literary studies.* Melbourne, Australia: Melbourne University Press.

Gupta, S., & Umar, A. (1994). Barriers to achievement faced by immigrant women of colour. In J. Gallivan, S. D. Crozier, & V. M. Lalande (Eds.), *Women, girls, and achievement* (pp. 56–62). North York, Ontario, Canada: Captus University Press.

Hall, K. (2002). "Unnatural" gender in Hindi. In M. Hellinger & H. Bussman (Eds.), *Gender across languages* (Vol. 2, pp. 133–162). Amsterdam: John Benjamins.

Hall, S. (1992). The question of cultural identity. In S. Hall, D. Held, & T. McGrew (Eds.), *Modernity and its futures* (pp. 273–299). Cambridge: Polity Press/Open University.

Hammersley, M. (1992). *What's wrong with ethnography.* London: Routledge.

Hammersley, M. (1998). *Reading ethnographic research: A critical guide* (2nd ed.). Essex, England: Addison Wesley Longman.

Hammersley, M. (2000). The relevance of qualitative research. *Oxford Review of Education, 26,* 393–405.

Harris, M. (1997). Cultural conflicts in the writing center: Expectations and assumptions of ESL students. In C. Severino, J. C. Guerra, & J. E. Butler (Eds.), *Writing in multicultural settings* (pp. 220–233). New York: Modern Language Association.

Heller, M. (2001). Gender and public space in a bilingual school. In A. Pavlenko, A. Black-ledge, I. Piller, & M. Teutsch-Dwyer (Eds.), *Multilingualism, second language learning, and gender* (pp. 257–282). Berlin: Mouton de Gruyter.

Herbert, R. (1990). Sex-based differences in compliment behavior. *Language in Society, 19,* 201–224.

Herring, S. C. (1999). The rhetorical dynamics of gender harassment on-line. *The Information Society, 15,* 151–167.

Herring, S. C., Johnson, D. A., & DiBenedetto, T. (1995). "This discussion is going too far!": Male resistance to female participation on the Internet. In K. Hall & M. Bucholtz (Eds.), *Gender articulated: Language and the socially constructed self* (pp. 67–96). New York: Routledge.

Hesse-Biber, S., & Gilbert, M. K. (1994). Closing the technological gender gap: Feminist pedagogy in the computer-assisted classroom. *Teaching Sociology, 22,* 19–31.

Holbrook, S. E. (1991). Women's work: The feminizing of composition. *Rhetoric Review, 9,* 201–229.

Holcomb, C. (1997). A class of clowns: Spontaneous joking in computer-assisted discussions. *Computers and Composition, 14,* 3–18.

Holliday, A. (1999). Small cultures. *Applied Linguistics, 20,* 237–264.

Holmes, J. (1984). "Women's language": A functional approach. *General Linguistics, 24,* 149–178.

Holmes, J. (1988). Paying compliments: A sex-preferential politeness strategy. *Journal of Pragmatics, 12,* 445–465.

Holmes, J. (1997). Women, language and identity. *Journal of Sociolinguistics, 1,* 195–223.

hooks, b. (1992). *Black looks: Race and representation.* Boston: South End Press.

hooks, b. (1994). *Teaching to transgress: Education as the practice of freedom.* New York: Routledge.

hooks, b. (1996). *Reel to real: Race, sex, and class at the movies.* New York: Routledge.

Hsiao, C. S. (1998). The interplay of a biology teacher's beliefs, teaching practices and gender-based student-teacher classroom interaction. *Journal of Teacher Education, 14,* 100–110.

Hyde, K. A. L. (1993). Sub-Saharan Africa. In E. M. King & M. A. Hill (Eds.), *Women's education in developing countries* (pp. 100–135). Baltimore: The Johns Hopkins University Press for the World Bank.

Hymes, D. (1972). Introduction. In C. B. Cazden, V. P. John, & D. Hymes (Eds.), *Functions of language in the classroom* (pp. xi–lvii). New York: Teachers College Press.

Ibrahim, A. (1999). Becoming black: Rap and hip-hop, race, gender, identity, and the politics of ESL learning. *TESOL Quarterly, 33,* 349–369.

Ide, S., & McGloin, N. H. (Eds.). (1990). *Aspects of Japanese women's language.* Tokyo: Kurosio.

IIUM directory. (2002). Kuala Lumpur: International Islamic University Malaysia.

I want to become an American: Changing race through cosmetic surgery [Television broadcast]. (1998). *World Reports.* Tokyo: Japan Broadcasting Corporation.

Jaeger, J. (1998). Brain and language: Does sex make a difference? In S. Wertheim, A. Bailey, & M. Corston-Oliver (Eds.), *Engendering communication: Proceedings of the Fifth Berkeley Women and Language Conference* (pp. 221–233). Berkeley, CA: Berkeley Women and Language Group.

Jamaluddin, N., Nongshah, N., Taufek, N. A. R., & Zulkifli, N. (1986). *Inappropriate questions.* Paper presented in a seminar in sociolinguistics, University of Pennsylvania, Philadelphia.

Janangelo, J. (1991). Technopower and technoppression: Some abuses of power and control in computer-assisted writing environments. *Computers and Composition, 9*(1), 47–64.

Jarratt, S. C. (2001). Feminist pedagogy. In G. Tate, A. Rupiper, & K. Schick (Eds.), *A guide to composition pedagogies* (pp. 113–131). Oxford: Oxford University Press.

Jaworski, A. (1993). *The power of silence.* London: Sage.

Jewell, J. B. W. (1998). A transgendered ESL learner in relation to her class textbooks, heterosexist hegemony and change. *Melbourne Papers in Applied Linguistics, 10,* 1–21.

Jones, A. (1993). Becoming a "girl": Post-structuralist suggestions for educational research. *Gender and Education, 5,* 157–166.

Julé, A. (1998). *"Christmas is your guru's birthday": Practices which build a community of learners in a Punjabi Sikh classroom.* Unpublished master's thesis, Simon Fraser University, Burnaby, British Columbia, Canada.

Julé, A. (2001, September). *Linguistic space: An ethnographic look at gender in an ESL classroom.* Paper presented at the Oxford Ethnography and Education Conference, Oxford, England.

Julé, A. (2002, May). *Use of linguistic space.* Paper presented at the Canadian Association for the Study of Women in Education/Canadian Society for the Study of Education conference, Toronto, Ontario, Canada.

Kappra, R. (1998/1999). Addressing heterosexism in the IEP classroom. *TESOL Matters, 8*(6), 19.

Kawashima, Y. (1995). Female workers: An overview of past and current trends. In K. Fujimura-Fanselow & A. Kameda (Eds.), *Japanese women: New feminist perspectives on the past, present, and future* (pp. 271–294). New York: The Feminist Press.

Kenway, J., & Modra, H. (1992). Feminist pedagogy and emancipatory possibilities. In C. Luke & J. Gore (Eds.), *Feminisms and critical pedagogy* (pp. 138–166). New York: Routledge.

Kilbourn, J. (1979). *Killing us softly* [Videotape]. Cambridge, MA: Cambridge Documentary Films.

Kiura, J. M. (1995). *Women's dignity*. Nairobi, Kenya: Paulines.

Kobayashi, Y. (2002). The role of gender in foreign language learning attitudes: Japanese female students' attitudes toward English learning. *Gender and Education, 14,* 181–197.

Kouritzin, S. (2000). Immigrant mothers redefine access to ESL classes: Contradiction and ambivalence. *Journal of Multilingual and Multicultural Development, 21,* 14–32.

Kramsch, C., & von Hoene, L. (2001). Cross-cultural excursions: Foreign language study and feminist discourses of travel. In A. Pavlenko, A. Blackledge, I. Piller, & M. Teutsch-Dwyer (Eds.), *Multilingualism, second language learning, and gender* (pp. 283–306). Berlin: Mouton de Gruyter.

Kubo, K., & Gelb. J. (1994). Obstacles and opportunities: Women and political participation in Japan. In J. Gelb & M. Palley (Eds.), *Women of Japan and Korea: Continuity & change* (pp. 120–149). Philadelphia: Temple University Press.

Kwesiga, J. C. (2002). *Women's access to higher education in Africa: Uganda's experience.* Kampala, Uganda: Fountain.

Lakoff, R. (1975). *Language and woman's place.* New York: Harper & Row.

Lakoff, R. (1995). Cries and whispers: The shattering of the silence. In K. Hall & M. Bucholtz (Eds.), *Gender articulated: Language and the socially constructed self* (pp. 25–50). London: Routledge.

Land, R., & Whitley, C. (1989). Evaluating second language essays in regular composition classes: Toward a pluralistic U.S. rhetoric. In D. Johnson & D. Roen (Eds.), *Richness in writing: Empowering ESL students* (pp. 284–294). New York: Longman.

Lang, S. (1997). Various kinds of two-spirit people: Gender variance and homosexuality in Native American communities. In S. Jacobs, T. Wesley, & S. Lang (Eds.), *Two-spirit people: Native American gender identity, sexuality, and spirituality* (pp. 100–118). Urbana: University of Illinois Press.

Langerman, C. (1990). Books and boys: Gender preferences and book selection. *School Library Journal, 36,* 132–136.

Lather, P. (1991). *Getting smart: Feminist research and pedagogy with/in the postmodern.* London: Routledge.

Latterell, C. G. (2000). Decentering student-centeredness: Rethinking tutor authority in writing centers. In L. C. Briggs & M. Woolbright (Eds.), *Stories from the center: Connecting narrative and theory in the writing center* (pp. 104–120). Urbana, IL: National Council of Teachers of English.

Law, G. (1995). Ideologies of English language education in Japan. *JALT Journal, 17,* 213–224.

Le Page, R. B., & Tabouret-Keller, A. (1985). *Acts of identity.* Cambridge: Cambridge University Press.

Leung, C., Harris, R., & Rampton, B. (1997). The idealised speaker, reified ethnicities, and classroom realities. *TESOL Quarterly, 31,* 543–576.

Liddle, J., & Nakajima, S. (2000). *Rising suns, rising daughters: Gender, class, and power in Japan.* London: Zed Books.

Livia, A., & Hall, K. (1997). "It's a girl!": Bringing performativity back to linguistics. In A. Livia & K. Hall (Eds.), *Queerly phrased: Language, gender, and sexuality* (pp. 3–18). New York: Oxford University Press.

Lochhead, A. (1990). *Abakyala mu mirimu gyeby'obusuubuzi* [Women in business]. Kampala, Uganda: Quaker Service Norway & Development Network of Indigenous Voluntary Associations.

Losey, K. (1995). Gender and ethnicity as factors in the development of verbal skills in bilingual Mexican-American women. *TESOL Quarterly, 4,* 635–661.

Luke, C. (1992). Feminist politics in radical pedagogy. In C. Luke & J. Gore (Eds.), *Feminisms and critical pedagogy* (pp. 25–53). New York: Routledge.

Luke, C., & Gore, J. (Eds.). (1992a). *Feminisms and critical pedagogy.* New York: Routledge.

Luke, C., & Gore, J. (1992b). Introduction. In C. Luke & J. Gore (Eds.), *Feminisms and critical pedagogy* (pp. 1–14). New York: Routledge.

Luke, C., & Gore, J. (1992c). Women in the academy: Strategy, struggle and survival. In C. Luke & J. Gore (Eds.), *Feminisms and critical pedagogy* (pp. 192–210). New York: Routledge.

MacGregor, L. (Ed.). (1998). [Special issue]. *The Language Teacher, 22*(6).

Maffi, L., Skutnabb-Kangas, T., & Andrianarivo, J. (2000). Language diversity. In D. Posey & G. Dutfield (Eds.), *Cultural and spiritual values of biodiversity: A complementary contribution to the global diversity assessment* (pp. 19–57). New York: United Nations Environmental Programme; Cambridge: Cambridge University Press.

Mahony, P. (1985). *Schools for the boys?: Co-education reassessed.* London: Hutchinson.

Markley, P. (1998). Empowering students: The diverse roles of Asians and women in the ESL computer classroom. In J. Swaffar, S. Romano, P. Markley, & K. Arens (Eds.), *Language learning online: Theory and practice in the ESL and L2 computer classroom* (pp. 81–96). Austin, TX: Labyrinth.

Marofsky, M., & Grote, K. (1991). *The mosaic: Men and women working together* [Videotape]. Princeton, NJ: Films for the Humanities.

Mason, L. D., Duin, A. H., & Lammers, E. (1994). Linking learners: Structuring mentoring via a telecommunications course. *Computers and Composition, 11,* 123–135.

Matsuda, P. K. (1999). Composition studies and ESL writing: A disciplinary division of labor. *College Composition and Communication, 50,* 699–721.

Matsumoto, Y. (1996). Does less feminine speech in Japanese mean less femininity? In N. Warner, J. Ahlers, L. Bilmes, M. Oliver, S. Wertheim, & M. Chen (Eds.), *Gender and belief systems: Proceedings of the Fourth Berkeley Women and Language Conference* (pp. 455–467). Berkeley, CA: Berkeley Women and Language Group.

McArthur, T. (Ed.). (1981). *Longman lexicon of contemporary English.* Essex, England: Longman.

McKay, S., & Wong, S. L. (1996). Multiple discourses, multiple identities: Investment and agency in second-language learning among Chinese adolescent immigrant students. *Harvard Educational Review, 66,* 577–608.

McLaren, P. L., & Lankshear, C. (1993). Critical literacy and the postmodern turn. In C. Lankshear & P. McLaren (Eds.), *Critical literacy: Politics, praxis, and the postmodern* (pp. 375–425). Albany: State University of New York Press.

McMahill, C. (1997). Communities of resistance: A case study of two feminist English classes in Japan. *TESOL Quarterly, 31,* 612–622.

McMahill, C. (2001). Self-expression, gender, and community: A Japanese feminist English class. In A. Pavlenko, A. Blackledge, I. Piller, & M. Teutsch-Dwyer (Eds.), *Multilingualism, second language learning, and gender* (pp. 307–344). Berlin: Mouton de Gruyter.

McVeigh, B. (1996). Cultivating "femininity" and "internationalism": Rituals and routine at a Japanese women's junior college. *Ethos, 24,* 314–349.

Mercer, N. (1995). *The guided construction of knowledge: Talk amongst teachers and learners.* Clevedon, England: Multilingual Matters

Meunier, L. E. (1997). Affective factors and cyberteaching: Implications for a postmodern pedagogy. In K. A. Murphy-Judy (Ed.), *The convergence of language teaching and research using technology* (pp. 122–132). Durham, NC: Computer Assisted Language Learning and Instruction Consortium.

Mickleburgh, R. (2003, December 6). Two teens arrested in fatal B.C. beating. *The Globe and Mail*. Retrieved December 8, 2003, from http://www.globeandmail.com/servlet /story/RTGAM.20031205.wdead-teen06/BNStory/Front/

Mignolo, W. D. (2000). The many faces of cosmo-polis: Border thinking and critical cosmopolitanism. *Public Culture, 12,* 721–748.

Miller, S. (1991). The feminization of composition. In R. Bullock & J. Trimbur (Eds.), *The politics of writing instruction: Postsecondary* (pp. 39–53). Portsmouth, NH: Heinemann.

Ministry of Education. (1999). *School basic survey*. Tokyo: Ministry of Education.

MonoConc Pro (Version 2.0) [Computer software]. (1999). Houston, TX: Athelstan.

Moulton, J. (1997). *Formal and nonformal education and empowered behavior: A review of the research literature*. Washington, DC: Support for Analysis and Research in Africa Project.

Najjemba, E. N. (n.d.). *How Busulwa became a street boy*. Kampala, Uganda: Children's Joy to Learn.

Nelson, C. (1999). Sexual identities in ESL: Queer theory and classroom inquiry. *TESOL Quarterly, 33,* 371–391.

Nelson, C. D. (in press). *Out to educate? Sexual identities in language education*. Mahwah, NJ: Erlbaum.

Nelson, G., & Echols, E. (1991, October). *A cross-cultural comparison of Egyptian and American compliments*. Paper presented at the meeting of the Southeast Regional TESOL Convention, Atlanta, GA.

Nelson, M. W. (1991). *At the point of need: Teaching basic and ESL writers*. Portsmouth, NH: Heinemann.

Nilsen, A. P. (1999). *Living language: Reading, thinking, and writing*. Boston: Allyn & Bacon.

North, S. M. (1984). The idea of a writing center. *College English, 46,* 433–446.

Norton, B. (1997). Language, identity, and the ownership of English. *TESOL Quarterly, 31,* 409–429.

Norton, B. (2000). *Identity and language learning: Gender, ethnicity and educational change*. Harlow, England: Pearson Education.

Norton, B., & Toohey, K. (2001). Changing perspectives on good language learners. *TESOL Quarterly, 35,* 307–321.

Norton, B., & Toohey, K. (Eds.). (2004). *Critical pedagogies and language learning*. New York: Cambridge University Press.

Norton Peirce, B. (1995). Social identity, investment, and language learning. *TESOL Quarterly, 29,* 9–31.

Norton Peirce, B., Harper, H., & Burnaby, B. (1993). Workplace ESL at Levi Strauss: "Dropouts" speak out. *TESL Canada Journal, 10*(2), 9–30.

Nunan, D. (1992). *Research methods in language learning*. Cambridge: Cambridge University Press.

O'Barr, W. M., & Atkins, B. K. (1998). "Women's language" or "powerless language"? In J. Coates (Ed.), *Language and gender: A reader* (pp. 377–387). Oxford: Blackwell.

O'Brien, M. (1981). *Politics of reproduction*. Boston: Routledge.

Ohara, Y., Saft, S., & Crookes, G. (2001). Toward a feminist critical pedagogy in a beginning Japanese-as-a-foreign-language class. *Japanese Language and Literature, 35,* 105–33.

Okamoto, S. (1995). "Tasteless" Japanese: Less "feminine" speech among young Japanese women. In K. Hall & M. Bucholtz (Eds.), *Gender articulated: Language and the socially constructed self* (pp. 297–325). New York: Routledge.

Okamoto, S., & Sato, S. (1992). Less feminine speech among Japanese females. In K. Hall, M. Bucholtz, & B. Moonwomon (Eds.), *Locating power: Proceedings of the Second Berkeley Women and Language Conference* (pp. 478–488). Berkeley, CA: Berkeley Women and Language Group.

O'Loughlin, K. (2001). (En)gendering the TESOL classroom. *Prospect: An Australian Journal of TESOL, 16*(2), 33–44.

Ó'Móchain, R., Mitchell, M., & Nelson, C. D. (2003). Dialogues around "Heterosexism in ESL: Examining Our Attitudes" and "Sexual Identities in ESL: Queer Theory and Classroom Inquiry" by Cynthia Nelson (1993, 1999). In J. Sharkey & K. E. Johnson (Eds.), *The* TESOL Quarterly *dialogues: Rethinking issues of language, culture, and power* (pp. 123–140). Alexandria, VA: TESOL.

Omoding-Okwalinga, J. (1985). *Literacy and the learning and practice of rural off-farm occupations.* Unpublished doctoral dissertation, University of Wisconsin, Madison.

O'Neill, R. (1970). *Kernel lessons intermediate.* Essex, England: Longman.

Orner, M. (1992). Interrupting the calls for student voice in "liberatory" education: A feminist post-structuralist perspective. In C. Luke & J. Gore (Eds.), *Feminisms and critical pedagogies* (pp. 74–89). New York: Routledge.

Oxford, R. (2002). Sources of variation in language learning. In R. Kaplan (Ed.), *The Oxford handbook of applied linguistics* (pp. 245–252). Oxford: Oxford University Press.

Pagnucci, G. S., & Mauriello, N. (1999). The masquerade: Gender, identity, and writing for the Web. *Computers and Composition, 16,* 141–151.

Parry, K. (2000). *Language and literacy in Uganda: Towards a sustainable reading culture.* Kampala, Uganda: Fountain.

Parry, K. (2002). Literacy for development? A community library project in Uganda. *Language Matters, 33,* 142–68.

Parry, S. (1996). Feminist pedagogy and techniques for the changing classroom. *Women's Studies Quarterly, 24,* 45–54.

Pavlenko, A. (2001). Bilingualism, gender, and ideology. *The International Journal of Bilingualism, 5,* 117–151.

Pavlenko, A. (2004). Gender and sexuality in foreign/second language education: Critical and feminist approaches. In B. Norton & K. Toohey (Eds.), *Critical pedagogies and language learning* (pp. 53–71). Cambridge: Cambridge University Press.

Pavlenko, A., Blackledge, A., Piller, I., & Teutsch-Dwyer, M. (Eds.). (2001). *Multilingualism, second language learning, and gender.* Berlin: Mouton de Gruyter.

Pavlenko, A., & Piller, I. (2001). New directions in the study of multilingualism, second language learning, and gender. In A. Pavlenko, A. Blackledge, I. Piller, & M. Teutsch-Dwyer (Eds.), *Multilingualism, second language learning, and gender* (pp. 17–52). Berlin: Mouton de Gruyter.

Penelope, J. (1990). *Speaking freely: Unlearning the lies of the fathers' tongues.* New York: The Athene Series.

Pennycook, A. (1994). *The cultural politics of English as an international language.* New York: Longman.

Pennycook, A. (1997). Cultural alternatives and autonomy. In P. Benson & P. Voller (Eds.), *Autonomy and independence in language learning* (pp. 35–53). London: Longman.

Pennycook, A. (1998). *English and the discourses of colonialism.* New York: Routledge.

Pennycook, A. (1999). Critical approaches to TESOL [Special-topic issue]. *TESOL Quarterly, 33*(3).

Pennycook, A. (2001). *Critical applied linguistics: A critical introduction.* Mahwah, NJ: Erlbaum.

Phillips, H. M. (1970). *Literacy and development.* Paris: United Nations Educational, Scientific, & Cultural Organization.

Phillipson, R. (1992). *Linguistic imperialism.* New York: Oxford University Press.

Plakans, B. (1997). Undergraduates' experiences with and attitudes toward international teaching assistants. *TESOL Quarterly, 31,* 95–119.

Razack, S. (1998). *Looking white people in the eye: Gender, race, and culture in courtrooms and classrooms.* Toronto, Ontario, Canada: University of Toronto Press.

Reynolds, K. A. (Ed.). (1993). *Onna to nihongo* [Women and language in Japanese]. Tokyo: Yuushindoo.

Rilling, S. (2000). A teacher preparation course for computer assisted language learning. In E. Hanson-Smith (Ed.), *Technology-enhanced learning environments* (pp. 149–161). Alexandria, VA: TESOL.

Ritter, J. J. (2000). Recent developments in assisting ESL writers. In B. Rafoth (Ed.), *A tutor's guide: Helping writers one to one* (pp. 102–110). Portsmouth, NH: Heinemann.

Rivera, K. (1999). Popular research and social transformation: A community-based approach to critical pedagogy. *TESOL Quarterly, 33,* 485–500.

Roberts, G. (1994). *Staying on the line: Blue-collar women in contemporary Japan.* Honolulu: University of Hawaii Press.

Rwakasisi, R. (1996). *How friends became enemies.* Kampala, Uganda: Fountain.

Said, E. (1984). Reflections on exile. *Granta, 13,* 157–172.

Saint Pierre, R. (1994). On being out in the classroom: Dilemma or duty? In K. Jennings (Ed.), *One teacher in ten: Gay and lesbian educators tell their stories* (pp. 164–167). Boston: Alyson.

Sandler, B., & Hall, R. (1986). *The campus climate revisited: Chilly for women faculty, administrators and graduate students.* Washington, DC: Association of American Colleges, Project on the Status and Education of Women.

Sarangi, S. (1995). Culture. In J. Verschueren, J. Östman, & J. Blommaert (Eds.), *Handbook of pragmatics* (pp. 1–30). Amsterdam: John Benjamins.

Schmied, J. (1991). *English in Africa: An introduction.* Harlow, England: Longman.

Searle, J. R. (1969). *Speech acts.* Cambridge: Cambridge University Press.

Silveira, J. (1979). Generic masculine words and thinking. In C. Kramarae (Ed.), *The voices and words of women and men* (pp. 165–178). New York: Pergamon Press.

Simon, R. (1992). *Teaching against the grain: Texts for a pedagogy of possibility.* New York: Bergin & Garvey.

Simon-Maeda, A. (2002). *A critical ethnographic investigation of Japanese junior college female learners' attitudes towards gender issues and education.* Unpublished doctoral dissertation, Temple University, Philadelphia.

Simpson, A. (1996). Fictions and facts: An investigation of the reading practices of girls and boys. *English Education, 28,* 268–279.

Simpson, R. C., Briggs, S. L., Ovens, J., & Swales, S. L. (1999). *The Michigan corpus of academic spoken English.* Ann Arbor: The Regents of the University of Michigan. Retrieved October 10, 2003, from http://www.lsa.umich.edu/eli/micase/micase.htm

Singh, R., Lele, J., & Martohadjono, G. (1988). Communication in a multilingual society: Some missed opportunities. *Language and Society, 17,* 433–459.

Skutnabb-Kangas, T. (2000a). *Linguistic genocide in education—or worldwide diversity and human rights?* Mahwah, NJ: Erlbaum.

Skutnabb-Kangas, T. (2000b). Linguistic human rights and teachers of English. In J. K. Hall & W. G. Eggington (Eds.), *The sociopolitics of English language teaching* (pp. 22–44). Clevedon, England: Multilingual Matters.

Smith, S., & Yamashiro, A. (Eds.). (1998). Gender issues in language teaching [Special issue]. *The Language Teacher, 22*(5).

Soukup, C. (1999). The gendered interactional patterns of computer-mediated chatrooms: A critical ethnographic study. *The Information Society, 15,* 169–176.

Spender, D. (1980). Talking in the class. In D. Spender & E. Sarah (Eds.), *Learning to lose: Sexism and education* (pp. 148–154). London: The Women's Press.

Spielberg, S. (Producer/Director). (1997). *Amistad* [Motion picture]. Glendale, CA: Dreamworks SKG/United International Pictures.

Spivak, G. C. (1988). *In other worlds: Essays in cultural politics.* New York: Methuen.

Spivak, G. C. (1990). *The post-colonial critic: Interviews, strategies, dialogues.* New York: Routledge.

Stake, R. E. (1995). *The art of case study research.* London: Sage.

Stanworth, M. (1981). *Gender and schooling: A study of sexual divisions in the classroom* (Explorations in Feminism No. 7). London: Women's Research and Resources Centre.

Statistical data on international students. (2002). Retrieved December 7, 2003, from http://www.international.psu.edu/international_students/intl_enroll_growth.htm

Stevenson, R. L. (1995). *Kidnapped* (retold by V. Thomas). Bombay, India: Better Yourself Books. (Original work published 1886)

Stone, A. R. (1995). *The war of desire and technology at the close of the mechanical age.* Cambridge, MA: MIT Press.

Street, B. (Ed.). (1993). *Cross-cultural approaches to literacy.* Cambridge: Cambridge University Press.

Stubbs, M. (1976). *Language, schools and classrooms.* London: Methuen.

Summerhawk, B. (1998). From closet to classroom: Gay issues in ESL/EFL. *The Language Teacher, 22*(5), 21–23.

Sunderland, J. (Ed.). (1994). *Exploring gender: Questions and implications for English language education.* New York: Prentice Hall.

Sunderland, J. (1995). "We're boys, miss!": Finding gendered identities and looking for gendering of identities in the foreign language classroom. In S. Mills (Ed.), *Language and gender: Interdisciplinary perspectives* (pp. 160–178). New York: Longman.

Sunderland, J. (1998). Girls being quiet: A problem for foreign language classrooms. *Language Teaching Research, 2*(1), 48–62.

Sunderland, J. (2000). Issues of language and gender in second and foreign language education. *Language Teaching, 33,* 203–223.

Suzuki, M. (1995). Genjitsu o tsukuridasu soochi: Imeeji CM [Reality-making devices: Image commercials]. In T. Inoue, C. Inoue, & Y. Ehara (Eds.), *Hyoogen to media* [Expressions and the media] (pp. 150–165). Tokyo: Iwanami Shoten.

SyllaBase [Computer software]. (2001). North Logan, UT: 3GB Technologies.

Takashi Wilkerson, K. (1998). Feminist linguistic innovations on loan: Japan's borrowing privileges. In S. Wertheim, A. C. Bailey, & M. Corston-Oliver (Eds.), *Engendering communication: Proceedings of the Fifth Berkeley Women and Language Conference* (pp. 613–624). Berkeley, CA: Berkeley Women and Language Group.

Talbot, M. (1998). *Language and gender: An introduction.* Cambridge, MA: Blackwell.

Tamale, S. (1998). *When hens begin to crow: Gender and parliamentary politics in Uganda.* Kampala, Uganda: Fountain.

Tanaka, K. (1993). Shinbun ni miru koozooka sareta seisabetsuhyoogen [The systematization of sexual discrimination in newspapers]. In K. A. Reynolds (Ed.), *Onna to nihongo* [Women and language in Japanese] (pp. 98–122). Tokyo: Yuushindoo.

Tannen, D. (1990). *You just don't understand.* New York: Morrow.

Taylor, L. (2003). *Longing to become, coming to belong: ESL students' engagement of integrative antiracism social justice education.* Unpublished doctoral dissertation, University of Toronto, Ontario, Canada.

Taylor, L. (in press). Transcreation, transformation and the fertility of difference: Reading ESL students' negotiations of language difference through the lens of translation. In P. Trifonas (Ed.), *Pedagogies of difference.* New York: Routledge.

Thornborrow, J. (2002). *Power talk.* London: Longman.

Toohey, K. (2000). *Learning English at school: Identity, social relations and classroom practice.* Clevedon, England: Multilingual Matters.

Toronto District School Board. (2000). *Every student survey: Executive summary.* Toronto, Ontario, Canada: Author.

Toronto District School Board. (2001). *Equity foundation statement.* Toronto, Ontario, Canada: Author.

Treichler, P. A. (1994). A room of whose own?: Lessons from feminist classroom narratives. In D. B. Downing (Ed.), *Changing classroom practices: Resources for literary and cultural studies* (pp. 75–103). Urbana, IL: National Council of Teachers of English.

Tyler, A. (1994). Sexual harassment and the ITA curriculum. *Journal of Graduate Teaching Assistant Development, 2,* 31–41.

Tyler, A., & Boxer, D. (1996). Sexual harassment? Cross-cultural/cross-linguistic perspectives. *Discourse and Society, 7,* 107–133.

Uganda Bureau of Statistics & ORC Macro. (2002). *Uganda DHS EdData survey 2001: Education data for decision-making.* Kampala: Author, Uganda Ministry of Education and Sports, & U.S. Agency for International Development.

Uganda Change Agent Association. (n.d.). *Gender issues.* Kampala, Uganda: Author.

Uganda National Commission for UNESCO. (2001). Education and poverty eradication. *Uganda and UNESCO Information Magazine, 1,* 1–2.

Uganda Women's Network. (2000). *Abakyala mumanye eddembe lyammwe ku ttaka* [Women know your land rights]. Kampala, Uganda: Author.

United Nations Educational, Scientific, and Cultural Organization. (1990). *World declaration of education for all and framework for action to meet basic learning needs.* Jomtien, Thailand: World Conference on Education for All.

United Nations Educational, Scientific, & Cultural Organization. (1995). *World education report.* Oxford: Author.

Usher, R., & Edwards, R. (1994). *Postmodernism and education: Different voices, different worlds.* London: Routledge.

Vandrick, S. (1994). Feminist pedagogy and ESL. *College ESL, 4*(2), 69–92.

Vandrick, S. (1997a). Heterosexual teachers' part in fighting homophobia. *TESOL Matters, 7*(2), 23.

Vandrick, S. (1997b). The role of hidden identities in the postsecondary ESL classroom. *TESOL Quarterly, 31,* 153–157.

Vandrick, S. (1999a). The case for more research on female students in the ESL/EFL classroom. *TESOL Matters, 9*(2), 16.

Vandrick, S. (1999b). Who's afraid of critical and feminist pedagogies? *TESOL Matters, 9*(1), 9.

Vandrick, S. (2000). The need for more research on female language learners in the classroom. In A. Yamashiro (Ed.), *Temple University Japan Working Papers in Applied Linguistics: Gender Issues in Language Education* (Vol. 17, pp. 11–25). Tokyo: Temple University Japan.

Vieira, E. R. P. (1999). Liberating Calibans: Readings of *Antropofagia* and Haroldo de Campos' poetics of transcreation. In S. Bassnett & A. Lefevere (Eds.), *Post-colonial translation: Theory and practice* (pp. 95–113). New York: Routledge.

Walker, B. G. (1983). *The woman's encyclopedia of myths and secrets.* New York: Harper & Row.

Walkerdine, V. (1990). *Schoolgirl fictions.* London: Verso.

Wallace, C. (1992). Critical literacy awareness in the EFL classroom. In N. Fairclough (Ed.), *Critical language awareness* (pp. 59–92). London: Longman.

Wasike, A. (2002, October 5). 24 million Ugandans. *New Vision,* pp. 1–2.

Watkins, K. (2000). *The Oxfam education report.* Oxford: Oxfam.

Weedon, C. (1987). *Feminist practice and poststructuralist theory.* Oxford: Blackwell.

Weiler, K. (1988). *Women teaching for change: Gender, class and power.* Westport, CT: Bergin & Garvey.

Weiler, K. (1991). Freire and a feminist pedagogy of difference. *Harvard Educational Review, 61,* 449–474.

Weis, L. (1988). High school girls in a de-industrializing economy. In L. Weis (Ed.), *Class, race, and gender in American education* (pp. 183–208). Albany: State University of New York Press.

Werner, D., with Thuman, C., Maxwell, J., & Pearson, A. (1979). *Where there is no doctor: A village health care handbook for Africa.* London: Macmillan.

West, C., & Zimmerman, D. H. (1983). Small insults: A study of interruptions in cross-sex conversations between unacquainted persons. In B. Thorne, C. Kramarae, & C. N. Henley (Eds.), *Language, gender and society* (pp. 103–118). Rowley, MA: Newbury House.

West, C., & Zimmerman, D. H. (1987). Doing gender. *Gender and Society, 1,* 125–151.

Willett, J. (1995). Becoming first graders in an L2: An ethnographic study of L2 socialization. *TESOL Quarterly, 29,* 473–503.

Willinsky, J. (1998). *Learning to divide the world: Education at empire's end.* Minneapolis: University of Minnesota Press.

Wolfe, J. L. (1999). Why do women feel ignored? Gender differences in computer-mediated classroom interactions. *Computers and Composition, 10*(3), 153–166.

Wolfe, J. L. (2000). Gender, ethnicity, and classroom discourse: Communication patterns of Hispanic and white students in networked classrooms. *Written Communication, 17,* 491–519.

Wolfe, P. (1998). Best supporting actress: Gender and language across four secondary ESL/bilingual classrooms. *Current Issues in Education, 1,* 1–12.

Wolfson, N. (1989). *Perspectives: Sociolinguistics and TESOL.* Rowley, MA: Newbury House.

Wolfson, N., D'Amico-Reisner, L., & Huber, L. (1983). How to arrange for social commitments in English: The invitation. In N. Wolfson & E. Judd (Eds.), *Sociolinguistics and language acquisition* (pp. 116–28). Rowley, MA: Newbury House.

Wolfson, N., & Manes, J. (1978). Don't "dear" me. In S. McConnell-Ginet, R. Borker, & N. Furman (Eds.), *Women and language in literature and society* (pp. 79–92). New York: Praeger.

Yamashiro, A. (Ed.). (2000). Gender issues in language education [Special issue]. *Temple University Japan Working Papers in Applied Linguistics, 17.*

Yepez, M. (1994). An observation of gender-specific teacher behavior in the ESL classroom. *Sex Roles, 30,* 121–133.

Yin, R. K. (1994). *Case study research: Design and methods* (2nd ed.). Thousand Oaks, CA: Sage.

Your companion in the absence of a doctor. (2000). Kampala, Uganda: Femrite.

Index

Page numbers followed by *f, t,* and *n* refer to figures, tables, and footnotes, respectively.

A

Abadzi, H., 81
Abstract topics, dealing with, gender differences in, 63
Academic performance, gender differences in, 61–62, 62*t*
Acceptable-use policy statement, for computer-mediated communication, 124
Access, to linguistic and interactional resources, 4
Adelman, C., 69
The Adventures of Pinocchio (Collodi), 88
Africa, literacy as gendered issue in, 84–85
African students, and feminism, 103–105
Agency, gendered, 3
Alexander, M., 71
American Association of University Professors, sexual harassment guidelines of, 31
Amin, N., 4
Amistad (Spielberg), 104
Anderson, F., 145
Andrianarivo, J., 108
Andrianson, L., 121
Angelo, M., 69, 70
Anzaldúa, G., 44, 47, 51, 53
Arai, S., 132
Aries, E., 69
Arnold, R., 96
Asian students, classroom interactions of, 62

B

Bagneski, M., 8, 115
Bains, C., 70
Ballara, M., 85
Bannerji, H., 69
Barber, C., 157
Barndt, D., 96
Barrett, E., 119
Barrett, F. J., 101
Bauer, D., 84
Bean, J., 46
Bedford Bibliography for Teachers of Writing (Bizzell, Herzberg, & Reynolds), 43
Bell, S., 134
Benesch, S., 17, 47
Bergvall, V., 2
Bernstein, B., 24
Bhopal, K., 69
Biases, in textbooks, 161
Biles, Rebecca, 8, 124
  Explorations of Language and Gender in a Graduate Technology Course, 111–124
Bing, J., 2
Birat, K., 147

Assessment
  in gender and language issues program, 138–139
  of Intensive English Studies Program, 160–161, 169
Atkins, B. K., 121
Auerbach, E., 143
Autonomous learning, 155

Bisexual issues. *See* Gay/lesbian/bisexual/ transgendered issues
Bizzell, P., 43
Blackledge, A., 1
Bonvillain, N., 2
Boraks, N., 84
Borrowing patterns, in Kitengesa Community Library Project, 87–90, 88*t*, 89*t*
Bourdieu, P., 107
Boxer, Diana, 6, 42
  Gender, Sexual Harassment, and the International Teaching Assistant, 29–42
Brah, A., 69, 71
Brain, sex differences in, 2
Brember, I., 84
Briggs, S. L., 117
British Columbia, Punjabi Sikh community in, 69–78
Britzman, D. P., 18, 105
Brooke, J., 70
Brush, S. G., 30
Bucholtz, M., 130
Burke, B., 96
Burnaby, B., 4
Burns, A. A., 91
Butler, J., 101
Byamugisha, H., 81, 90

◈ C

Cameron, D., 2, 73, 119, 130, 146, 156
Campo-Flores, A., 61
Canada, 7, 8
  ESL Antidiscrimination Camp in, 95–109
  Punjabi Sikh community in, 69–78
Canagarajah, S., 98, 108
Canale, M., 29
Candlin, C. N., 19
Cao, Y., 95
Casanave, C. P., 5, 10
Chaika, E., 157, 164
Cherry, K., 131, 157
Clarke, M. A., 17
Class, and oppression, 2
Class discussions, on gay/lesbian/bisexual/ transgendered issues, 21–23
Classroom(s), 10
  differences from writing centers, 49–50, 52

empowerment in, 11
interactions in
    gender differences in, 60–61, 62–63, 71–72
    importance of, 69
  language structures specific to, 71
  linguistic space in, 73–74, 73*f*
  power relations in, 128–129
  speech acts in, type and direction of, 74–75, 76*t*, 77*t*
  turn taking in, gender differences in, 62–63, 63*t*
CMC. *See* Computer-mediated communication
Coates, J., 132
Code switching, 47, 53
Cohen, Tamarah, 9, 163
  Critical Feminist Engagement in the EFL Classroom: From Supplement to Staple, 155–169
College Assistance Migrant Program, 48
Collodi, C., 88
Community(ies)
  imagined, gendered, 3
  intercultural frame of, 100–101
  student-constructed understandings of, 99
Community of difference, 99–100, 107–108
Community outreach, of Kitengesa Community Library Project, 90
Compliments, and sexual harassment perceptions, 38–39
Composition. *See* ESL tutoring, feminist composition pedagogies in; Writing
Computer-mediated communication (CMC), 115
  acceptable-use policy statement for, 124
  controversial topics in, 124
  e_Chat for, 115, 118, 122–123
  gender and, 119
  MonoConc Pro for, 116–117, 121–122
  multiple forms of, 123
  online behavior in, teachers' control of, 119
  to solve teaching problems, 122–123
  students' awareness in, 123
  students' personal experiences in, 123
  suitability of, 118
  SyllaBase for, 114–115, 118, 119, 121–122
  Tapped In for, 116, 120
  teacher's power in, 117–118

transcripts from, 123
and virtual rape, 120
women's language in, 121–122
Corson, D., 4, 5, 71
Course evaluations, in Intensive English
    Studies Program, 160–161, 169
Crawford-Lange, L., 143
Cristall, F., 96
Critical consciousness, in EFL classes at
    Japanese university, 150–152
Critical feminism
  in EFL classroom, 155–169
  in TESOL, common themes of, 10–11
Critical pedagogy, 143
Critical perspective, on racialized gender,
    105–106, 107
Critical reflection, by students, on writing
    assignments, 52
Crookes, G., 143, 144, 145
Cultural feminism, 1–2
Culture
  and gay/lesbian/bisexual/transgendered
        issues, 18–19, 24–25
  and gender, 2
  poststructuralist theories of, 18–19
  and sexual harassment, 30
  and sexual identity, 24–25
Cumming, A., 71
Curriculum
  and critical feminist praxis in TESOL, 10
  in EFL classes, at Japanese university,
        144–145
  flexibility of, in ESL tutoring, 51

◈ D

Daisley, M., 119
Daly, M., 159
D'Amico-Reisner, L., 37
David, M. K., 67
David, Maya Khemlani, 68
  Investigating the Male Voice in a
        Malaysian ESL Classroom, 59–68
Davies, B., 129
Davies, J., 84
de Campos, H., 100
Dei, G. J. S., 96
DELL. See Department of English Language
    and Learning
Delpit, L., 47
Department of English Language and

Learning (DELL), at International Islamic
    University Malaysia, 59–68
Derrida, J., 108
Dibbell, J., 120
DiBenedetto, T., 119
Difference
  community of, 99–100, 107–108
  intercultural frame of, 100–101
  multidimensional, intersecting model of,
        99
  student-constructed understandings of, 99
Disability, and oppression, 2
Discussions
  whole class, on gay/lesbian/bisexual/
        transgendered issues, 21–23
  of writing assignments, in ESL tutoring,
        50
Dobson, B. K., 17
Double translation, 100
Duin, A. H., 117
Dyer, B., 134
Dzeich, B., 31

◈ E

Eastern and Central Africa Women in
    Development Network, 91
e_Chat, 8, 115, 118, 122–123
Echols, E., 32
Eckert, P., 129, 130
Editing, in ESL tutoring, 54
Edwards, R., 18
EFL classes
  critical feminist engagement in (See
        Intensive English Studies Program)
  at Japanese university, 143–154
    context of, 144–145
    critical consciousness in, 150–152
    cultural concerns in, 145
    curriculum in, 144–145
    description of, 147–148
    dialogue on gender in, 148–150
    distinguishing features of, 148–152
    institutional constraints on, 152
    language and gender in, 145–146
    participants in, 144
    practical ideas from, 152–153
    setting of, 144
Ehrlich, S., 1, 4, 32, 120, 129
Ellis, R., 145
Ellsworth, E., 128, 134

Employment-gaining skills, importance of, gender differences in, 66, 66t
Empowerment
  in classroom, 11
  English as language of, 3
Engaged pedagogy, 131
English, as language of empowerment, 3
The English Language (Barber), 157
Equity Leadership Retreats, 96
Equity Studies Office, 96, 97, 99, 109
ESL Antidiscrimination Camp (Canada), 95–109
  community in, 99–101
  context of, 95–98
  description of, 101–105
  difference in, 99–101
  distinguishing features of, 105–106
  identity in, 99–101
  and language and gender, 98–101
  participants in, 97–98
  practical ideas from, 106–108
  program of, 96–97
  sample activity from, 109
  student-constructed understandings in, 99, 106–107
  student profiles from, 101–105
ESL classes, at International Islamic University Malaysia, 7, 59–68
ESL tutoring, feminist composition pedagogies in, 6, 43–56
  context of, 44–45
  critical thinking in, 52
  curriculum flexibility in, 51
  description of, 48–49
  discussions in, 50
  distinguishing features of, 49–51
  editing in, 54
  language and gender in, 45–47
  levels of need of students in, 50–51
  mechanics in, 54
  pace of students in, 50–51
  practical ideas in, 51–54
  slowing down of writing process in, 53
  survey in, 48–49, 55–56
Essed, P., 96
Ethnicity, and oppression, 2
Etymology, 161
Evaluation
  in gender and language issues program, 138–139
  of Intensive English Studies Program, 160–161, 169

F

Face-to-face discussions, in graduate level technology course, 117, 120, 122–123
Fader, S., 30
Faigley, L., 117
Fairclough, N., 108
Femininity, racialized images of, 105
Feminism
  cultural, 1–2
  and English as language of empowerment, 3
  in Japan, 146, 160n
  material, 1–2
Feminist pedagogy, 9
  for composition, 43–56
Feminist poststructuralism, 2–3
Fitzgerald, L. F., 31, 32
Flyvbjerg, B., 69
Foote, C., 60, 63
Foss, K. A., 45, 47
Foss, S. K., 45, 47
Foster, P., 67
Foucault, M., 129
Fox, W., 29
Framing, of questions, in gay/lesbian/bisexual/transgendered issues, 24
Freeman, R., 129
Freire, P., 128, 143, 145
Frye, D., 4
Fujimura-Fanselow, K., 5, 10, 129, 134, 146
Funding, for library projects, 92

G

Gal, S., 72
Gay, G., 29
Gay/lesbian/bisexual/transgendered issues, 5–6, 15–28
  and ambiguities of sexual identity, 25
  and class discussions, 21–23
  context of, 16
  culture and, 18–19, 24–25
  description of, 19–23
  distinguishing features of, 23–25
  framing of questions about, 24
  and group work, 21–23
  and identity, 18
  and language and gender, 16–19
  practical ideas from, 26–27
  and risk taking, 23–24

and stereotyping, 19–23, 20*f*
topics in, 16–17
Geertz, C., 70
Gelb, J., 146
Gender
  and access to linguistic and interactional
      resources, 4
  in Canadian Punjabi Sikh community, 71–
      72
  in composition, 45–46
  in computer-mediated communication,
      119
  culture and, 2
  definition of, 1–3
  dialogue about, fostering of, 152–153
  differentiation from sex, 2
  dynamic nature of, dialogue on, 149–150
  in EFL classes, at Japanese university,
      145–146
  in ESL Antidiscrimination Camp, 98–101
  in ESL classes, at International Islamic
      University Malaysia, 60–61
  in gender and language issues program,
      129
  in graduate level technology course, 113–
      114
  in Intensive English Studies Program,
      156–157
  in Kitengesa Community Library Project,
      84–85
  and oppression, 2
  race and, 8, 95–109
  social nature of, 2
  and technology, 8
  and TESOL, 3–5
Gender and language issues (GALI)
    program, 127–141
  assessment in, 138–139
  classroom of, power relations in, 128–129
  context of, 127–128
  course plan for, 140–141
  course requirement for, 140
  description of, 130–136, 140
  distinguishing features of, 136–137
  journal writing in, 130, 132–136
  language and gender in, 129
  politically incorrect reactions in,
      acceptance of, 137
  practical ideas from, 137–139
  student participation in, 137–138
  textbook criticism in, 134–136

topic introduction in, 130–131
worksheets in, 131–132, 141
Gender differences
  in academic performance, 61–62, 62*t*
  in classroom interactions, 62–63, 71–72
  in dealing with abstract topics, 63
  in goal orientations, 64–66
  in importance of employment-gaining
      skills, 66, 66*t*
  in importance of oral communication
      skills, 65–66, 65*t*
  in importance of writing skills, 64–65, 64*t*
  research on, 60–61
  in turn taking in classrooms, 62–63, 63*t*
Gender Issues (Uganda Change Agent
    Association), 91
Gendered agency, 3
Gendered interaction, 4–5
Gendered resistance, 3
Ghuman, P. A. S., 69
Gibbon, M., 1, 156
Gilbert, M. K., 118
Gill, J., 71
Girls, silence of, in Canadian Punjabi Sikh
    community, 69–78
Gitlin, A., 128
Goal orientations, in ESL classes, at
    International Islamic University Malaysia,
    64–66
Goldberger, N., 72
Goldstein, T., 4, 98
Gore, J., 2, 47, 96, 99, 128, 132, 134, 137,
    156
Govindasamy, Subra, 7, 68
  Investigating the Male Voice in a
      Malaysian ESL Classroom, 59–68
Graddol, P., 72, 73
Graduate technology course. *See*
    Technology course, at graduate level
Grammar rules, questioning of, 161
Griffin, C. L., 45, 47
Grote, K., 133
Group work, on gay/lesbian/bisexual/
    transgendered issues, 21–23
Gruber, S., 117, 122
Gumperz, J. J., 70
Gunew, S., 162
Gupta, S., 71

❖ H

Hall, K., 2, 120
Hall, R., 29, 31
Hall, S., 18, 19
Hammersley, M., 70
Harper, H., 4
Harris, M., 44, 46, 48, 51
Harris, R., 98
Heller, M., 4, 5
Herbert, R., 38
Herring, S. C., 119, 120
Herzberg, B., 43
Hesse-Biber, S., 118
Hidden identities, 10
High school, ESL Antidiscrimination Camp
   for. *See* ESL Antidiscrimination Camp
Hoffman, A., 84
Holbrook, S. E., 44, 45, 46
Holcomb, C., 119
Holliday, A., 18, 19
Holmes, J., 38, 130
hooks, b., 6, 43, 44, 51, 53, 103, 131
How Busulwa Became a Street Boy
   (Najjemba), 88
How Friends Became Enemies (Rwakasisi), 88
Hsiao, C. S., 60–61, 62
Huber, L., 37
Hyde, K. A. L., 82, 84
Hymes, D., 77

❖ I

Ibrahim, A., 98
Ide, S., 146
Identity
   intercultural frame of, 100–101
   lesbian/gay/bisexual/transgendered issues
      and, 18
   multidimensional, intersecting model of, 99
   poststructuralist theories of, 18
   student-constructed understandings of,
      99, 107
Ideology, and language, 132
IES Program. *See* Intensive English Studies
   Program
IIUM. *See* International Islamic University
   Malaysia
Imagined communities, gendered, 3
Inclusion, pedagogies of, 18
Initiation-response-follow-up (IRF)
   exchanges, in classroom interactions, 71

Inquiry, pedagogies of, 18
Institutional constraints, dealing with, 152
Intensive English Studies (IES) Program,
   155–169
   context of, 155–156
   course evaluations in, 160–161, 169
   critical analysis exercise in, 164–166
   description of, 157–160
   distinguishing features of, 160–161
   interpretive skills in, 160
   language and gender in, 156–157
   neologism exercises in, 166–168
   practical ideas from, 161–162
   sample textbook exercise in, 163–164
   teaching sequences in, 158–160
   textbooks in, 157–158
Interactional resources, gendered access to, 4
Interactions, gender differences in, 4–5,
   60–61
Intercultural perspective, on racialized
   gender, 105–106, 107
Interculture, 41
International Islamic University Malaysia
   (IIUM), 7, 59–68
   ESL classes in
      academic performance in, 61–62, 62*t*
      classroom interactions in, 62–63
      context of, 59–60
      description of, 61
      distinguishing features of, 61–67
      goal orientations in, 64–66
      language and gender in, 60–61
      practical ideas from, 66–67
      students in, 60
      students' needs in, 66–67
International teaching assistants (ITAs), 6
   and sexual harassment, 29–42
      context of work on, 29–31
      description of work on, 32–33
      distinguishing features of work on,
         33–39
      perceptions of, 34–40
      practical ideas from work on, 39–40
      video prompts and interviews, 33
      written scenario reactions, 32–33
   teaching journals of, 40
   training of, 30
   work with U.S. undergraduates, 40
Internships, for students, 67
Interpretive skills, development of, 160
Invitations, and sexual harassment
   perceptions, 37–38

IRF exchanges. *See* Initiation-response-follow-up exchanges
Islamic cultures, sexual connotations in, 30
ITAs. *See* International teaching assistants

🔷 J

Jaeger, J., 2
Jamaluddin, N., 30
Janangelo, J., 117
Japan, 8–9
  English as language of empowerment in, 3
  feminism in, 3, 146, 160*n*
  gender and language issues program in, 127–141
  gender inequality in, 145–146
  Intensive English Studies Program in, critical feminist engagement in, 155–169
  sexual harassment in, 133–134
  university EFL class in, 143–154
Japan Association for Language Teaching, 129
Jarratt, S. C., 44, 46, 47, 53
Jaworski, A., 71
Jewell, J. B. W., 17
Johnson, D. A., 119
Jones, A., 2
Jordan, Jay, 6, 55
  Feminist Composition Pedagogies in ESL Tutoring, 43–56
Journals
  in gender and language issues program, 130, 132–136
  teaching, of international teaching assistants, 40
Julé, Allyson, 7, 78
  Speaking in Silence: A Case Study of a Canadian Punjabi Girl, 69–78

🔷 K

Kappra, R., 17
Kawashima, Y., 146
KCSS. *See* Kitengesa Comprehensive Secondary School
Kenway, J., 138, 157
Kernel Lessons Intermediate (O'Neill), 135
Kidnapped (Stevenson), 88
Kitengesa, Uganda
  Community Library Project in, 81–93
  literacy in, 82–83
  role of English in, 83–84

Kitengesa Community Library Project, 81–93
  books borrowed in, 86, 87–90, 88*t*, 89*t*, 91
  community outreach of, 90
  context of, 82–84
  description of, 85–90
  distinguishing features of, 90–91
  girls as agents for literacy and development in, 85
  language and gender in, 84–85
  participants in, 86–87, 87*t*
  practical ideas from, 91–92
  rural focus of, 90
Kitengesa Comprehensive Secondary School (KCSS), 7–8, 83–84
Kiura, J. M., 91
Kobayashi, Y., 3
Kouritzin, S., 4
Kramsch, C., 10
Kubo, K., 146
Kwesiga, J. C., 82

🔷 L

Lakoff, R., 72, 121
Lally, V., 119
Lammers, E., 117
Land, R., 53
Lang, S., 2
Langerman, C., 84
Language
  in Canadian Punjabi Sikh community, 71–72
  in EFL classes at Japanese university, 145–146
  in ESL Antidiscrimination Camp, 98–101
  in ESL classes, at International Islamic University Malaysia, 60–61
  in gender and language issues program, 129
  in graduate level technology course, 113–114
  and ideology, 132
  in Intensive English Studies Program, 156–157
  in Japan, 146
  in Kitengesa Community Library Project, 84–85
  and sexual harassment, 31
Language: The Social Mirror (Chaika), 157
Language differences, as strengths, 53

Language for Occupational Purposes (LOP), 66–67

Lankshear, C., 19

Larazin, M., 95

Lather, P., 18, 128, 129

Latterell, C. G., 45, 47, 54

Law, G., 145

Le Page, R. B., 25

Learning, autonomous, 155

Lele, J., 30

Lesbian issues. *See* Gay/lesbian/bisexual/ transgendered issues

Lessons, structure of, 77–78

Leung, C., 98

Levels of needs, of students, in ESL tutoring, 50–51

Library projects
  base of, 92
  books for, 92
  funding for, 92
  Kitengesa Community Library Project, 81–93
  local support for, 92
  location of, 92

Liddle, J., 129

Linguistic Genocide in Education—or Worldwide Diversity and Human Rights (Skutnabb-Kangas), 157

Linguistic resources, gendered access to, 4

Linguistic space, 71
  division of, in classroom, 73–74, 73*f*

Literacy, as gendered issue, in Africa, 84–85

Livia, A., 120

Living Language (Nilsen), 157

Lochhead, A., 91

Looking Inward, Looking Outward (Birat), 147

LOP. *See* Language for Occupational Purposes

Losey, K., 5

Lovich, R., 91

Luke, C., 2, 96, 99, 129, 132, 134, 137, 156

❧ M

MacGregor, L., 5, 10

Maffi, L., 108

Mahony, P., 71, 73

Malaysia, ESL classes in, male students in, 7, 59–68

Manes, J., 33, 38

Marino, D., 96

Markedness, 162

Markley, P., 118

Marofsky, M., 133

Martohardjono, G., 30

Masaka District, of Uganda, Kitengesa Community Library Project in, 81–93

Mason, L. D., 117

Material feminism, 1–2

Matsuda, P. K., 48

Matsumoto, Y., 146

Mauriello, N., 120

Maxwell, J., 91

McArthur, T., 130

McConnell-Ginet, S., 129, 130

McElhinny, B., 129

McGloin, N. H., 146

McKay, S., 98

McLaren, P. L., 19

McMahill, C., 3, 5, 10, 146

McVeigh, B., 146

Mechanics, in ESL tutoring, 54

Meetings, led by students, 67

Men, in Malaysian ESL classrooms, 59–68

Mercer, N., 28

Meunier, L. E., 119

Michigan Corpus of Spoken Academic English (MICASE), 116–117

Mickelburgh, R., 70

Mignolo, W. D., 100

Miller, S., 44, 46

Minhas, R., 71

Ministry of Education, 99, 129

Mitchell, M., 17

Modra, H., 138, 157

Mohamed, I., 60

MonoConc Pro, 116–117, 121–122

Morrow, M., 134

The Mosaic: Men and Women Working Together (Marofsky & Grote), 133

Moulton, J., 85

Multivoiced consciousness, 10

Muslim students, classroom interactions of, 62

❧ N

Najjemba, E. N., 88

Nakajima, S., 129

National Education Association (NEA), sexual harassment guidelines of, 31

Nelson, Cynthia D., 5–6, 28
  Beyond Straight Grammar: Using Lesbian/

Gay Themes to Explore Cultural
Meanings, 15–28
Nelson, G., 32
Nelson, M. W., 46, 52, 53
Neologism exercises, in Intensive English
Studies Program, 166–168
Nilsen, A. P., 157
Nongshah, N., 30
North, S. M., 46, 54
Norton, Bonny, 11, 19, 98, 143
Gender and English Language Learners:
Challenges and Possibilities, 1–11
Norton Peirce, B., 4, 98
Nunan, D., 15

◈ O

O'Barr, W. M., 121
O'Brien, M., 156
Ohara, Yumiko, 9, 154
Promoting Critical Reflection About
Gender in EFL Classes at a Japanese
University, 143–154
Okamoto, S., 146
O'Loughlin, K., 17, 18
Ó'Móchain, R., 17
Omoding-Okwalinga, J., 81
O'Neill, R., 135
Oppression, 2
Oral communication skills, importance of,
gender differences in, 64–65, 64t
ORC Macro, 81, 83
Orner, M., 128
Ovens, J., 117
Oxford, R., 2

◈ P

Pace, of students, in ESL tutoring, 50–51
Pagnucci, G. S., 120
Parry, Kate, 7–8, 93
Opportunities for Girls: A Community
Library Project in Uganda, 81–93
Parry, S., 130
Paulines Publishers, 88
Pavlenko, Aneta, 12
Gender and English Language Learners:
Challenges and Possibilities, 1–11
Pedagogy
critical, 143
engaged, 131
feminist, 9

feminist composition, 43–56
of inclusion, 18
of inquiry, 18
Penelope, J., 162
Pennsylvania State University, University
Park campus of, Undergraduate Writing
Center at, 44–45, 48. See also ESL
tutoring
Pennycook, A., 10, 98, 108, 122, 139
Personal questions, and sexual harassment
perceptions, 39
Phillips, H. M., 81
Phillipson, R., 108
Physical contact, with student, and sexual
harassment perceptions, 35–36
Piller, I., 1
Plakans, B., 29
Positionality, and power relations, 128
Poststructuralist feminism, 2–3
and power relations in classroom, 128
Poststructuralist theories
of culture, 18–19
of identity, 18
Power relations, in classroom, 128–129
Pseudogenerics, 156–157, 161
Punjabi Sikh community, in Canada, 7, 69–
78
context of, 70–71
language and gender and, 71–72
schools and, 70
silence of girls in, 69–78
work with
description of, 72–73
distinguishing features of, 73–77
practical ideas from, 77–78

◈ Q

Qualitative educational research, 69–70,
152
Questions
framing of, in gay/lesbian/bisexual/
transgendered issues, 24
personal, and sexual harassment
perceptions, 39
printed, prior to dialogue, 152
variety of, 161

◈ R

Race
and femininity, 105

Race (*continued*)
  and gender, 8, 95–109
  and oppression, 2
Rampton, B., 98
Razack, S., 96
Reading aloud, in Kitengesa Community
  Library Project, 86–87, 87*t*
Reading culture, 81
Reasonable person, in sexual harassment
  definition, 31
Reasonable woman, in sexual harassment
  definition, 31
Research, qualitative, 69–70, 152
Research Methodology course, at
  International Islamic University Malaysia,
  60
Resistance, gendered, 3
Reynolds, K. A., 146
Reynolds, N., 43
Rilling, Sarah, 8, 124
  Explorations of Language and Gender in a
    Graduate Technology Course, 111–
    124
Risk taking, on gay/lesbian/bisexual/
  transgendered issues, 23–24
Ritter, J. J., 44, 51
Rivera, K., 4
Roberts, G., 146
Role playing, by students, 67
Rwakasisi, R., 88

◈ S

Saft, Scott, 9, 154
  Promoting Critical Reflection About
    Gender in EFL Classes at a Japanese
    University, 143–154
Said, E., 162
Saint Pierre, R., 17
Sandler, B., 29, 31
Sarangi, S., 19
Sato, S., 146
Schmied, J., 83
Searle, J. R., 73, 75
Sex, differentiation from gender, 2
Sexual harassment
  in computer-mediated communication,
    120
  culture and, 30
  divergent views of, in action and
    language, 31
  guidelines of, 31

international teaching assistants and (*See*
  International teaching assistants)
in Japan, 133–134
legal definitions concerning, 40
perceptions of
  compliments and, 38–39
  invitations and, 37–38
  personal questions and, 38–39
  physical contact with student and,
    35–36
  telephone calls and, 34–35
  unannounced visits and, 36–37
reasonable person *versus* reasonable
  woman in, 31
Sexual identity
  ambiguities of, 25
  culture and, 24–25
  and oppression, 2
  of teachers, 25
Shapiro, K., 91
Silberstein, S., 17
Silence
  definition of, 72
  of girls
    in Canadian Punjabi Sikh community,
      69–78
    examples of, 76–77
  purposes of, 72
Silveira, J., 156
Simon, R., 19
Simon-Maeda, Andrea, 8–9, 140
  Transforming Emerging Feminist
    Identities: A Course on Gender and
    Language Issues, 127–141
Simpson, A., 84
Simpson, R. C., 117
Singh, R., 30
Skutnabb-Kangas, T., 108, 157, 163
Smith, S., 5, 10, 129, 146
Soukamneuth, H. S., 95
Soukup, C., 120
Speech acts, in classroom, type and
  direction of, 74–75, 76*t*, 77*t*
Spender, D., 71
Spielberg, S., 104
Spivak, G. C., 18, 137
Stake, R. E., 69
Stanworth, M., 71
Stereotyping
  and gay/lesbian/bisexual/transgendered
    issues, 19–23, 20*f*
  in textbooks, 134–136

Stevenson, R. L., 88

Stimulated recall, 15

Stone, A. R., 120

Street, B., 91

Stubbs, M., 69, 73

Students

critical reflection by, on writing
assignments, 52

internships of, 67

meetings led by, 67

needs of

in ESL tutoring, 50–51

responding to, 66–67

pace of, in ESL tutoring, 50–51

personal gender and language issues of,
132–134, 136

physical contact with, and sexual
harassment perceptions, 35–36

talk of, in classroom, 73–74, 73f

Summerhawk, B., 17

Sunderland, J., 1, 69, 130

Survey, in feminist composition pedagogies,
for ESL tutoring, 48–49, 55–56

Suzuki, M., 146

Swain, M., 29

Swales, S. L., 117

Swann, J., 72, 73

SyllaBase, 8, 114–115, 118, 119, 121–122

◈ T

Tabouret-Keller, A., 25

Takashi Wilkerson, K., 160

Takayoshi, P., 124

Talbot, M., 119, 146

Tamale, S., 84

Tanaka, K., 146

Tannen, D., 130

Tapped In, 8, 120

Tastsoglou, E., 134

Taufek, N. A. R., 30

Taylor, Lisa, 8, 108

Creating a Community of Difference:
Understanding Gender and Race in
a High School ESL
Antidiscrimination Camp, 95–109

TDSB. *See* Toronto District School Board

Teachers, 11

role in classroom, 73–74, 73f

sexual identity of, 25

Teaching assistants. *See* International
teaching assistants

Teaching journals, of international teaching
assistants, 40

Technology, gender and, 8

Technology course, at graduate level

context of, 111–113

description of, 114–117

distinguishing features of, 117–123

e_Chat in, 8, 115, 118, 122–123

face-to-face discussions in, 117, 120,
122–123

language and gender in, 113–114

MonoConc Pro in, 116–117, 121–122

participants in, 112–113

practical ideas from, 123–124

SyllaBase in, 8, 114–115, 118, 119, 121–
122

Tapped In in, 8, 116, 120

Telephone calls, and sexual harassment
perceptions, 34–35

TESOL

critical feminist praxis in, common
themes in, 10–11

gender and, 3–5

Teutsch-Dwyer, M., 1

Text, dialogic engagement with, 161

Textbooks

biases in, 161

criticism of, in gender and language issues
program, 134–136

in Intensive English Studies Program,
157–158

Thompson, A., 128

Thornborrow, J., 71, 75

Toohey, K., 10, 70, 98, 143

Toronto District School Board (TDSB), 95,
96

Transcreation, 100

Transformative classroom practices, 11

Transgender issues. *See* Gay/lesbian/
bisexual/transgendered issues

Treichler, P. A., 47

Turn taking, in classroom interactions,
gender differences in, 62–63, 63t

Tutoring. *See* ESL tutoring

Tyler, Andrea, 6, 42

Gender, Sexual Harassment, and the
International Teaching Assistant,
29–42

◈ U

Uganda
   gender disparity in, 81–82
   Kitengesa Community Library Project in, 81–93
   role of English in, 83–84
Uganda Bureau of Statistics, 81, 83
Uganda Change Agent Association, 91
Uganda National Commission for UNESCO, 83
Uganda Women's Network, 91
Umar, A., 71
Undergraduate Writing Center, at University Park campus, of Pennsylvania State University, 44–45, 48. *See also* ESL tutoring
United Nations Education, Scientific, and Cultural Organization (UNESCO), 81, 92
Usher, R., 18

◈ V

Vandrick, S., 10, 17, 51, 69, 129, 143
Vaughn, D., 5, 10, 129
Vieira, E. R. P., 100
Violence Against Women (Eastern and Central Africa Women in Development Network), 91
Visits, unannounced, and sexual harassment perceptions, 36–37
von Hoene, L., 10

◈ W

Walker, B. G., 157
Walkerdine, V., 71
Wallace, C., 162
Wasike, A., 83
Watkins, K., 81, 84, 85
Websters' First New Intergalactic Wickedary of the English Language (Daly), 159
Weedon, C., 2, 18
Weiler, K., 99, 129, 143
Weiner, L., 31
Weis, L., 84, 132

Werner, D., 91
West, C., 72
Where There Is No Doctor (Werner), 91
Where Women Have No Doctor (Burns, Lovich, Maxwell, & Shapiro), 91
Whitehead, S., 101
Whitley, C., 53
Willett, J., 5
Willinsky, J., 108
Wolfe, J. L., 119, 121, 122
Wolfe, P., 60, 63
Wolfson, N., 33, 37, 38
The Woman's Encyclopedia of Myths and Secrets (Walker), 157
Womansword: What Japanese Words Say About Women (Cherry), 157
Women in Business (Lochhead), 91
Women Know Your Land Rights (Uganda Women's Network), 91
Women's Dignity (Kiura), 91
Wong, S. L., 98
Writing
   critical reflection on, by students, 52
   gender and, 45–46
   importance of skills in, gender differences in, 64–65, 64*t*
   language differences as strengths in, 53
   process of, in ESL tutoring, 53
Writing centers
   differences from classrooms, 49–50, 52
   ESL tutoring in (*See* ESL tutoring)
   feminism and, 46

◈ Y

Yamashiro, A., 5, 10, 129, 146
Yepez, M., 69
Your Companion in the Absence of a Doctor, 91

◈ Z

Zain, A., 60
Zimmerman, D. H., 72
Zulkifli, N., 30

Also Available From TESOL

Academic Writing Programs
Ilona Leki, Editor

Action Research
Julian Edge, Editor

Bilingual Education
Donna Christian and Fred Genesee, Editors

Community Partnerships
Elsa Auerbach, Editor

Content-Based Instruction in Higher Education Settings
JoAnn Crandell and Dorit Kaufman, Editors

Distance-Learning Programs
Lynn E. Henrichsen, Editor

English for Specific Purposes
Thomas Orr, Editor

Grammar Teaching in Teacher Education
Dilin Liu and Peter Master, Editors

Implementing the ESL Standards for Pre-K–12 Students Through Teacher Education
Marguerite Ann Snow, Editor

Integrating the ESL Standards Into Classroom Practice: Grades Pre-K–2
Betty Ansin Smallwood, Editor

Integrating the ESL Standards Into Classroom Practice: Grades 3–5
Katharine Davies Samway, Editor

Integrating the ESL Standards Into Classroom Practice: Grades 6–8
Suzanne Irujo, Editor

Integrating the ESL Standards Into Classroom Practice: Grades 9–12
Barbara Agor, Editor

Intensive English Programs in Postsecondary Settings
Nicholas Dimmit and Maria Dantas-Whitney, Editors

Interaction and Language Learning
Jill Burton and Charles Clennell, Editors

Internet for English Teaching
Mark Warschauer, Heidi Shetzer, and Christine Meloni

Journal Writing
Jill Burton and Michael Carroll, Editors

Mainstreaming
Effie Cochran, Editor

Teacher Education
Karen E. Johnson, Editor

Technology-Enhanced Learning Environments
Elizabeth Hanson-Smith, Editor

For more information, contact
Teachers of English to Speakers of Other Languages, Inc.
700 South Washington Street, Suite 200
Alexandria, Virginia 22314 USA
Tel 703-836-0774 • Fax 703-836-6447 • publications@tesol.org •
http://www.tesol.org/